The International Sweethearts of Rhythm

by

D. Antoinette Handy

WITHDRAW

THE SCARECROW PRESS, INC.
METUCHEN, N.J., & LONDON
1983

Library of Congress Cataloging in Publication Data

Handy, D. Antoinette, 1930–
   The International Sweethearts of Rhythm.

   Bibliography: p.
   Includes index.
   1. International Sweethearts of Rhythm.
2. Afro-American women musicians. I. Title.
ML421.I6H36 1983   785'.06'276259   83–3185
ISBN 0–8108–1619–9

This book is dedicated to the
International Sweethearts of Rhythm,
their original teacher, Consuella Carter,
and
their creator, Laurence Clifton Jones.

TABLE OF CONTENTS

PREFACE

While preparing my book Black Women in American Bands &
Orchestras (Scarecrow, 1981), the International Sweethearts
of Rhythm emerged as a band warranting more research.
Such an investigation necessitated extensive travel, continuous
correspondence, frequent telephone calls, and many hours
reading microfilm. The findings justified the effort for me
and I hope the rewards of these experiences will also be enjoyed by the reader.

From the beginning, it has been my intention to write
the definitive history of the ladies' jazz band from Piney Woods
Country Life School in Piney Woods, Mississippi. To what
extent this has been accomplished, only time can determine.
Surely there are those who will recall some event or issue
that I have omitted or understated, but I have intentionally
limited the coverage to inclusion of information that could be
substantiated. On controversial issues, I have tried to give
both sides of the story, recognizing that all behavior can be
rationalized (and perhaps justified) after the fact.

The band's creator, Laurence Clifton Jones, brought
meaning to the old adage "nothing attempted, nothing gained."
His school needed money; Piney Woods had discovered in the
past that utilizing the innate talents of student singers and
athletes was a successful method for securing funds. With
many female instrumentalists then enrolled, it was only natural that Jones, the school's founder/president, would in the
late 1930s involve band members in the fund raising process.
Not only would he send out a group of female jazz players
as emissaries of Piney Woods Country Life School, but he
would have a second band in reserve.

In this era of internships and distributive and cooperative education, it is worth noting that a little Mississippi Country Life School successfully employed such programs several decades earlier. Unfortunately, most of those who recall the band know little about its point of origin, its organizational purpose, or its fascinating journey from relative obscurity to national fame. Also unfortunate is the fact that the school itself has virtually eliminated the band's existence from its history.

The 1940s brought increased opportunities for women, particularly in the world of jazz. But for the most part, both opportunities and recognition vanished with the return of men from the war. The only real survivors were female vocalists. Corrective measures began in the late 1970s (following International Women's Year--1975), though often as a mere token bow to feminism, considering the continuation of the division of jazz instrumentalists into male and female spheres. But the Sweethearts' story is noteworthy regardless of any sexual division.

No effort has been made to evaluate the band along musical lines. However, it should be obvious to the reader that the International Sweethearts of Rhythm were certainly competitive with other prominent bands between the years 1939 and 1949. What it lacked in one department was compensated for in another. Management understood the importance of arrangers, so they secured the services of the best in the business: Eddie Durham, Jesse Stone, and Maurice King. Management knew the significance of discipline, so they established strict rules and enforced them. After listening to recordings and viewing several film clips, I am convinced that no discussion of the big band era is complete without inclusion of the International Sweethearts of Rhythm.

Acknowledgments

I was privileged to have been directed to Claude Phifer (who, along with Nellie Jones Bass, was an agent for the Sweethearts) and Pauline Braddy (the band's original drummer) early in the writing stage. They were on opposite sides of the controversy that developed, but they remained friends, loyal to Piney Woods Country Life School and respectful of the band's organizer. In retrospect, both were found to be most objective. Without their information, photographs, and consistent responses to my many requests (over a period of four years), this publication could hardly have been realized. I am grateful to all the Sweethearts who responded to my request for information and for the spirit in which those in attendance at the Women's Jazz Festival, 1980 (Kansas City, Missouri) "counted me in."

I am greatly obliged to Johnston Memorial Library (Virginia State University), Omaha (Nebraska) Public Library, Nebraska State Historical Society, and the Mississippi Department of Archives and History. A special thanks to five black newspapers, the Pittsburgh Courier, the Chicago Defender, the Afro-American, the New York Age, and the Jackson Advocate and to the jazz periodical Down Beat.

For additional assistance, many others deserve acknowledgment. Preeminent are Nellie Jones Bass, Consuella Carter, and Yvonne Plummer Terrelongue. I offer very special thanks to Dr. Eileen Southern for her constant encouragement and the high standards of scholarship that she established for all to follow. For their critical reading and helpful suggestions, I am indebted to Dr. Jeannette Jennings and William E. Terry. Without the understanding, tolerance, patience, and support of my husband, Calvin, and our children--Zanda Michelle, Blaine, and Obiora--this project could neither have been launched nor completed.

D. A. H.

FOREWORD

If one were to ask the average jazz enthusiast to name twenty
first-rate jazz instrumentalists, the answer would probably be
given without much hesitation. The list, however, would probably include only one or two women. If one asked the same
person to name twenty women who were first-rate jazz instrumentalists, it would take much longer to get an answer. Despite the fact that from the earliest days of jazz to the present women have made important and lasting contributions to
the common vocabulary and the evolution of the music, their
efforts have not been given the attention they deserve.

Duke Ellington admired the talents of trombonist/con-
ductor Marie Lucas; King Oliver hired Lillian Hardin Armstrong as the regular pianist in his legendary Chicago band;
Cleo Brown replaced Fats Waller on CBS radio; and Mary
Lou Williams was billed as "The Lady Who Swings the Band"
when Andy Kirk brought his Clouds of Joy east from Kansas
City. These four exceptionally talented women were respected
and admired by their peers because their creative efforts
were comparable to the giants they worked with; but because
they were women, their stories have not been documented
with the same care and frequency as the stories of their male
counterparts. The possible exception is Mary Lou Williams.
Though she received considerable attention during her lifetime,
the full story of her remarkable achievements is yet to be
told.

Though women performed side by side with men as far
back as the Minstrel Show days, there was such a general
bias against hiring them that many fine musicians organized
all-female orchestras to provide talented women an opportunity
to perform the same repertory in venues similar to all male
orchestras.

One of the best all-female bands got its first big break in my hometown, Washington, D.C. The International Sweethearts of Rhythm created a sensation when they made their debut at the Howard Theatre in 1940. Though for years there had been several excellent female pianists who performed in all the professional circles, it was unusual to see women playing all the instruments in the orchestra. The biggest surprise was their sound and the way they swung. The Howard Theatre audiences were accustomed to hearing the best black bands--Duke Ellington, Count Basie, Jimmy Lunceford, Earl Hines, and many more; so they judged the Sweethearts by those standards and were enthralled with the music made by this group of enthusiastic women from Mississippi.

Who were they? How did they get together? How did they learn to play so well? What made them special?

It took many years for some of these questions to be answered and it took an exceptional woman with talents both scholarly and musical to document the history of this important group. With sensitivity stemming from her own experiences in the music field, D. Antoinette Handy tells the story of the musicians who individually and collectively made the International Sweethearts of Rhythm the important musical organization it was to the black community at large and to the world of jazz in general.

> BILLY TAYLOR
> Jazz Pianist, Composer,
> Historian, Radio Commentator,
> and Educator

CHAPTER I

PROLOGUE

A SALUTE TO THE INTERNATIONAL
SWEETHEARTS OF RHYTHM,
MARCH 1980

For female supporters and jazz aficionados, Kansas City,
Missouri has become the place to be during the month of
March. It all began in 1978 (March 17-19) with a Women's
Jazz Festival, the brainchild of Dianne Gregg, program di-
rector for National Public Radio outlet KCUR, and Carol
Comer, local singer/pianist/songwriter and Kansas City cor-
respondent for Down Beat magazine.

According to several sources, Gregg and Comer set
out to find where the women jazz players were following their
visit to the 1977 jazz festival in Wichita. They instantly put
together a board of directors, composed of "women and men
sympathetic to the goal of publicizing the accomplishments of
women artists in the jazz idiom." Gregg served as president
of the Women's Jazz Festival Incorporated and Comer as
executive director; nationally known jazz pianist Marian
McPartland served as a member of the board of directors.
As early as November 1977, the following announcement appeared:

> A group of jazz partisans [in Kansas City] is or-
> ganizing what may become a major annual festival.
> The first event is scheduled for next March. The
> festival's focus will be jazz, but with a different
> touch: the featured musicians will be women....
> "We'd like to bring some attention to the women in

jazz," said Dianne Gregg.... "Most people can
think of women as singers and piano players, but
they are more than that."[1]

The first Women's Jazz Festival was dedicated to the
memory of recently deceased black Kansas City vocalist/
pianist Bettye Miller.   Persons came from thirty-six states
and despite the fact that attendance reached only seventy-five
percent of the anticipated number, the first Women's Jazz
Festival was deemed an overwhelming success.   As one festival board member assessed the situation, "the sponsors
weren't making money but they were making history."[2]   The
only controversy was the threat of a demonstration from those
who opposed the playing involvement of a few males who were
there primarily as backups.

Featured performers were Marian McPartland, pianist/
composer/arranger Mary Lou Williams, vocalist/song stylist
Betty Carter and numerous other experienced, though lesser
known, artists.   The veterans managed well to blend their
musical gifts with those of the talented late- and newcomers.
Particularly conspicuous were young women, several participating but many simply enjoying the fellowship--listening to
and rubbing shoulders with jazz legends.

Support for this ambitious undertaking came from such
sources as the Missouri Arts Council, the Kansas Arts Commission, the National Endowment for the Arts, local corpora-
tions, and numerous individuals.   Jazz encyclopedist, critic,
and record producer Leonard Feather, an endorser and promoter of women jazz musicians since the late 1930s, wrote
of the first festival:

It's long overdue....   All these years people have
been trying to eliminate racism in jazz, but nobody's
done much to get rid of sexism.   This ought to attract enough attention to help women musicians who
deserve the publicity....

The event needs all the publicity it can get.   I'm
sure that there will be plenty of media attention
paid to it, and people will, perhaps, begin to realize that women definitely have an important place
in jazz.[3]

McPartland waged a one-woman campaign, realizing
that the event was supportive of both her personally and of

feminist causes which she sanctioned. She released on her
own Halcyon label the album "Now Is the Time" (featuring
women performers) and further plugged female jazz activities
on National Public Radio. Simultaneously, Stash Records released three discs featuring women in jazz between 1926 and
1961. 4

New York Times critic John S. Wilson wrote of the
year 1978:

> The consciousness raising that has accompanied the
> rise of the women's movement has been relatively
> slow in penetrating the jazz world. But this year
> it is beginning to build a head of steam. 5

Of the Stash record releases, Wilson added:

> They provide a very convincing demonstration that
> women, singly and in groups, have been making im-
> pressive contributions to jazz since its earliest re-
> corded days and doing it, for the most part, in
> relative anonymity....

> Aside from the occasional singing, there is nothing
> on any of these disks to indicate that the performers
> are women. Or men. They are just musicians and
> their playing is as good as--and often better than
> the performances you hear on other records of the
> same periods and styles. 6

As preparations were underway for the second festival
to be held on March 23-25, 1979, Kansas City Star's entertainment editor Shifra Stein wrote:

> A year ago this week, against overwhelming odds,
> a major step was taken to ensure that the role of
> women in forming this native American art form is
> not forgotten.... [T]he Women's Jazz Festival ...
> proved beyond argument the ability of women to per-
> form jazz.... Until last year's event, no major
> festival had included women musicians within its
> format--let alone dedicated itself to showcasing
> women musicians. 7

Though prior to 1978 no festival had featured women
musicians exclusively, several earlier events seemed to be
harbingers of renewed interest in women musicians.   The

spotlight was turned on women on November 4, 1973, when
a female jazz sextet of top professionals were specially selected to appear at the New York Jazz Museum. As part of
the series the Calvert Extra Sunday Concerts, the performance was believed to be the first major presentation of an
all-women's jazz band in twenty-five years. [8] Later, in July
1975, International Musician's "Pop and Jazz Scene" reporter
Burt Koball recalled a program titled "Women in Jazz," which
had recently been presented at the Executive Sweet [sic] in
New York City's Alden Hotel. According to Koball, "[The
program] provided telling proof of the aptitude of at least
seven women"--all instrumentalists. [9] This was the year proclaimed International Women's Year by the United Nations,
"highlight[ing] the importance of eliminating discrimination
against women all over the world."

        Following the First Women's Jazz Festival in Kansas
City, the New York City-based Universal Jazz Coalition initiated a five-night Salute to Women in Jazz during June 1978.
As promoter Cobi Narita explained, "This [was] a salute to
women artists, an opportunity to show that women are artists
and should be treated as artists." The 1978 Salute was re-
gional, focusing on jazz women in the New York City area.
Plans called for a national and international focus in two subsequent events. [10]

        The momentum was high; the market was increasing
for female jazz artists; and as jazz critic Nat Hentoff wrote
of the times, "male bastions [were] falling to female talent
and determination."[11] A second festival was guaranteed to
be a winner. Headliners for the 1979 event were Marian
McPartland and the incomparable vocalist Carmen McRae.

        No sooner was the Second Women's Jazz Festival com-
pleted before plans were underway for the Third. Kansas
City would remain as the site and the three-day event was
extended to four days (March 20-23, 1980). Upon the festival
committee's request, Mayor Richard Berkley proclaimed the
month of March 1980 as Jazz Month. The activities were
launched at the Bennett-Marak Gallery, where a Smithsonian
Institution exhibit, chronicling the struggles of working women
from 1824 to 1976, was installed. The Commission on the
Status of Women and Elected Officials from eight area counties designated March 22 through March 29 as Women's Week
in Kansas City, "designed to increase public awareness of the
particular problems and needs of area women. [12] Obviously
Kansas City, Missouri was "tuned in" to the equal rights for

women/equal rights for jazz movement, if perhaps only for
the month of March.

The site for the Third Women's Jazz Festival, Crown
Center, was alive with jazz--formal and informal concerts,
clinics and workshops (on vocal jazz, beginning and advanced
reeds, brass, and rhythm sections, and the business aspects
of music), and jam sessions. National Public Radio's "Jazz
Alive" production crew was on hand, recording the events for
future broadcasts over its more than 200 affiliated stations
throughout the country.

Since its inception, the stated purpose of the Women's
Jazz Festival Incorporated has been "to create a market for
the increasing number of female jazz artists and to stimulate
an interest in jazz in general." A weekend celebration each
year during the month of March was to be the principal show-
case, commemorating decades of female achievement in jazz,
promenading current female jazz musicians, and projecting a
jazz future where sex and race would be of no import.

In March 1980, emphasis was placed on "commemorating decades of female achievement in jazz." On the fourth
day, the Women's Jazz Festival hosted a Salute to the "Original" International Sweethearts of Rhythm, a black women's
jazz band that "earn[ed] a reputation (that still stands) as the
best all-women swing band ever to perform."[13]

To honor the International Sweethearts of Rhythm was
to begin the long and tedious path of rectifying a pattern of
omission, neglect, and perhaps sheer prejudice, both racial
and sexual. I recall so well my first contact with Pauline
Braddy (September 1977), the band's drummer. A willing
provider of personal and International Sweethearts of Rhythm
information, photographs, and clippings, she commented,
"I'm so glad that someone is going to give us some recognition. I thought the world had forgotten us." Such thoughts
were certainly justified; the band had been forgotten, even by
those chroniclers of jazz history who somehow managed to
remember the much less successful Ina Ray Hutton, Ada
Leonard, Phil Spitalny, and other "white only" female aggregations of the period.

To my knowledge, only Hollywood script writer, college professor, and band leader Gene Fernett gave any consideration to the International Sweethearts of Rhythm, and
this in his second swing band publication. Swing Out: Great

Negro Dance Bands (1970) devoted a chapter each (half narra-
tion, half photographs) to "twenty-five Negro bands" and one
to "Other Voices." The Sweethearts was one of the "other
voices," meriting inclusion of a photograph and accompanying
caption. Wrote Fernett, "The Sweethearts of Rhythm ...
produced some remarkably fine dance music, and developed
a large following of fans, particularly among Harlem audiences."[14] It is worth noting that Fernett's first book, entitled A Thousand Golden Horns (The Exciting Age of America's Greatest Dance Bands), included only Ina Ray Hutton's
all-girl orchestra, "one of a number ... which proliferated
during the swing era."[15]

I first heard of the International Sweethearts of Rhythm
as a high school student in Dallas, Texas (1942). The Sweethearts were particularly attractive to this young trumpet student (I later abandoned the trumpet for the flute), though I
was never privileged to hear the group play. "Their type of
music" could only be listened to in the privacy of one's room,
a reality in most upwardly mobile black homes.

Local and national newspapers were in great abundance
in the Handy household. Regularly there appeared photographs
of an attractive group of young black females who were gain-
ing wide followings across the country. The group reflected
an air of respectability; their physical stance seemed to du-
plicate all of the elements of correct playing posture that my
trumpet instructor had been emphasizing.

The years passed; the group's name disappeared from
the press, and neither jazz nor general music history books
discussed their existence. I did not recall the name International Sweethearts of Rhythm until my curiosity about black
women instrumentalists arose a few years ago.

The band, composed of fourteen to seventeen young
ladies between the ages of fourteen and nineteen, originated
at Piney Woods Country Life School, Piney Woods, Mississippi. Organized by the school's founder/president Laurence
C. Jones, the band performed under the auspices of the school
from 1937 until April 1941, at which time the girls, their
chaperon/manager, and their tutor turned professional and
severed all connections with the Piney Woods School. "As
their musical proficiency grew so did their fame and they
were soon in demand far beyond the periphery of their Mississippi homeland."[16]

In April 1941, the International Sweethearts of Rhythm moved to Arlington, Virginia. From there the Sweethearts, often referred to as "the darlings of swing," journeyed by way of their own luxury bus to such revered halls as the Apollo Theatre in New York City; the Howard Theatre in Washington, D. C.; the Regal Theatre in Chicago; the Cotton Club in Cincinnati; the Riviera in St. Louis; the Dreamland in Omaha; and Club Plantation and the Million Dollar in Los Angeles. The Sweethearts' talent and audience appeal even carried them as far away as the Olympia Theater in Paris. Over a twelve-year period, the band developed a large following, participated in "Swing Battles of Music" with name bands, established a reputation, broke box-office records, and ensured its place in history (so one would have thought).

While researching her forthcoming book "Jazzwomen," Marian McPartland encountered what Leonard Feather termed "the extraordinary saga" of the International Sweethearts of Rhythm. Her curiosity was further stimulated by meetings with me in 1977 and 1978 in Richmond, Virginia, since I was by then very familiar with the lady musicians from Piney Woods. According to Feather, McPartland proposed to Gregg and Comer that a reunion of the Sweethearts would be a unique idea for the 1980 festival. McPartland would also use this occasion to release her article "The Untold Story of the International Sweethearts of Rhythm," based on material to be used in her forthcoming publication.

Fifteen former Sweethearts--nine original members and six later ones--were located through a miraculous tracking system. I have since discovered that another "original," Nina de La Cruz, was within easy reach in Kansas City, Kansas, but evidently was not contacted. Though she was best remembered as front for the Swinging Rays of Rhythm (Piney Woods' other ladies jazz band), photographs--including one in the festival's souvenir program--confirm the fact that Nina de La Cruz was indeed an "original" Sweetheart. Another original, though absent member, saxophonist Ina Belle Byrd (Little), has since been found in Los Angeles, California. She was with the band through its 1945 sojourn to France and Germany. Unfortunately, recent correspondence to Byrd has brought no response.

An undated (but perhaps late February) letter from Executive Director Comer detailed the Kansas City arrangements:

Dear Sweetheart,

We have arranged for your round trip air transportation, as you know, and your hotel accommodations
--all as guests of the Women's Jazz Festival, Inc.
The accommodations are at Crown Center Hotel,
Kansas City's most luxurious facility; in fact, you
may have seen the Republican Party's headquarters
during their 1976 National Convention. A lot nicer
than sleeping on the bus, huh?!

We ask only that you be responsible for food/bever-
ages during your stay. Everyone on our board is
a "soft touch" though, and maybe some of us can
take you to lunch or dinner as our guests at some
point during our four-day Jazzwomen '80.

As we've told you, one of our board members will
be picking you up at the airport. We have men on
our board as well as women, ... so don't be surprised if a guy wearing one of our T-shirts greets
you when you arrive! We also have several volun-
teers who are not on our board who will be helping
to pick up our Festival guests....

Some of you have asked whether you'll be expected
to perform or not. We are bringing you in to honor
you and not put you on display. If you want to perform, we would LOVE it--but we don't want any of
you to think that performing is a part of the deal.
Whatever you feel like doing--that's what we want
you to do.... At the actual Salute on Sunday afternoon, if any of you want to--again--it's up to you.
We only want you to have a super time. [17]

Pianist Johnnie Mae Rice (Graham) and drummer Pauline Braddy (Williams) arrived in K.C. from Washington, D.C.;
vocalist Evelyn McGee (Stone) from Jamaica, New York; saxophonists Irene Grisham (Veal) from Broomfield, Colorado and
her twin sister Ione Grisham (Miller) from Tougaloo, Mississippi, Helen Saine (Coston) from Chicago, and Willie Mae
Wong (Scott) from Spencerville, Maryland; and trombonists
Judy Bayron (Cammarota) from Buena Vista, California and
Helen Jones (Woods) from Omaha, Nebraska.

These nine were members of the band before the group
severed its relationship with Piney Woods Country Life School;

these were indeed key representatives of "the originals."
However, unlike the other eight, vocalist/temporary leader
Evelyn McGee was not a former student at the school. As
she later explained,

> I was considered an "original" because when I
> joined the group, it was still Piney Woods' band.
> The group played one night in my hometown of
> Anderson, South Carolina. The manager let me
> sing with the group that night. She liked what she
> heard and accompanied me to my house to convince
> my mother that she should let me join the band.
> We were very poor. I'd completed only the ninth
> grade. But as you well know, "You can't study
> when you're hungry." So I left that night [some-
> time in 1940] with all my clothes in a cardboard
> box. [18]

Later members of the group (formally introduced at
the Sunday Salute as special guests) were trumpeter Ernestine
"Tiny" Davis from Chicago; leader/vocalist Anna Mae Winburn (Pilgrim) from Louisville, Kentucky; saxophonist Rosalind Cron from Los Angeles; trumpeters Mim Garfield (Polak)
from Arlington, Massachusetts and Nancy Brown (Pratt) from
Sea Girt, New Jersey; and trumpeter/bassist Toby Butler
from Tacoma, Washington. Cron, Garfield, Brown, and Butler, who are white, provided proof that the group became
truly integrated in the later years.

The band's integration by including white musicians
was a product of the post-Piney Woods years. However,
prior to that time, "international" was the keyword, since
many Piney Woods students and Sweetheart members were of
mixed parentage--American Black and Native American, Mexican, Chinese, or Puerto Rican--which was quite unique for
the state of Mississippi in the 1930s. This fact was visually
verified at the Sunday celebration. It was the belief of or-
ganizer/promoter/director-general Laurence C. Jones that
since all popular female groups of the day were exclusively
white, the mixed blood of his group would be a selling point.
Jones firmly believed that his girls' "emotions, rhythmic
sense and musical tendencies found natural expression in
swing music."[19]

I missed the first two Women's Jazz Festivals, but
was determined not to miss the third. One of the "originals"
was kind enough to alert me to the scheduled Sweethearts
(cont. on page 21)

Left to right: Pianist Johnnie Mae Rice, Women's Jazz
Festival volunteer, and drummer Pauline Braddy.

Relaxing in the Festival's hospitality suite are Braddy, Cron,
Bayron, and Polak (left to right, forefront); and Irene Grisham
and Rice (rear).

Saxophonist Rosalind Cron (left) with trumpeter Mim Polak.

Leader/vocalist
Anna Mae Winburn.

Vocalist Evelyn McGee shares a photograph as pianist Johnnie Mae Rice comments.

A period of listening for
Evelyn McGee at the open
jam session.

Seated: drummer Pauline Braddy, guest host Leonard
Feather, and pianist Johnnie Mae Rice.   Standing: saxophonist Rosalind Cron and trumpeter Mim Polak.

Cron, Rice, and Winburn.

Musical director Jesse Stone listens at the open jam session.

Relaxing in the lobby are (left to right) Braddy, Winburn, Polak, Rice, and Wong.

Saxophonist Cron (left) and trombonist Judy Bayron flank
women's jazz historian/pianist Marian McPartland.

Saxophonist Willie Mae Wong
and her husband, Scotty.

Twins Ione and Irene Grisham, saxophonists.

"Salute" narrator Leonard Feather and a member of National
Public Radio's "Jazz Alive" crew.

"It's been more than thirty years ..." recalled a spectator to trumpeter/vocalist Ernestine "Tiny" Davis.

Pauline Braddy "takes to the skins."

A capacity crowd, with Sweethearts occupying reserved front seats.

Trombonist Helen Jones with one of her three accompanying children.

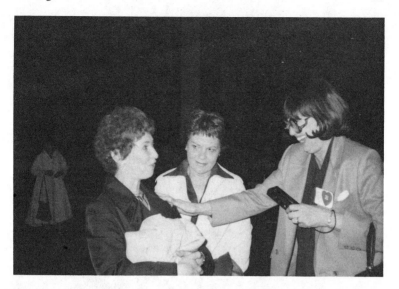

Meeting in the lobby en route to the evening main concert
are (left to right) Cron, Polak, and Saine.

Left to right: Author Handy, Cleo Laine, and Mim Polak.

Posing for "Salute" photographs are all fifteen Sweethearts and narrator Leonard Feather. Left to right: Nancy Brown, Irene and Ione Grisham, Mim Polak, Johnnie Mae Rice, Evelyn McGee, Pauline Braddy, Helen Saine, Rosalind Cron, Judy Bayron, Helen Jones, Ernestine Davis, Toby Butler, Willie Mae Wong, Leonard Feather, and Anna Mae Winburn.

tribute and another shared with me the previously mentioned
letter from Comer. Of my two possible plane routings to
Missouri--through either Chicago or Washington, D. C.--I
fortunately chose the former. The result was a chance meeting with Sweethearts drummer Pauline Braddy and pianist
Johnnie Mae Rice at O'Hare Airport, a shared flight into
Kansas City, and a "formal" welcome at Kansas City International by a festival board member. Our arrival coincided
with the arriving flight of trombonist Helen Jones from Omaha,
Nebraska and the daughter and son-in-law of Jesse Stone, of
whom more will be said later. What a beginning for two and
a half memorable days! Though I had corresponded or talked
by telephone with many of the Sweethearts while preparing the
book Black Women in American Bands and Orchestras, I had
met with only Pauline Braddy.

My two-day visit allowed for interaction with all former Sweethearts on the scene. The personal benefits were
both immediate and long-range. In addition to much artistic
and wholesome fellowship, as well as good music listening,
I was able to prepare another edition of my public affairs
broadcast "Black Virginia" for radio station WRFK-FM (Richmond, Virginia),* establish valuable contacts, and gather much
information for this book.

Since it is the purpose of this publication to fill in the
gaps, to present other sides of the Sweethearts' history and
to tell the story from a black perspective, I am limiting my
discussion here to the Kansas City event--Sunday afternoon,
2:00 to 4:00 p.m., March 23, 1980, at The Meeting Place,
Crown Center Hotel ("A Salute to the Original Sweethearts of
Rhythm")--and to those few hours preceding and immediately
following the event.

I report as one whose parents, grandparents, and
great-grandparents are natives of a Mississippi town (Hazlehurst) less than forty-five minutes away from Piney Woods,
Mississippi; as one who spent many summers in Hazlehurst
throughout childhood and lived in the area for two years as
an adult; as one who has an understanding of, affiliation with,
and commitment to the traditionally black institution; as one
who has carefully researched the International Sweethearts of
Rhythm over a period of years; and as one who has made

---

*Wherever the program's host was, so were "Black Virginia"
listeners.

several visits to Piney Woods, talking with "those who were
there when" and still remember. This will be the commen-
tary of one who rejoiced over the idea of the Women's Jazz
Festival, was dismayed that the black press gave the event
almost no coverage (ironic, in view of the fact that the black
press followed the Sweethearts so avidly during the group's
heyday), and was distressed that so few blacks were in attendance.

        Once at Crown Center, the former Sweethearts began
to seek the whereabouts of other Sweethearts, most of whom
had not seen each other for several decades. I stayed close
to Braddy, who started the chain of introductions to the honorees. The gathering place was the festival's hospitality suite,
where I was able to spend Saturday afternoon talking with and
listening to members of the group. It was there that I met
vocalist Evelyn McGee's husband, Jesse Stone, who was at-
tending for reasons other than mere support of his spouse.

        Jesse Stone, a native of Kansas, was the Sweethearts'
coach and arranger for two years (c. 1942-44). Now in his
seventy-ninth year, Stone had been very much a part of the
Kansas City jazz scene in the 1920s and early 1930s, as band
organizer and leader, pianist, composer, and arranger. Much
of the Sweethearts' success was attributable to his musicianship, experience, and coaching skills.

        I asked Stone to explain the nature of his connection
with the Sweethearts. He responded,

            I was hired to improve their reading abilities, ar-
            range for them and help with presentation ideas.
            I taught them how to bow and taught Anna Mae Win-
            burn [the band's leader] how to properly hold the
            baton.

        Stone also shed some light on his early infatuation
with his current wife, Evelyn McGee, whom he married in
1975.

            When I first met Evelyn, I thought she was about
            fourteen years old. Only later did I discover that
            she was a bit older. She was real tiny and even
            though I had a crush on her then, I had to wait.
            The girls were well protected by Rae Lee Jones
            (chaperon/manager) from everybody but me. Mrs.
            Jones trusted me and I never mixed business with
            pleasure.

Anna Mae Winburn and I had corresponded and con-
versed by telephone, but now we were to meet face to face.
Since I had already documented her personal and career facts,
I was simply curious about how she felt with regard to the
weekend experience. She offered,

> It's the most fantastic thing that ever happened in
> my life--to see these girls after all these years.
> It's simply beautiful.

The ladies were the center of attention throughout the
weekend. They were easily recognized by badges worn on
their lapels--a red heart carrying the name "Sweetheart, "
secured on a white background. Understandably, most of the
time they spent together, generally allowing me to "tag along. "
Three and a half decades of separation was a long time for
a group as closely knit as the Sweethearts of Rhythm. Closeness was essential for the landmark women's group, if for
no other reason than survival.

This was a weekend of sharing and reminiscing, discussing events in their lives since a member left for marriage,
another musical assignment, or, ultimately, since the group
disbanded. Photographs of their children, grandchildren, and
places of residence were passed around. They recalled in-
cidents that only they could fully appreciate, such as the time
a member fell off the bandstand or the time Stone wacked
Braddy across the knuckles in search of percussion perfection.
The Sweethearts discussed work activities (musical and other-
wise), current interests, and ambitions. They also compared
wardrobes and reached agreement on what they would wear to
the grand Salute. Former leader Winburn assembled the girls
in her room for final briefings prior to the appointed hour.
They had class in the late thirties and forties; class they
would exhibit at the two o'clock hour.

Interesting updates came from Jones, Bayron, and
McGee. Helen Jones had married, given birth to four children, completed her bachelor's degree (1977), and was currently working as a social worker. Judy Bayron had finished
high school after marrying and becoming the mother of three.
She finished college after giving birth to her fourth child and
was currently teaching English as a second language.

Following marriage and two children, high school dropout Evelyn McGee secured her GED certificate and was currently enrolled at the Kingsboro Community College, with the

goal of securing a college degree. These educational achievements and pursuits would have made Laurence C. Jones very
proud. For as McGee pointed out, "Jones was a man of vision. To him, education was essential."

   Sunday morning afforded me an opportunity to talk in
the hotel lobby with Bayron, Wong, and Jones, as they sat
anxiously awaiting the arrival of Helen Saine. Speaking of
the festival and the involvement of the International Sweethearts of Rhythm, Bayron said,

> This is a most fantastic thing. We didn't think
> we'd ever be able to see each other again--after
> such a long time, after we've all married and have
> grown children--to talk about our past and the fun
> that we had on the road. We should have been
> here earlier.

Willie May Wong, whose husband was also on hand to share
in the festivities, expressed herself accordingly,

> A wonderful feeling. Really a surprise. I never
> dreamed that we could get together. But as my
> daughter said, "Better late than never."

Added Jones, who was accompanied by three of her four children,

> I'm very pleased and I'm flattered that they thought
> this much of us, because sometimes people go for-
> ever and never receive any type of recognition for
> what they've done. Just think, it's been thirty some
> years since we've seen each other collectively.

Bayron threw some light on those early years.

> Being very young, we were naive. We were seeing
> so many places. We were missing a lot of educa-
> tion, though we had a tutor. Many of us hadn't
> even graduated from high school. But we learned
> from the experience. Our music has opened a lot
> of doors for women. It's an honor being here and
> being praised so highly. We didn't give ourselves
> the credit we're getting these four days.

Jones continued,

For what we had to offer then, we were ahead of
our time. The rock 'n roll they're playing today
we played in the '30s and '40s. People paid it no
attention then. I think we were real trailblazers.

Seats were at a premium as early as sixty minutes
prior to the long-awaited hour of 2:00 p.m. The first rows
(to the left of the stage and near the main entrance) were
reserved for the rejoined, now celebrated International Sweethearts of Rhythm--the honorees.

McPartland was the scheduled narrator, but relinquished
the position to Leonard Feather and instead, positioned herself with the Sweethearts. Music was provided by the Bonnie
Janofsky-Ann Patterson Big Band from Los Angeles (since re-
named "Maiden Voyage"). The band included one black, saxo-
phonist/flutist Fostina Dixon, who we have since learned was
a substitute.[20] According to narrator Feather, the Janofsky-
Patterson band was "an example of what is happening in
terms of this kind of orchestra today--a sort of logical continuation of what happened back in those days."[21]

The Salute began with two numbers from the Janofsky-
Patterson band, as people continued to arrive and the Sweethearts made their grand entrance. The only missing Sweetheart was Ernestine "Tiny" Davis, who was expected but had
not yet appeared. Feather began,

> This is a very special, unique and sentimental oc-
> casion for a number of us here today and most
> particularly for the women I want to introduce--
> nine original members in our midst, and the other
> members, including their conductor Anna Mae Win-
> burn.

He then acknowledged the presence of Marian McPartland, "a
one woman source of research, one without whose efforts this
whole thing may not have ever happened."

All nine "originals" were individually asked to the
microphone, presented a sweetheart rose and invited to make
comments about the glorious years. Trombonist Helen Jones,
the adopted daughter of Laurence C. Jones, pointed out that
Dr. Jones wanted her to learn the violin but finally consented
to let her study the trombone. She added,

> Dr. Jones loved music--all kinds. He was a

musician himself. Following a trip to Chicago
where he heard the Ina Ray Hutton Melodears, he
began selecting girls from the forty-five piece all-
girl marching band that existed at Piney Woods
Country Life School.

Drummer Pauline Braddy added that before long thereafter, the girls were on the road with a manager, chaperon,
and tutor.   Filling the assignment of chaperon/manager/head
mistress was Rae Lee Jones, who was brought in from Omaha,
Nebraska.   When Feather asked if the band was run more
like a school than an orchestra, Braddy responded:

Young ladies don't smoke; young ladies don't sit at
the bar; young ladies always carry their gloves and
wear their hats. Young ladies never dance with
fellows without jackets and ties. It was kind of
rough on the fellows and tough on the girls, too.

With a glance toward Willie Mae Wong's husband, she added,

Scotty knew because he married one. You didn't
break many rules without [Mrs. Jones] knowing.

Braddy had pointed out earlier that it was probably this "Rae
Lee Jones control" that made the orchestra as strong as it
was and held it together for so many years.

The Grisham twins made a joint trip to the microphone.
A bit surprising to master of ceremonies Feather and the capacity crowd was the response they gave to the question,
"What were the first really important things that happened on
the road, once you got away from the school?" First there
was silence; then came, "When the band left, our sister came
and got us. " Neither the Salute nor McPartland's "The Untold Story of the International Sweethearts of Rhythm" revealed
the fact that not all the Sweethearts deserted Laurence C.
Jones and Piney Woods School in 1941, and that the Grisham
twins returned to Piney Woods when the band decided to strike
out on its own. One of the twins worked at the school (following graduation) until 1975. Saxophonist Helen Saine also
returned to Piney Woods, though not by personal choice. Her
return was dictated by the Virginia Welfare Department because she was a minor. Once of age however, she rejoined
the group at its Arlington, Virginia home base.

Feather then moved on to the matter of finances. He

properly called on the group's treasurer, Willie Mae Wong,
who joined the band at age sixteen.   Feather asked if the
group made a satisfactory living.   Wong replied,

> The originals started out receiving one dollar a
> day for food and a one dollar a week allowance,
> for a total of eight dollars.   That continued for
> years.   We got a substantial raise to fifteen dol-
> lars a night, which for three nights was forty-five
> dollars a week.   Financially, the originals didn't
> make anything.   We were incorporated.   Whenever
> the bus that we traveled on needed a new tire or
> there was engine trouble, we had to donate out of
> our money.   But some of the professionals I under-
> stand were making one hundred and one hundred-
> fifty dollars a week.

Sighs of disbelief could be heard from the audience.
Feather commented, "I guess mostly you stayed on for the
joy of being a part of it all."   He then inquired about the
girls' earnings from the RCA record that he produced in
1946.   Responded Wong, "I wasn't treasurer then, but I was
still getting my fifteen dollars.   For the record sessions,
we didn't get anything extra."

An interesting update of personal activities was offered
by saxophonist Helen Saine, who upon leaving the Sweethearts
followed briefly a career as a model.   Then came marriage
and a family (one son accompanied her to Kansas City), followed by a return to the classroom.   She completed the bachelor's degree (Magna Cum Laude), earned membership in the
prestigious Phi Beta Kappa, and was currently working on
her master's degree at the University of Chicago.   This
represents quite a feat for one who was denied her transcript
from Piney Woods and of necessity entered college with a
GED certificate.

Rosalind Cron, one of the white members, elaborated
on what it was like traveling as a racially mixed group
throughout the U.S.A. in the 1940s.

> We white girls were supposed to say "My mother
> was black and my father was white."   I swore to
> this sheriff in El Paso that I was black.   But he
> went through my wallet and found this photo of my
> mother and father and it just didn't jell.   So I
> spent my night in jail.

To this Anna Mae Winburn added,

> We had so many types in the band. Down South
> they couldn't tell whites from blacks. The white
> girls had to put on dark makeup, but of course
> we couldn't paint their blue eyes.

And then came vocalist Evelyn McGee, the only original Sweetheart still musically active. Accompanied by
McPartland, the gifted songbird gave a spellbinding rendition
of "Unforgettable," dedicated to her sisters, the International
Sweethearts of Rhythm. In the second verse she called
names: "Sweethearts, you're unforgettable"; "Marion McPartland, you're unforgettable"; "Carol Comer, you're unforgettable"; "Dianne Gregg, you're unforgettable." The audience
loved it.

McGee next started to sing "I Cried for You." Drummer Pauline Braddy could contain herself no longer. More
than twelve years had passed since she touched the skins,
but only she was aware of this. Nancy Brown (Pratt) bor-
rowed a trumpet from a Janofsky-Patterson band member and
lent her artistry to the tune. The crowd became ecstatic.
This truly was a nostalgic trip for drivers (the Sweethearts)
and passengers (the audience) alike. As Feather later indicated, "It was less the performance than the good vibes that
established this as a memorable event."[22]

It was regrettable that latercomer Ernestine "Tiny"
Davis didn't share her talents with the audience (for reasons unknown). Her "ready" mouthpiece was clearly evident and Festival correspondence had expressed the hope
that she would bring her trumpet. From early reviews
of Sweetheart performances and reports from those who
have heard her recently in Chicago, she too could have
set the house ablaze.

In the closing moments, Feather shared telegrams to
the honorees from then President Jimmy Carter, jazz
promoter/producer Norman Granz, trumpeter Clark Terry,
and former Sweetheart member (as well as a 1978 and 1979
Women's Jazz Festival participant) bassist/vocalist Carline
Ray. For the Salute finale, a joyous fifteen ladies were surrounded by hundreds of wellwishers and were then swept to
the lobby for official Festival Salute photographs.

Wanting nothing to dispel the memory, I accepted the

Salute as my Festival finale. More conversation with small
groups and individual Sweetheart members was my only remaining desire. During the course of such meetings, I encountered one of my all-time favorite vocalists, Cleo Laine,
who kindly consented to pose for pictures with a few of the
Sweethearts as well as with me. Forgoing the "live" Cleo
Laine performance that was to take place a few hours later
was a real sacrifice for me, but she had been in attendance
at the afternoon Salute and understood.

Billboard journalist Paul Hohl designated the Third
Women's Jazz Festival superior by far to the first two and
designated the Salute as one of the Festival's most memorable events. 23   The Sweethearts had indeed fulfilled the wish
of Festival organizers and planners: they had enjoyed a
"super time." Leaving the Salute area, I overheard one
member exclaim, "That was like being in the Twilight Zone."

The following morning, still concerned over the poor
turnout by blacks at the special event and the lack of publicity in the black press, I placed a call to the Kansas City
Call office. The paper's advertising manager offered this
explanation:

> If you want the black audience, you must contact
> the black press. This has been true historically
> and is still true today.   If you don't advertise with
> us, we don't publicize. 24

Master of Ceremony Feather's review of the Salute
[with additional historical data] was carried in the Sunday,
April 13, 1980, issue of the Los Angeles Times. His opening sentence read as follows: "It was a school reunion unlike
any other in recorded history." The same article was carried one week later by Jackson, Mississippi's Clarion-Ledger/
Jackson Daily News. The headlines read: "The Sweetheart[s]
Hold School Reunion at Piney Woods" [emphasis added]25--
perhaps Mississippi's first reminder of its late 1930s-1940s
musical gift to America. My copy of the Mississippi reprint
was provided by a proud Piney Woods alumnus.

Weeks later, I asked all fifteen ladies, "What are
your feelings about the event?" Five responded:

> I thought it was the greatest thing that could have
> happened to us, even though we were old before
> they made us famous. [Pauline Braddy]

It was an experience I'll never forget and will
cherish forever. [Johnnie Mae Rice]

I thought it was great. The event made me realize
that I must keep singing. [Evelyn McGee]

It was a catalyst in making my dream of seeing my
beloved sisters again come true. [Toby Butler]

I know of no other musical group--male or female--
that has ever been honored in such a way. So we
are forever grateful for the moments we had together and the tribute itself. [Rosalind Cron]

NOTES

1. "Jazz Festival Will Feature Women" Richmond Times
    Dispatch, November 20, 1977, p. J-10.

2. Maryanne Vollers, "Women's Jazz Festival Makes a
    Joyful Noise," Rolling Stone, May 18, 1978, p. 19.

3. Shifra Stein, "Festival Proves Jazz Prowess of Women,"
    The Kansas City Times, March 17, 1978, p. 8C.

4. Stash Records: ST-111, "All Women Groups"; ST-112,
    "Pianists"; ST-109, "Jazz Women: A Feminist Retro-
    spective."

5. John S. Wilson, "Women in Jazz, Past and Present,"
    The New York Times, June 11, 1978, pp. D25, 38.

6. Ibid.

7. Shifra Stein, "Jazz Festival Gives Women Performers a
    Showcase," The Kansas City Star, March 18, 1979,
    pp. 1E, 9E. The statement "no major festival had
    included women musicians within its format" is, of
    course, false.

8. "Women's Lib in New York," The Black Perspective in
    Music, Spring 1974, p. 107.

9. Burt Koball, "Women in Jazz," International Musician,
    July 1975, p. 12.

10. John S. Wilson, "Salute to Women in Jazz to Open,"

The New York Times, June 25, 1978, p. 39; and "UJC
Salutes Women in Jazz at Birdland June 26-29," The
Jazz Catalyst, June, 1978, pp. 1, 8.

11. Nat Hentoff, "The Women of Jazz," The Chronicle Review, April 30, 1979, p. R20.

12. Lorraine Shalvoy, "Women's Week Will Stress Job
Goals," The Kansas City Star, March 20, 1980, p. 9.

13. Women's Jazz Festival Program, 1980, p. 16.

14. Gene Fernett, Swing Out: Great Negro Bands. Midland, Mich.: Pendell Company, 1970, p. 166.

15. Gene Fernett, A Thousand Golden Horns. Midland,
Mich.: Pendell Company, 1966, p. 107.

16. Women's Jazz Festival Program, March 1980.

17. Correspondence from Carol Comer (Women's Jazz Festival, Inc.) to "Original" International Sweethearts of
Rhythm, undated.

18. Telephone conversation with McGee (Stone), July 25,
1981.

19. "Sweethearts of Rhythm," The Chicago Defender, June
22, 1940, p. 20.

20. Leonard Feather, "Women's Jazz Festival," Down Beat,
July 1980, p. 58.

21. It was more of "a logical continuation of what happened
back in those days" when Maiden Voyage appeared on
the NBC Tonight Show a few weeks following the Salute
to the International Sweethearts of Rhythm event. In
recalling names of pioneering all-women's big bands,
Maiden Voyage spokesperson and host Johnny Carson
could remember only two names: Phil Spitalny and
Ina Ray Hutton.

22. Feather, "Women's Jazz Festival," op. cit.

23. Paul Hohl, "Kansas City's Women's Jazz Fest Superior
by Far to First Two," Billboard, April 5, 1980,
pp. 66, 69.

24. Telephone conversation with James R. Benton, March
    24, 1980.

25. Leonard Feather, "The Memories of Sweethearts," Los
    Angeles Times--Calendar, April 13, 1980, p. 64; and
    "The Sweetheart[s] Hold School Reunion at Piney
    Woods," The Clarion Ledger/Jackson Daily News,
    April 20, 1980, Section I, p. 4.

CHAPTER II

For a fuller appreciation of the International Sweethearts of
Rhythm and their many accomplishments, it is essential that
we place their creation and existence in a historical context.
The reader must first understand the mood of the times when
Piney Woods Country Life School came into existence (1909);
when founder/president Laurence C. Jones began sending out
his first musical messengers (singing groups--early 1920s);
and the years of instrumental training, early tours, and the
break into the "big time" (1935-1941).   One must understand
the state of affairs in terms of race relations and know some
of the historical paradoxes that affected black Americans.

It will also be helpful to know something about the
Sweethearts' home State--Mississippi, often referred to as
"The Closed Society."   Still other essential background information relates to how black Americans fitted into the
scheme of things artistic; what roles women (generally) and
black women (specifically) assumed in the work force; and the
status of women in the music world.   Finally, the question
arises, what was the Big Band era all about and who were
the International Sweethearts of Rhythm's competitors?

MOOD OF THE TIMES / RACE RELATIONS

Following the Civil War, American blacks were largely illit-
erate.   Black literacy in 1870 was 18.6 percent; by 1880,
30 percent; and by 1890, 42.9 percent, thanks to the efforts
of the Freedmen's Aid Societies, missionary associations,
churches, and blacks themselves.   Various philanthropic

33

agencies provided buildings, endowment scholarships, and
support for teacher training and industrial education. Always,
"Christianization of the Negro" was deemed the necessary
first step.

Moving into the twentieth century, blacks represented
11. 5 percent of the population and 89. 7 percent of all blacks
lived in the South.   Illiteracy among the race stood at 44. 5
percent. The black leader of the times was Booker T. Washington (1856-1915), who in his Cotton States Exhibition speech
in Atlanta, Georgia, September 18, 1895, placed equality of
the races on the back burner and advanced to the forefront
economics and vocational education. Washington expressed
himself accordingly:

> No race can prosper until it learns there is as
> much dignity in tilling a field as in writing a poem.

>   . . .

> In all things purely social we can be as separate
> as the five fingers, and yet one as the hand in all
> things essential to mutual progress.

Washington promoted the gospel of industrial education,
believing that from a mastery of trades, skilled wage earners
could acquire the necessary wealth to prepare for the profes-
sions. His educational philosophies were put into practice at
Tuskegee Institute in Alabama, which he founded in 1881.

Washington's economic philosophies were realized
through the organization of the National Negro Business
League, often referred to as the black man's Chamber of
Commerce. The organizational meeting took place in 1900
in Boston, with four hundred delegates from thirty-four states
in attendance. In less than a decade, membership of the
league (both male and female) had grown to represent every
section of the country and every department and phase of
business life. At a 1909 meeting in Louisville, Kentucky,
Washington announced in his annual address:

> We have at least 500 Negro Business Leagues
> scattered throughout the country. When we began
> work there were few drug stores under the control
> of black people; now we have nearly 200. A few
> years ago, there were only about half a dozen
> Negro banks in the country; now there are 47.

> Dry-good stores, grocery stores and industrial
> enterprises to the number of nearly 10, 000 have
> sprung up in all parts of the country. [1]

Not all agreed with Washington's philosophies. His
most vocal critic and challenger was sociologist/civil rights
activist W. E. B. DuBois (1868-1963), who expressed his views
about the man and his ideas in his book The Souls of Black
Folk, published in 1903. DuBois referred to Washington's
philosophy in the following pronouncement:

> Mr. Washington distinctly asks that black people
> give up, at least for the present, three things--
>   First, political power;
>   Second, insistence on civil rights;
>   Third, higher education of Negro Youth--
> and concentrate all their energies on industrial
> education, the accumulation of wealth, and the
> conciliation of the South.

DuBois continued by objecting strenuously,

> Mr. Washington's programme practically accepts
> the alleged inferiority of the Negro race. . . .
> [T]he reaction from the sentiment of war time
> has given impetus to race-prejudice against Ne-
> groes and Mr. Washington withdraws many high
> demands of Negroes as men and American citi-
> zens. [2]

The educational points of view of these two dynamic
personalities represented a continuing philosophical controversy, still debated in the last decades of the twentieth century. We shall note Laurence C. Jones' assessment of the
two philosophies later.

The "Committee on Work Among Negroes" of the
International Sunday-School Association convened an important
conference at Clifton, Massachusetts during the summer of
1908. Of the seventy-five guests, fifty were white and
twenty-five were black. Representatives from thirty-seven
black colleges and schools, nine missionary organizations,
and twelve religious denominations were in attendance.

For three days the participants considered how to coordinate the Sunday-School movement with the educational
work among blacks. The connection was understandable

since, as Booker T. Washington pointed out, "The first
schools for Negroes in this country were Sunday-Schools,
and the first school book the Negro knew was the Bible."[3]
Conference proceedings were reported two years later, under
the title An Era of Progress and Promise: 1863-1910 (The
Clifton Conference). The editor, also the conference con-
vener, included testimony from white teachers who had given
"fifteen to forty years of service in the education of the Negro." The following represents shared thinking on the subject of "The Kind of Education the Negro Needs" at the time
Piney Woods Country Life School was founded:

> What the Negro masses need is to have communi-
> cated to them the largest possible number of im-
> pulses towards true religion, temperance, thrift,
> better home life, and larger life in every way.
>
> . . .
>
> A good missionary in the homes of the Negroes
> will do more for the race than five Greek and
> Latin professors.
>
> . . .
>
> After thirty-five years' experience in educational
> work in the South, I believe in this outline of
> policy for the Negro.
> 1) For the relative few: Preparation for leader-
>   ship, by education in the best schools avail-
>   able.
> 2) For the many: Industrial and economic effi-
>   ciency, through acquaintance and practice with
>   the best forms of manual training.
> 3) For all: Religious and social betterment,
>   with property ownership, that we may have
>   a general uplift of society, home and church.[4]

The Superintendent of Education of the American Baptist Home Mission Society, at the time aiding twenty-six "Institutions for the Education of the Negro" in thirteen different
states, wrote the following as his recommendations: 1) common school training for all; 2) training for spiritual leadership; and 3) training for industrial and agricultural leadership. [5]

In 1909, twenty-six-year-old Laurence Clifton Jones,

a University of Iowa (Iowa City) educated black man, arrived
in Braxton, Mississippi with a determination to found a school,
which he called Piney Woods Country Life School. He em-
braced fully the concept of "head, heart, and hands" education and was therefore more philosophically allied to those
theories preached and practiced by Booker T. Washington.

Schools were all but non-existent in the heart of Mississippi's piney-woods country, though for years area blacks
had been trying to develop one. Populist Governor James
Vardeman had only recently abolished the only black normal
school in the state, explaining that "Negro education is a
threat to white supremacy." Seventeen "Mississippi Institutions for the Education of the Negro" existed at the time,
many carrying the name College or University (though most
were little more than good elementary schools), but absolutely
nothing existed in the vicinity of Braxton, on the border of
Rankin and Simpson counties.

There were other events of the early twentieth century
worth noting. W. E. B. DuBois called a conference of black
leaders in 1905, held at Niagara Falls, Canada. Twenty-nine
members of the "Talented Tenth," from thirteen states and
the District of Columbia, were represented. Their Declara-
tion of Principles demanded equal economic opportunity, equal
education, a fair administration of justice, and an end to
segregation. The Niagara Falls Movement represented the
genesis of the National Association for the Advancement of
Colored People (NAACP), which formally began in 1909. The
following year, DuBois represented the NAACP at the International Congress of Races meeting in London, primarily to
counteract Booker T. Washington, who was also in attendance.

Also at this time the Committee on Urban Conditions
Among Negroes (1910), The National League for the Protec-
tion of Colored Women (1905), and The Committee on Industrial Conditions for Negroes in New York (1906) merged to
found The National Urban League in 1911. Its primary purpose was the improvement of living conditions and the
strengthening of family life. Both the NAACP and the Urban
League were founded in New York City, but their concerns
and programs were felt nationwide.

In 1915, the NAACP unsuccessfully tried to prevent
the showing of D. W. Griffiths' film "Birth of a Nation,"
wherein the Ku Klux Klan was glorified and blacks denegrated.
The same year, University of Chicago and Harvard trained

historian Carter G. Woodson (1875-1950) founded the Association for the Study of Negro Life and History. The following
year, Woodson began publishing the scholarly quarterly The
Journal of Negro History. In response to the first issue,
the Boston Herald reported,

> When men of any race begin to show pride in their
> own antecedents we have one of the surest signs of
> prosperity and rising civilization. ... Hitherto the
> history of the Negro race has been written chiefly
> by white men; now the educated Negroes of this
> country have decided to search out and tell the his-
> toric achievements of their race in their own way
> and from their own point of view. [6]

When the United States entered World War I in 1917,
DuBois, editor of the NAACP's official publication, The Crisis, wrote an editorial entitled "Close Ranks," suggesting
that "while this war lasts, forget our special grievances and
close our ranks shoulder to shoulder with our white fellow
citizens...."[7] More than 400,000 Blacks complied. During
the war, blacks purchased $250,000,000 worth of bonds and
stamps for the war effort, despite the fact that more than
1,000 had been lynched since 1900 and second class citizen-
ship was black status nationally.

Their efforts to "make the world safe for democracy"
were futile however, since during the second half of 1919,
seventy-six blacks were lynched, twenty-five race riots occurred, and a re-birth of the Ku Klux Klan was in evidence.
By 1920, Klan membership in twenty states had reached
100,000.

Black historian Benjamin Quarles gave this description
of the era of the twenties:

> [A]s never before, Negroes began to realize that
> their roots were deep in the land of their birth,
> and that colored men and women had contributed
> significantly to American history and culture. [8]

The chief spokesman for black masses was Marcus
Garvey who arrived in New York City in 1916 from Jamaica,
British West Indies and began immediately to gain support
for the nationalist organization he started in Jamaica, the
Universal Negro Improvement Association. Having expressed
interest in industrial training for the natives of Jamaica to

Booker T. Washington, Garvey was encouraged by Washington to come to America. Though Washington died before his arrival, Garvey traveled throughout the country studying conditions of blacks in America. Garvey's first convention of the UNIA was held in New York City in August 1919 and lasted for one month. Upon its conclusion, three thousand delegates unanimously passed a Bill of Rights for Negroes. Wrote essayist, novelist, poet, and diplomat James Weldon Johnson (1871-1938),

> [A]n embryo army was set up with Marcus Garvey as commander-in-chief. A mission was sent to Liberia to negotiate an agreement whereby the Universal Improvement Association would establish a colony.... Garvey became a world figure, and his movements and utterances were watched by the great governmental powers. [9]

Garvey's steamship company The Black Star Line (established to transport interested blacks to Africa) collapsed in December 1921; he was arrested and charged with use of the mails to defraud, was indicted by a Federal grand jury in February 1922, and was deported to Jamaica in December 1926. Nevertheless, Marcus Garvey, perhaps more than anyone else, caused black masses to take pride in their African heritage and rid themselves of all feelings of inferiority.

The 1920s saw a steady migration of Southern blacks to the North and West. In 1925, sixteen organizations convened a National Interracial Conference in Cincinnati, Ohio "to construct a reasonably faithful contemporary picture of Negro life and the status of race relations." The theme was "Race Problems in the United States in the Light of Social Research." Dr. Charles S. Johnson, former editor of the Urban League's journal Opportunity and then Head of Fisk University's Department of Social Science, served as research secretary and was charged with the responsibility of compiling the data for publication. [10]

As a final note about this decade, it should be recalled that Negro History Week was established in 1926 by Carter G. Woodson. Dominating the twenties were the Harlem Renaissance and black women blues singers, both of which will be discussed later in this chapter.

The collapse of the stock market in October 1929

obviously had the greatest impact on the country's black citizens, who by 1930 represented 9.7 percent of the total population, with 78.7 percent of the black population now residing in the South.   But new hope came in 1932 with the election of President Franklin D. Roosevelt and his pledge of a "new deal."

The Civilian Conservation Corps (CCC), a relief measure, was established in 1933 and though blacks represented almost 10 percent of the population, participation by them in the CCC was only 5.3 percent.   By 1935, black families receiving relief represented 21.5 percent of the total black population, compared with 12.8 percent of the white population. The Work Projects Administration (WPA) was created in 1935 by executive order of President Roosevelt to provide useful public work for needy unemployed persons.   Originally called the Works Progress Administration, the program lasted for eight years and though sponsored primarily by state or local agencies, the cost was borne chiefly by the federal government.   Establishment of the Federal Arts Project of the WPA gave work to creative artists and performers.

On Easter Sunday, 1939, world famous black contralto Marian Anderson sang to an audience of more than 75,000 gathered on the steps of the Lincoln Memorial when the Daughters of the American Revolution denied her performance rights to appear at Constitution Hall, which they owned. Eleanor Roosevelt withdrew her D.A.R. membership in protest and two thirds of the American public approved of her action.

By 1940, blacks represented 9.8 percent of the population and most still lived in southern rural areas.   Per capita expenditure for public education for blacks was $18,82; for whites, $58.69.   Mississippi was expending five times as much per white child as per black child.   At Piney Woods, Mississippi (by this time the school had acquired its own post office), Laurence C. Jones' International Sweethearts of Rhythm was reaching heights far exceeding the president's original dreams and manager Rae Lee Jones was negotiating the band's movement into the "big time."   America was on the brink of World War II and black/white relationships were of secondary importance.

FOCUS ON MISSISSIPPI

It may be recalled that in Mississippi state government,

moderates and liberals alike inevitably asked for "more time" on all federal, state, and local rulings that positively affected her black residents, and consistently proclaimed "NEVER" to all suggestions of integration. This state that joined the Union in 1817 is the one that most opposed blacks exercising the right of franchise under the guarantees of the so-called "War Amendments" and paved "the way of intervention" legally for other Southern states to follow.

In 1879, Mississippi threatened to close the Mississippi River "by sinking all boats carrying Negroes." Shipping companies resumed service only under threats of Federal intervention. This is the state whose elected governor in 1903 (Vardeman) proudly earned the title "The Great White Father," and whose white citizens were angered by President Theodore Roosevelt's having invited Booker T. Washington to dinner at the White House. When Roosevelt appointed a black postmistress at Indianola, the post office had to be closed because the white citizens there boycotted it.

It was Mississippi's U.S. Senator (Theodore G. Bilbo) who introduced Senate Bill 2231 in 1939, proposing resettlement of American Blacks in Africa. The following year he wrote:

> If we could effect the resettlement of from five to eight million Negroes who are now ready to go to Africa, we could solve the unemployment problem and would be able soon to do away with the necessity of these large annual appropriations for relief. [11]

Until most recently, Mississippi had been justifiably labeled the prime example of institutional racism, the tragedy of the South and the nation's most unattractive image.

School attendance by blacks in Mississippi between the ages of seven and twenty in 1910 was 52.7 percent; in 1920, 55.8 percent; and in 1930, 66.1 percent. Of course the emphasis was on elementary training, where the program lasted under six months per year for both races and still less for blacks alone. Public secondary training was practically nil.

According to the United States Census of 1920-32, the illiteracy rate among blacks in Mississippi was 23.2 percent, as compared with 2.7 percent among whites. Only the states of South Carolina, Alabama, and Louisiana had higher rates of black illiteracy. Almost three quarters of all blacks

"gainfully employed" were engaged in agriculture, with 11. 5
percent in domestic and personal service, 7. 4 percent in
manufacturing and mechanical industries and 1. 3 percent in
professional service. Of the farm operators, 87. 6 percent
were tenants. Only 13. 3 percent of the black population was
urban, compared with 20. 5 percent of the white population.
Home ownership among black families was 17. 1 percent, compared with 48. 5 percent among white families.

By the end of the 1920s, Mississippi had ten black
colleges, of which seven were four-year institutions and three
were two-year institutions. Only two were publicly supported.
For every 1, 000 blacks of college age, only 8. 7 percent were
enrolled.

When Laurence C. Jones founded his school, the State
was paying $10. 60 for each white child and $2. 26 for each
black child. Following several years of research, the Bureau
of Education investigating "Negro Education--Private and
Higher Schools for Colored People in the United States" released a report in 1917 recommending the following for Mississippi:

1) Strengthen and extend the elementary school
   system;
2) Increase teacher-training facilities;
3) More provisions for instruction in gardening,
   household arts, and simple industries;
4) More instruction in agriculture and in the problems of rural life, so that teachers and leaders
   may be developed for a people primarily rural;
   and
5) The maintenance of industrial high schools in
   cities. [12]

The report, prepared in cooperation with the Phelps-
Stokes Fund, indicated that Piney Woods Country Life School
was supported largely by Dr. Jones' energy in securing funds,
receiving very small appropriations from Simpson and Rankin
County school funds. Enrollment had reached one hundred
fifty-eight students (all elementary), with seventy boarders.
Eight faculty members taught the basic elementary courses,
in addition to carpentry, blacksmithing, shoemaking, and
printing to the boys and sewing and broommaking to the girls.
All worked on the farm.

Financial accounting for the school year 1912-13 dis-

closed the following: Income, $3,269; Expenditures, $3,617;
Indebtedness, $348; Value of Plant, $9,300.   Expenditures
included $645 for teachers' salaries.   The Bureau of Educa-
tion recommended for Piney Woods Country Life School:

1) That the institution be developed as a county
   training school;
2) That industrial training be limited to manual
   training in wood and iron theory and practice
   of gardening for boys and cooking and sewing
   for girls; and
3) That aid be provided to build a simple, substan-
   tial plant. [13]

W. E. B. DuBois reacted not so favorably to the Bureau's
report and wrote a few months following its release:

Thinking Negroes ... and other persons who know
the problem of educating the American Negro will
regard the ... report, despite its many praise-
worthy features, as a dangerous and in many respects unfortunate publication.

In typical DuBois fashion, he opposed the insistence on
manual training, industrial education, and agricultural training.   He questioned what the results would be when philanthropic agencies such as the Jeanes Fund sent in a person to
introduce "shuck mat work, simple sewing, patch quilting for
girls, repair of buildings and woodworking for boys."[14]

Embracing both Washington's and DuBois' philosophies
of education, in view of his awareness of the realities around
him, Laurence Jones continued on his course and by the end
of the 1930s he had extended Piney Woods' services to include
grades kindergarten through junior college and courses beyond
the scope of those recommended by the Bureau of Education
in 1917.   DuBois objected to the report's suggestion that private schools in the South should "cooperate" with Southern
whites, but Jones contended that much of his and Piney Woods'
success was the result of a cooperative effort of both races,
the beneficiaries being Piney Woods students.   This black/
white relationship was a point always stressed by Jones and
other chroniclers of the school's history.

BLACK AMERICANS IN THE SCHEME
OF THINGS ARTISTIC

Blacks laid claim to legitimate theater as early as 1821,
with the establishment of the African Grove Theatre at the
corner of Bleecker and Mercer Streets in New York City.
Productions included "Othello," "Richard III," and other classic plays, with music provided by an integrated three-piece
orchestra--violin, clarinet, and bass fiddle. But the conduct
of whites (accommodated at the rear), "out for a lark and
causing disorder" led to the theatre's closing after only a few
months. The company was back in business, however, by
1823 and was known to have existed (in some form) until 1832.
From this company came the names James Hewlett and Ira
Aldridge, the latter of whom distinguished himself at a later
date as one of the greatest Shakespearean actors of his era
in the leading capitals of Europe.

That blacks were skilled entertainers was evident from
the additional duties they assumed as slaves. According to
James Weldon Johnson,

> Every plantation had its talented band that could
> crack Negro jokes, and sing and dance to the ac-
> companiment of the banjo and the bones.... When
> the wealthy plantation-owner wished to entertain
> and amuse his guests, he needed only to call for
> his troupe of black minstrels. [15]

White actors realized the commercial value of black
theatrics, so they blackened their faces and took to the road
with black imitations early in the 1840s. By the late 1860s,
blacks were to follow the "on stage" patterns established by
whites and, also with blackened faces, they embarked on the
professional minstrel stages impersonating themselves. From
this era came such names as Billy Kersands, Sam Lucas,
Gussie Davis, and James Bland. Again in the words of
James Weldon Johnson,

> Minstrelsy ... fixed the tradition of the Negro as
> only an irresponsible, happy-go-lucky, wide-grinning,
> loud-laughing, shuffling, banjo-playing, singing,
> dancing sort of being. Nevertheless, these com-
> panies ... provide[d] stage training and theatrical
> experience for a large number of coloured men.
> They provided an essential training and theatrical
> experience which, at the time, could not have been
> acquired from any other source. [16]

Subsequent developments in terms of black theatrical directions and achievements--musical comedy and vaudeville-- is the topic of Henry T. Sampson's book <u>Blacks in Blackface: A Source Book on Early Black Musical Shows</u> (Scarecrow Press, 1980). Sampson premises the need for his report on the fact that

> many of the songs, dances, comedy routines, and
> music which eventually became an integral part of
> the American musical theatre originated in pioneer
> black musical shows, [and] omission of the informa-
> tion has resulted in a significant gap in the history
> of the growth and development of this art form. [17]

The skill of black craftpersons is still recognizable (particularly in the Old South) if not often acknowledged. Utilizing talents carried over from ancestral Africa, early blacks labored as carpenters, weavers, woodcarvers, black-smiths, and harness and cabinet makers. Tom Day the Cabinetmaker had established his own workshop in North Carolina as early as 1818. Despite limited opportunities for development as sculptors and painters, the works of sculptress Edmonia Lewis and painters Robert Duncanson, Edward Bannister, and Henry O. Tanner must be included in America's list of contributions to world art of the era. America must also acknowledge that the nation's first art club was established by Bannister (its only member) in Providence, Rhode Island, around 1870.

By mid nineteenth century, blacks began claiming a stake in America's literary tradition in the form of slave narratives, protest and propaganda poems, and novels. Of particular importance was the name of reformer, historian, essayist, novelist, playwright William Wells Brown (1816-1884). National magazines were publishing the short stories of Charles Waddell Chesnutt as early as 1887. Paul Laurence Dunbar established himself as a gifted American poet with the publication of his first collection of poems, entitled <u>Oak and Ivy</u> (1893). Dunbar's novel <u>The Uncalled</u> (1898) and Chesnutt's short stories "The Conjure Woman" and "The Wife of His Youth and Other Stories of the Color Line" (1899) began es-tablishing black credibility in the area of prose fiction. Not-able contributors as essayists between the years 1903 and 1920 were W. E. B. DuBois and James Weldon Johnson, with such published collections as <u>The Souls of Black Folk</u> (DuBois, 1903) and <u>The Autobiography of an Ex-Coloured Man</u> (Johnson, 1912).

James V. Hatch edited <u>Black Theater USA</u> in support
of a black dramatic tradition. Seven of the forty-five plays
were written prior to the 1920s, a black literary heyday and
the decade in which the first full-length black-authored play
was to reach the Great White Way (Garland Anderson's <u>Ap-
pearances,</u> 1925). This anthology is also "the outgrowth of
need and neglect."[18]

With regard to acting, April 5, 1917, has been de-
signated as the most important date in the history of blacks
in the American theatre. On this date, three one-act plays
("The Rider of Dreams," "Granny Maumee," and "Simon the
Cyrenian"), by white poet Ridgeley Torrence, opened at the
Garden Theatre in downtown New York with an all-black cast.
This presentation marked "the first time anywhere in the
United States for Negro actors in the dramatic theatre to
command the serious attention of the critics and the general
press and public." Three years later, Eugene O'Neill's
<u>Emperor Jones</u> opened at the Provincetown Theatre in Green-
wich Village, featuring black actor Charles Gilpin in the title
role. The results included Gilpin's being named one of the
ten best actors of the year, Eugene O'Neill's ascent to fame,
and the beginning national acceptance of blacks in serious
drama.

For black Americans, the 1920s was a glorious era,
one variously designated as the Harlem or Black Renaissance
and the New Negro Movement. It was a period of racial
pride and cultural awareness. It was a period when a group
of black poets, based primarily in Harlem, sought to break
away from the gentility of earlier black writers.

The "new" literary group attempted "to express what
the masses of their race were then feeling and thinking and
wanted to hear. They attempted to make those masses articulate."[20] The NAACP's official journal <u>Crisis</u> and the Urban
League's <u>Opportunity</u> offered prizes to encourage black writers,
particularly the younger ones. The riotous summer of 1919
brought forth these words from Claude McKay:

> If we must die, let it not be like hogs....   Oh,
> Kinsmen! We must meet the common foe; ....
> Like men ... pressed to the wall, dying, but fight-
> ing back!

Arna Bontemps, one who joined the Harlem movement
from California midway through the decade, later referred to the

group as "a chorus of new voices" and in his essay "The
Negro Contribution to American Letters" (of a later date)
reminded us that Sir Winston Churchill was to use McKay's
"If We Must Die" as the conclusion to his speech before the
joint houses of the American Congress. Churchill, in seeking to draw the United States into World War II, made
McKay's poem "the voice of the embattled allies"--a clear
example of movement from racial to universal interpreta-
tion. [21]

There followed seventeen-year-old Countee Cullen's
"I Have a Rendezvous with Life" and nineteen-year-old Lang-
ston Hughes' "The Negro Speaks of Rivers" (1921). Other
leading Harlem Renaissance voices were those of Wallace
Thurman, Jean Toomer, Zora Neale Hurston, and Rudolph
Fisher. Chief interpreter of the movement was Washington,
D. C. -based philosopher and literary critic Alain Locke. His
epochal anthology of the young writers' verse, fiction, and
nonfiction was published in 1925, bearing the title The New
Negro.

But the movement had its critics. In mid-June 1926,
black journalist George Schuyler referred to the efforts as
"The Negro-Art Hokum. " In an article prepared for The
Nation, he wrote:

> Negro art there has been, is, and will be among
> the numerous black nations of Africa; but to sug-
> gest the possibility of any such development among
> the ten million colored people in this republic is
> self-evident foolishness. [22]

Schuyler suggested considering the names of the British Samuel Coleridge-Taylor; the Russian Alexander Puskin;
the Polish George Polgreen Bridgetower; and the Americans
Paul Laurence Dunbar, Charles W. Chesnutt, and James
Weldon Johnson--

> All Negroes; yet their work shows the impress of
> nationality rather than race. They all reveal the
> psychology and culture of their environment--their
> color is incidental. [23]

An opposing view was expressed by Langston Hughes
the following week. Hughes declared,

> Let the blare of Negro jazz bands and the bellowing

voice of Bessie Smith singing Blues penetrate the
closed ears of the colored near-intellectuals until
they listen and perhaps understand. Let Paul Robeson singing Water Boy, and Rudolph Fisher writing
about the streets of Harlem, and Jean Toomer holding the heart of Georgia in his hands, and Aaron
Douglas drawing strange black fantasies cause the
smug Negro middle class to turn from their white,
respectable, ordinary books and papers to catch a
glimmer of their own beauty. We younger Negro
artists who create now intend to express our individual dark-skinned selves without fear or shame.
If white people are pleased we are glad. If they
are not, it doesn't matter. We know we are beautiful. And ugly too. The tom-tom cries and the
tom-tom laughs. If colored people are pleased we
are glad. If they are not, their displeasure doesn't
matter either. We build our temples for tomorrow,
strong as we know how, and we stand on top of the
mountain, free within ourselves. [24]

Transplanted Blacks had kept their African music traditions alive in the New World for many decades. They occasionally went public, particularly with their demonstrations
at the Pinkster celebrations in the middle colonies, 'Lection
Day festivities in New England, and at Congo Square in New
Orleans. They vocalized in their African tongues and danced
to the accompaniment of crude instruments, constructed from
materials at hand--trees, reeds and bones. Gradually the
process of Americanization set in; cultural interchange led to
some conformation, but individuality persisted, particularly
in the folk and popular traditions.

Certainly the best chronicling of black musical activities in all traditions (i.e., folk, popular, and academic) was
provided by black musicologist Eileen Southern in her book
The Music of Black Americans: A History (W.W. Norton,
1971). Equally important is the journal that she began edit-
ing in 1973 entitled, The Black Perspective in Music, published by The Foundation for Research in Afro-American
Creative Arts.

The precedent was set by black music-biographer
James Monroe Trotter with his book Music and Some Highly
Musical People, published in 1881 by Lee and Shepard of
Boston and Charles T. Dillingham of New York (reprinted by
the Johnson Reprint Corporation, 1968). Trotter emphasized

the academic tradition and offered more than thirty "Sketches of the Lives of Remarkable Musicians of the Colored Race" (all achievers measured by world standards), musical families, the Colored American Opera Company (organized in 1872 at Washington, D. C.), The Fisk Jubilee Singers, and abbreviated reports on "musical people" of nineteen American cities scattered throughout the country.

Updating Trotter's documentary in 1936 were two extremely significant publications, also by black authors: Alain LeRoy Locke's The Negro and His Music and pianist/lecturer/ writer Maud Cuney-Hare's Negro Musicians and Their Music (The Associated Publishers). Trotter, Locke, and Cuney-Hare documented well the musical activities of American blacks with regard to a black musical presence, black musical participation, black musical initiation, and black musical collaboration.

We can here only highlight those black musical activities and personalities whose accomplishments had the greatest impact on the course of American music history. The great body of Afro-American folk music was first compiled and published in 1867 by William Allen, Charles Ware, and Lucy McKim Garrison (all of them white) under the title Slave Songs of the United States (Peter Smith). But the real Afro-American folk music messengers were the black Fisk University students who set out to save their school in 1871, when the American Missionary Association was considering abandoning it.

George L. White, the institution's treasurer, took four men and five women North to give concerts and raise money for the school. They returned to Nashville after six months with $25,000--enough money to buy the land on which Fisk University sits and to begin construction of Jubilee Hall. Within three years, the Fisk Jubilee Singers had performed at the White House, the World Peace Conference in Boston and toured Europe. After seven years, the group returned to Nashville with $150,000, valuable gifts and many friends for the University and the race. [25] To be sure, this was an experiment worthy of emulation by struggling Hampton and Tuskegee Institutes at a later date and Laurence C. Jones and Piney Woods Country Life School, half a century later.

Composers of a later period used these sorrow songs as the basis for more serious compositions, e. g. art songs, choral works, string quartets and symphonies. Beginning in the 1920s, concert artists Harry T. Burleigh, Roland Hayes, Paul Robeson, Marian Anderson, and Dorothy Maynor, to name a few, sang the songs of their people (as well as the mainstream repertoire), with no apologies offered. Professional choruses led by Hall Johnson and Eva Jessye, both strong believers in "preserving the integrity of the Negro spiritual," contributed immensely to the legacy of the Negro spiritual, concertizing throughout the country in a grand manner.

The secular side was publicly rendered first by black minstrel troupes that began touring the country in 1865. It was "Clorindy, or The Origin of the Cakewalk" that bridged the gap between minstrelsy and the musical. With lyrics by Paul Laurence Dunbar and music by the conservatory-trained Will Marion Cook, "Clorindy" was produced at the Casino Theatre in New York City in 1898 and was an instant success. The following year, Bert Williams and George Walker's "Sons of Ham" opened at the Grand Opera House in New York City. This collaboration existed for a decade, setting a trend to be continued by the white composer/lyricist teams of Rodgers and Hart, Rodgers and Hammerstein, and Lerner and Lowe.

A black musical comedy first was established with Will Marion Cook's "In Dahomey" which in 1902 opened in Times Square on Broadway. The show was an artistic and financial success, running for three years and later touring Europe. Other important names associated with musical theatre at the turn of the century were Robert Cole, J. Rosamond and James Weldon Johnson, Alex Rogers, Jesse Shipp, and J. Lubrie Hill.

The most glorious era for black musical theatre was the 1920s, the Black Renaissance. Eubie Blake and Noble Sissle's "Shuffle Along" opened at the Sixty-third Street Theatre, May 23, 1921. Other successful all-black shows on Broadway were Perry Bradford, Tim Brymn and Spencer Williams' "Put and Take" (1921); Luckey Roberts' "This and That" (1922); Blake and Sissle's "The Chocolate Dandies" (1924); Will Vodery's "From Dixie to Broadway" (1924); Ford Dabney's "Rang and Tang" (1927); and Fats Waller's "Keep Shuffling" (1928) and "Hot Chocolates" (1929). During the 1930s, shows with all-black casts were written by whites, with the exception of Hall Johnson's folk play "Run Little Chillun" (1933).

The first decades of the twentieth century found touring vaudeville companies replacing the minstrel troupes, offering work for the black professional as well as the black entertainment neophyte. One agency of great importance to black performers and black audiences, particularly in the South and Midwest, was the Theater Owners Booking Agency, also known as "Tough on Black Artists. " TOBA gave work to hundreds of black entertainers "whose offerings ranged from blackface comedy and blues to one-act plays, opera arias, adagio dancing and magic. " Ethel Waters, Mary Lou Williams, Ma Rainey, and countless others--long before their names went up in lights at the nation's finest theaters, clubs and concert halls--worked the vaudeville circuit under auspices of TOBA.

There are those who believe that all that can be called "American music" derives its most distinctive characteristics from the blues. There are also those who believe the blues, a music firmly rooted in worldly black folk experiences, existed from the day blacks arrived on American soil. As an old fiddler once explained, "The blues! Ain't no first blues! The blues always been. " Nevertheless, it was W. C. Handy who recognized their musical uniqueness and began writing them down. His "Memphis Blues" was written in 1909 (the same year that Piney Woods Country Life School came into being) and published in 1912. Two years later, Handy released his "St. Louis Blues. " But despite the importance of W. C. Handy, generally designated as "Father of the Blues, " it was black women singers of the 1920s who made blues history.

By the turn of the century, another distinctly black musical expression had developed--ragtime. Though the chief exponents originally were self-taught "piano thumpers, " the jagged rhythms were soon to be picked up by various instrumental combinations. The shift had long since been made to European instruments and skillful instrumental ensemble playing was now generally accepted.

The first public concert of syncopated music in America was given in the spring of 1905, at the Proctor Twenty-third Street Theatre in New York City. About twenty experienced entertainer-instrumentalists made up the playing-singing-dancing orchestra. Will Dixon was the dancing conductor of an orchestra comprised of banjos, mandolins, guitars, saxophones, a violin, a double bass, a couple of brass instru-

ments, and drums. The group called itself The Memphis
Students, though not one was a student and not one was from
Memphis.

James Reese Europe, a member of the group, organized the Clef Club in 1910, essentially a black musicians'
union. This was the source of contact for dance orchestras
of from three to thirty men for any occasion. In May of
1912 Europe's Clef Club Orchestra of 145 black men gave a
concert at Carnegie Hall. The instrumentation included (in
addition to violins, violas, 'cellos, and string basses) mandolins, guitars, banjos and ukuleles, as well as ten upright
pianos in five pairs.

Two other Carnegie Hall concerts were milestones in
black music programming. The first was W.C. Handy's
Concert of April 27, 1928, wherein all black music traditions
(folk, popular, academic) were represented: spirituals; blues;
plantation, work and character songs; ragtime and jazz.
Composers and performers of the first magnitude were included in the offering: Handy, Samuel Coleridge-Taylor,
Nathaniel Dett, James Bland, Scott Joplin, Fats Waller, J.
Rosamond Johnson, and Clarence Williams.

Then there was the evening of American Negro music,
conceived and produced by John Hammond, December 23,
1938, called "From Spirituals to Swing." Hammond dedicated
the concert to the recently deceased (1937) classic blues
singer Bessie Smith. The concert included a recording of
African tribal music, spirituals, "holy roller hymns," "soft
swing," blues, boogie-woogie piano playing, early New Orleans jazz, and swing by Count Basie and His Orchestra.
All participants--Sister Rosetta Tharpe, Sanford Terry, James
Rushing, Helen Humes, and Sidney Bechet among them--have
since claimed permanent places in American music history.
One featured group was The Kansas City Six, with Eddie
Durham, an arranger for Count Basie's orchestra, on electric guitar. Durham brought his experience in arranging to
the International Sweethearts of Rhythm when he became musical director a few years later. [26]

Surveying the situation for blacks artistically at the
commencement of the fifth decade was the 1942 released
Negro Handbook. [27] Recalled in the area of music and art
(music of course being divided along "classical" and "non-
classical" lines) was the following:

CLASSICAL MUSICIANS IN THE NEWS:

Baritone Paul Robeson sang at the annual banquet of Phi Beta Kappa Honorary Society and at Lewisohn Stadium with the New York Philharmonic.

Black conductor Dean Dixon conducted the NBC Symphony Orchestra in two concerts broadcast over a nation-wide radio network.

Two major works of composer William Grant Still were performed by the New York Philharmonic in New York City.

Presenting concerts at New York City's prestigious Town and Carnegie Halls were tenor Roland Hayes, A.J. Thomas's Negro Composers Study Group and the small choral ensembles The Southernaires and the Belmont Balladeers.

The Golden Gate Quartette sang at the White House.

Clarence Cameron White's opera "Quanga" (with an all-black cast) was performed at the New School for Social Research in New York City.

SWING MUSIC   (based on black-owned newspaper polls and one conducted by the white-owned music magazine Down Beat):

Leading bands were those carrying the names Count Basie, Jimmy Lunceford, Erskine Hawkins, Lucky Millinder, Ernie Fields, Andy Kirk, Cab Calloway, Ella Fitzgerald, Red Saunders, Claude Hopkins, Fats Waller, John Kirby, Tiny Bradshaw, Sunset Royals, SWEETHEARTS OF RHYTHM, Orlando Robeson, Louis Armstrong, Benny Carter and Noble Sissle.

"Six colored musicians were named to the 1941 All-American Band, in a contest ... in which nearly 15,000 votes were cast." The two leading bands were Benny Goodman and Tommy Dorsey [both white]. Duke Ellington placed third. Other black musicians named to the All-American Band were Cootie Williams and Roy Eldridge, trumpet; Johnny Hodges, saxophone; Jay C. Higginbottom, trombone; Charlie Christian, guitar; Fletcher Henderson and Sy Oliver, arranging.

ARTISTS IN THE NEWS:

Painters Charles Alston, Robert Blackburn,
Palmer Hayden, Lois Mailou Jones, Jacob Lawrence,
Horace Pippin, Charles White and Hale Woodruff;
Painter/Sculptress Elizabeth Catlett; Sculptors Richmond Barthe, Meta Warrick Fuller and Sargent
Johnson; Cartoonist E. Simms Campbell. Most
were cited for their participation in the 1940 American Negro Exposition, some for exhibits at leading
museums and galleries, and others for Fellowship
receiverships.

Attention was called to the collection of oils,
water-colors, and prints assembled to commemor-
ate the 75th Anniversary of passage of the Thir-
teenth Amendment and displayed at the Library of
Congress, emphasizing "the contribution of the
American Negro to American culture." Other parts
of the commemorative activities included a three-
day music festival featuring Dorothy Maynor, Roland Hayes and the Budapest String Quartet (white),
playing works based on Afro-American themes and
an exhibition of literature and photographs by outstanding Blacks.

THE RADIO:

Top black broadcasting orchestras were those
led by John Kirby and Cab Calloway, CBS; Jimmy
Lunceford, CBS and MBS; Erskine Butterfield, MBS;
Erskine Hawkins, Fats Waller, Lucky Millinder,
Andy Kirk and Coleman Hawkins, NBC. The weekly
broadcast Wings Over Jordan, featuring a black
speaker and a spiritual-singing choir, drew more
fan mail than any other black program on CBS,
averaging 8,000 letters a week. Band leader Cab
Calloway's quiz program "Quizzicale," with an all-
black cast and contestants, was fast rising in popularity on the MBS system.

Planned by the U.S. Office of Education and fi-
nanced by a Rosenwald Foundation Award, a series
of educational radio programs was broadcast in
1941 over NBC. "Freedom's People" focused on
"the role Negroes have played in American education, art, science, industry, sports and other
fields." Featured were profiles of baritone Paul
Robeson, scientist George Washington Carver, ex-

plorer Matthew Henson, and world heavyweight
champion Joe Louis. Featured musical participants
were ballad singer Joshua White, blues pioneer
W. C. Handy, band leaders Cab Calloway and Count
Basie, the Golden Gate Quartet, the Tuskegee Institute Choir and the Leonard DePaur Chorus.

STAGE AND SCREEN:

"During 1940, the Negro stage was in a process
of ferment trying to overcome the setbacks it had
suffered as the result of the economic depression,
competition from white plays and the death of the
Federal Theatre Project."
    The American Negro Theater was founded by
Abram Hill and Frederick O'Neal (later president
of Actor's Equity). One of its founding purposes
was "to destroy the remaining vestiges of minstrelsy
and stereotype in black acting, and demonstrate that
Blacks were capable of portraying human character
in all its diversity and complexity."
    Though black productions met with little success
at the turn of the decade, black actors and actresses
set box office records for white producers. Other
successful white produced-predominantly white casts
stage productions that gave relatively good spots to
black artists were "Gay New Orleans" and "The
Little Foxes." "Cabin in the Sky" was a relatively
popular 1941 Broadway production, featuring Ethel
Waters, Rex Ingram, J. Rosamond Johnson, Todd
Duncan, the J. Rosamond Johnson Singers and the
Katherine Dunham Dancers. Dunham was praised
by the critics for her departure from tradition, as
she drew upon the dance rhythms of Cuba, Mexico,
South America, the West Indies and southern United
States.

NEGROES IN WHITE PICTURES:[28]

    Rated motion picture stars and featured players
for 1940 in Hollywood's semi-official roster (compiled by the trade magazine Variety) were Hattie
McDaniel, Ben Carter, Mantan Moreland, Eddie
"Rochester" Anderson and Jack Randall. Hattie
McDaniel was the first black movie actress to receive the coveted Oscar from the Academy of Motion Picture Arts and Sciences, when in 1939 she

was so honored for her supporting role in David
Selznick's "Gone with the Wind." Nominated for
recognition was Butterfly McQueen for her role
played in the same movie.

Other "outstanding colored character performances
in major Hollywood productions" of the period were
those given by Leigh Whipper, Clarence Muse,
Louise Beavers, Theresa Harris, Willie Best,
Jesse Lee Brooks, Dorothy Dandridge and Ben
Carter. Over three hundred blacks were used in
Paramount's "Safari." Singer/stage actress Edith
Wilson was a newcomer in pictures. Vocalist/band
leader Ella Fitzgerald was signed for a role in
Universal's "Ride 'em Cowboy." The singing Ink
Spots made their first picture, appearing along with
the dancing Nicholas Brothers. Paul Robeson was
acclaimed for his role in the British film "Proud
Valley."

Blacks were involved in producing their own
films, building on the pioneering efforts of Oscar
Michaux (1920s) and continuing efforts of Ralph
Cooper, George Randal, F.E. Miller and Clarence
Muse, to name a few. The first Black Western
picture, "Harlem on the Prairie" was produced in
1939. Considered the best "all-colored" film of
1940 was "Mystery in Swing."

WOMEN GENERALLY AND BLACK WOMEN SPECIFICALLY

In the Work Force

The editor of Harper's Monthly Magazine voiced the opinion
in 1910 that if America received a visitor from another planet,
that

> visitant ... would infer from a casual survey of
> the things most obviously visible upon the surface
> of the earth ... that earthly civilization was pre-
> dominantly masculine, and that women were merely
> housekeepers and shoppers or the subordinate fac-
> tors of industry. [29]

Such an assessment of female status in American society was to improve only slightly in succeeding decades, despite a few gains achieved from time to time. Underscoring

this point is recollection of the fact that it was 1920 before
the 19th Amendment granted suffrage to women. The Amendment's changes were not the end of all women's problems
however, as evidenced by efforts at enforcement of Title IX
and the ultimate defeat of the Equal Rights Amendment (ERA).
Of the ten-year effort at ERA ratification and its June 30,
1982, death, journalist Henry Allen wrote, "Except for a
rally here and there, it went largely uncommemorated, that
June 30 crash following 10 years of lumbering down the run-
way. "30

By mid-1920s, a major problem for some American
women was the choice of home, job, or both? How to com-
bine a normal life of marriage and motherhood with a life of
intellectual activity, professional or otherwise--utilizing the
female's right to be an individual as well as to fulfill her
generic responsibility--was a dilemma facing a handful of
educated women. There were those who suggested that women
make marriage/parenthood and profession coordinate but independent (as with their male counterparts) and others who
suggested that marriage/parenthood be developed to a professional status. The compromise suggestion was that women
accept marriage/parenthood as the major profession while
continuing to "cherish and develop ... individual talents" as
a minor profession. 31 A few of the more elite women's colleges began making radical changes in their curricula, accommodating the two positions: bringing marriage/parenthood to
a professional status or making marriage/parenthood a major
and individual talents a minor.

As for black women, this problem was statistically in-
significant. With slavery just more than half-a-century past,
black women's problems (more closely linked to those of
black males) were far more basic. For example, the chief
concern of Spelman Seminary, the largest and most prestigious school for black girls, was still "intelligence, education,
culture and Christian character to replace stupidity, ignor-
ance, crudeness, and superstition. " The dominant thought
of its founders was "to win souls for Christ. "32

During the Bicentennial year, Life magazine saluted
one hundred sixty-six women, all "independent spirits who
broke free from passive home-hugging stereotypes, and made
a difference in American Life. " Twelve black women were
considered worthy of inclusion in the "American Album ...
One Side of the Family": Barbara Jordan, who exercised
"clout in the cloakroom of Congress"; "Mammy" Pleasant, a

successful bordello operator during the Gold Rush in San
Francisco, civil-rights activist, and abolitionist; Angela
Davis, philosopher and symbol of black rebellion; Mary
McLeod Bethune, founder of the National Council of Negro
Women and Bethune-Cookman College and President Roosevelt's official advisor on minority affairs; Harriet Tubman,
shepherder of more than three hundred slaves to freedom;
Leontyne Price, first lady of opera and "prima donna ab-
soluta"; Mary Lou Williams, pianist and composer who helped
improvise the history of jazz; Wilma Rudolph, sprinter and
gold medalist; Madame C.J. Walker (Sarah Breedlove), cos-
metologist, philanthropist and the nation's first black million-
aire; Bessie Smith, blues Empress; and Josephine Baker, ex-
patriate, Parisian legend and spokesperson against American
racism.   One of the "Five Great Spirits" was black contralto
Marian Anderson, cited for her attainment at the highest
realms of musical acclaim and her triumph over prejudice. [33]
The "visitant from another planet" could infer still more from
this Special Report, though by comparison with previous publications, some progress was evident.

        Black historian Lerone Bennett, in an August 1977 ar-
ticle entitled, "No Crystal Stair: The Black Woman In History," wrote the following:

        [T]o understand what Black woman has become ...
        one must walk with her a little while on the steep
        and tortuous stairs that made her what she is. [34]

Measurement of her progress warrants measurement of her
problems.   And as black journalist/attorney Marjorie McKenzie suggested, also to be considered is the "frustration she
has experienced and the aggression she has absorbed due to
practices of discrimination against her husband, father or
son."[35]   (It is beyond the scope of this book to provide a
full bibliography for the purpose of walking with black women
on the steep and tortuous stairs that have caused them to be
what they are, but the author commends to the reader those
works listed in Appendix A.)

        About the same time that Piney Woods founder Laur-
ence C. Jones and his wife were preparing to send out their
first musical messengers--the Cotton Blossoms--to assist in
fund raising, a rather comprehensive report on black women
in the work force was provided by an Examiner with the
United States Department of Labor's Employment Service.
Majority employment (for black women) could be categorized

under three broad headings: domestic and personal service, agriculture, and manufacturing and mechanical industries.

Domestic service generally included cooking, washing and ironing, the latter two being carried out in residences as well as laundries. From flat-work in laundries, some moved up to "finishing" shirt bosoms, which according to examiner Elizabeth Ross Haynes was really "artistic work."[36] She had this to say about residential labor in terms of employer/employee relationships:

> The bond between mistress and maid in many cases is not sufficiently strong for the mistress to learn her maid's surname or her address.... When one deeply interested in the whole problem analyzes the conditions and sympathizes with mistress and maid sufficiently to get the whole truth, she must con- clude that in too many cases the feeling of each borders on real dislike for the other. Neither has for the other that priceless possession--confidence.[37]

An element of gloom existed in the larger cities where many of the previous calls for black women domestic workers were now going to white females. In the nation's capital, with the fixing of a minimum wage in hotels and restaurants at $16.50 for a forty-eight-hour week "and the increasing number of available white women, Negro women were to a large extent displaced."[38]

The early 1920s found many thousands of black women on farms, eking out a bare existence. Wrote Haynes:

> They are out early in the morning afoot and on horseback going to near-by fields and, in many in- stances, on wagons going to fields four and five miles distant....
>
> ...
>
> [A]lmost the only recreational or social contacts enjoyed by such women came through the monthly church meeting, the occasional burial of a friend, or the annual trip to town at cotton-seed time.[39]

Some were engaged in manufacturing and mechanical pursuits, finding employment in cigar and tobacco factories, with wages ranging from $6 to $10 for a sixty-hour week.

Before the war, black women in small numbers were employed
in clothing, food, and metal industries; slaughtering and meat
packing houses; crab and peanut factories; and iron, steel,
and automobile industries. A few semi-skilled workers were
to be found in electrical-supply, paperbox, and rubber factories, and in the textile industries. A few skilled female
tailors, tinsmiths, coppersmiths, and upholsterers also
existed.

Nationally during the teens 62.6 percent of the gainfully employed black females ten years old and over were involved in domestic and personal service; 26.9 percent in
agriculture (farm labor primarily); 5.5 percent in manufacturing and mechanical industries; and 3.4 percent in professional
service. All others (less than 2 percent) were gainfully employed at clerical, public service, trade, transportation, and
communication occupations. The picture for black women in
the State of Mississippi was 69.1 percent gainfully employed
in agriculture (of which almost three-quarters were farm laborers); 27 percent in domestic and personal service; 2 percent in professional service; and one percent in manufacturing and mechanical industries. All others (less than one percent) were gainfully employed at clerical, public service,
trade, transportation, and communication occupations.

In the late 1930s, when Dr. Jones was considering future occupational outlets for his soon to be famous International Sweethearts of Rhythm, women constituted 28 percent
of the work force nationally, of which 26.5 percent were employed as clerical and kindred workers, 19 percent as operatives (users of large and small machines and equipment) and
kindred workers, and 12 percent as professional, technical,
and kindred workers. All others were employed as farmers
and farm managers, general managers, officials and proprie-
tors, salespersons, craftspersons or private household workers. The national picture for black women was drastically
different: 45 percent were employed as private household
workers, 18 percent as service workers (other than in private households), 14 percent as operatives and kindred workers, and 7 percent as farm laborers. All others were con-
sumed in the remaining occupations, with only 5 percent involved in professional and technical occupations. To be sure,
the picture was equally as dismal in the State of Mississippi,
understanding of course that there was a statistical shift between the private and household workers and farm laborers.

Participating in Things Musical

Musically speaking, a black vocal presence was established
by midway the nineteenth century.

> Black America's first concert singer was a woman--
> Elizabeth Taylor Greenfield, "The Black Swan"--
> and women dominated the concert stage throughout
> the nineteenth century.... The last quarter of the
> century saw the emergence of no fewer than five
> celebrated "prima donnas," as they were called by
> the press, and an additional half dozen or more
> singers of lesser fame.

The five celebrated prima donnas, most with sobriquets,
were Nellie Brown Mitchell (1845-1924), Marie Selika, "Queen
of Staccato" (c. 1849-1937); Flora Batson (Bergen), "Double-
Voiced Queen of Song" (1864-1906); M. Sissieretta Jones,
"Black Patti" (1869-1939); and Rachel Walker, "Creole Night-
ingale" (1873-192?). Both Batson and Jones continued their
careers in vaudeville, still singing their operatic arias.
Jones, following her retirement from the concert stage (1896),
continued as leader of Black Patti's Troubadours, touring the
nation for almost two decades. [40]

Early in the twentieth century, Gertrude "Ma" Rainey,
"Mother of the Blues," was touring with the Rabbit Foot Min-
strels. From time to time, she included in her act a type
of song that came to be known as the blues. The 1920s was
the era of classic blues, with black women reigning as queens
of the American popular music empire. From the traveling
minstrel and vaudeville shows, the rural and primitive blues
moved into theatres, concert halls, and recording studios,
often leaving the guitars and banjos behind.

Accompanying such stellar performers as Ma Rainey,
Chippie Hill, Ida Cox, Ethel Waters, Alberta Hunter, Sippie
Wallace, Lucille Hegamin, Lillyn Brown, Lavina Turner, and,
of course, the four Smiths--Mamie, Clara, Trixie, and Bes-
sie (no relation)--were small and large studio and theatre
bands, composed of the foremost instrumentalists of the day.
Female blues singers were in the forefront and the accom-
panying instrumental groups carried their names: Mamie
Smith and Her Jazz Hounds, Lucille Hegamin and Her Blue
Flame Syncopators, Ma Rainey and Her Georgia Band or Her
Tub Jug Washboard Band, Sara Martin and Her Jass Fools,

Ida Cox and Her Five Blue Spells, Lillyn Brown and Her
Jazz Bo Syncopators, Ethel Waters and Her Jazz Masters
or Her Ebony Four. Band membership was exclusively
male, with the exception of one back-up group led by
pianist Lovie Austin (Cora Calhoun). When Austin's all-
male groups provided backgrounds for singers, the label
carried the singer's name plus that of Lovie Austin and Her
Blues Serenaders.

The invention of the phonograph in 1877 and its mass
production beginning in 1888 were to play a significant role
in the development of black music. Though Victor had issued six single-sided records featuring the Dinwiddie Colored
Quartet in 1902, it was not until 1920 that the perfect marriage (recording industry and black recording artists) was to
take place. A 1920 Valentine's Day recording date found
black vocalist Mamie Smith substituting for white vocalist
Sophie Tucker, upon the persuasion of black songwriter and
music-store proprietor Perry Bradford. Issued on OKeh
(4113) in July 1920 was "That Thing Called Love" and "You
Can't Keep a Good Man Down," composed by Perry Bradford.
As Bradford wrote in his book Born with the Blues,

> I tramped the pavements of Broadway with the belief
> that the country was waiting for the sound of the
> voice of a Negro singing the blues with a Negro
> jazz combination playing for him or her. I felt
> strongly it should be a girl and that was what I
> was trying to sell. I was laughed at by all the
> wise guys in Tin Pan Alley. [41]

So successful was this first recording that Mamie
Smith pressed a second OKeh disc ("Crazy Blues") in August
1920, of which more than three million copies were sold.
Other record companies began cashing in on the money-
making idea, including Arto, Emerson, Paramount, and Columbia. The first black-owned recording company--Pace
Phonograph Corporation--was established in 1921. The company soon adopted the name "Black Swan," after the nineteenth-
century concert soprano Elizabeth Taylor Greenfield. For all
the record companies, promotion appeal and distribution were
geared to blacks, hence the label "race records."

Still living the era in the early 1980s and singing in
the classic blues tradition regularly was the ageless Alberta
Hunter and occasionally Sippie Wallace--the last of "the red-
hot mamas." To relive the era and follow its course of

development, the writer commends to the reader Rosetta
Reitz's Women's Heritage Series, Rosetta Records (1980).
In addition to the musical evidence, the accompanying
notes give new meaning to blues lyrics and the singers'
lives.

Establishing names for themselves in more sophisti-
cated circles were Abie Mitchell and Florence Cole Talbert.
Lillian Evanti was making history in the opera houses of
Europe.   The 1930s brought forth such black female superstars as Ella Fitzgerald, Billie "Lady Day" Holiday, Helen
Humes, and Maxine Sullivan, as well as concert artists Marian Anderson, "The Lady from Philadelphia." The beauty of
Anne Wiggins Brown's voice is said to have inspired the creation of the role of "Bess" in George Gershwin's folk opera
Porgy and Bess, produced in 1935.   Opera singer Caterina
Jarbora sang at the Puccini Opera House in Milan, Italy in
1930 and in 1933 she became the first black to perform with
a major opera company in the United States--The Chicago
Opera Company.   A few years later La Julia Rhea sang with
the Chicago Civic Opera Company (in 1937).   In 1939, concert singer Dorothy Maynor launched her career with an appearance at the Berkshire Music Festival.

It was in 1924 that Anderson came in first among a
group of three hundred contestants in a competition sponsored
by the New York Philharmonic.   In the early thirties, she
toured the leading capitals of Europe and in 1935, she appeared before a select audience in Salzburg.   In the audience
at this concert was maestro Arturo Toscanini, who declared
hers to be "a voice such as comes once in a hundred years."
By 1941, Anderson was one of the nation's ten highest paid
artists.

Florence B. Price acquired some credibility in composition circles when her Symphony in E Minor was performed
by the Chicago Symphony Orchestra at the Century of Progress
Exposition in 1933.   She had performed her piano concerto
with the same orchestra the prior year.   Price's pupil Margaret Bonds was also beginning to receive recognition for her
compositional abilities.

By the 1920s, concert pianists Helen Hagan and Hazel
Harrison had been lauded in Europe and were beginning to
acquire some recognition in their native America.   During
World War I, Yale University graduate Hagan was one of a
handful of blacks offering entertainment for black units in

France under auspices of the War Camp Community Service.
Harrison had appeared with the Berlin Philharmonic Orchestra
and was now beginning to tour the United States as a recitalist
and as soloist with symphony orchestras, including those of
Chicago, Minneapolis, and Los Angeles.

Black women were well represented in the area of
jazz piano playing, though naturally most utilized their talents
in ensembles. They had first claimed their right to exist or-
chestrally in family ensembles in the last decades of the nineteenth century. Moving into the twentieth century, they could
be found in any instrumental ensemble claiming the title "band"
or "orchestra"--whether minstrel, vaudeville, or ragtime.

The 1920s found Lovie Austin leading studio and theatre bands--primarily in Chicago--from the keyboard. Other
swinging pianists of the period, also affiliated with bands in
the Windy City, were Lottie Hightower, Ida Mae Maples, and
Garvinia Dickerson. Fisk University trained Lillian ("Lil")
Hardin Armstrong (second wife of trumpeter Louis Armstrong)
began her career as a piano song demonstrator for a Chicago
music store in 1918. Shortly thereafter she auditioned for
the position of pianist with a group from New Orleans. In
1921, she joined "King" Oliver's legendary Creole Jazz Band,
the same outfit that future husband Louis joined in 1922.
Lil Hardin Armstrong remained in the musical forefront for
many years to come, as pianist, composer, and vocalist.

There were other pianists filling early jazz band engagements. In New Orleans, Emma ("Sweet Emma") Barrett
and Jeanette Kimball worked with the Original Tuxedo Jazz
Band and Dolly Adams with her own band at the Othello Theatre. Appearing with her own combo in St. Louis and Minneapolis was Auzie Russell Dial. By the mid 1920s, Mary Lou
Williams was well on her way to earning the title "First
Lady of Jazz," having toured the vaudeville circuit and performed with Duke Ellington's Washingtonians and John Williams' (her future husband) Syncopators. Mary Lou Williams
officially joined the Andy Kirk Band in 1931, thus beginning
her long association with Kansas City. Also active with Kansas City Bands was Julia Lee. The 1930s brought into jazz
circles such gifted pianists as Cleo Patra Brown, Rose Murphy, Nellie Lutcher, Margaret "Countess" Johnson, Wilhemina
"Billie" Goodson Pierce, Gertrude Long, and the youthful
Hazel Scott.

Several black ladies utilized their piano talents with

"elite art" instrumental ensembles.   The early decades found both Ida Rose playing with the Bloom Philharmonic and Camille Nickerson playing with her father in William Nickerson's Ladies Orchestra in New Orleans.   Audiences in the 1920s enjoyed the pianistic skills of such persons as Olive Jeter (Jeter-Weir-Jeter Trio, New York City) and Gladys Bell (Harrison Ferrell Orchestra, Chicago) and 1930s' audiences enjoyed the talents of Bennie Parks (McKinney Symphony Orchestra, St. Louis), Mable Johnson, and Emma Martin (both in the Colonial Park String Ensemble, Baltimore).

Though society designated the piano as "appropriate for ladies," there were those who dared to play other instruments.   Further, bands and orchestras made up of black women exclusively were not as unusual as might be expected. (See Appendix B for a listing of all-female black groups, with known dates and places of existence.   See Appendix C for an abbreviated list of black female instrumental pioneers, all pacesetters for members of the International Sweethearts of Rhythm.)

Following the International Sweethearts of Rhythm years, Metronome's associate editor Jack Maher made an interesting observation.   Wrote Maher:

> Women have a way of always making themselves controversial.   Throughout history and in the personal relationships of people, men are forever having women troubles.   Jazz has women troubles too.
>
> What with the passing of the nineteenth amendment, women in ever increasing numbers have been taking the places of, and places beside, men....
>
> ...
>
> And so it is in jazz.   The female in jazz has this one basic attraction even before she begins to make music.   The guys ... look before they listen.
>
> But when they do begin to listen[,] what they hear is not always what they might want to hear.

Maher concentrated on singers, pianists, and vibraphonists, pointing out that these appeared to be the easiest musical roles for female adaptation.

> Two reasons pop immediately to mind to explain
> this: first the social unattractiveness families feel
> at seeing their young girl with a trombone or tenor
> saxophone obscuring her pretty little face and the
> ingrained belief that women should not be allowed
> to do things that seem indecorous or physically
> taxing. [42]

But, he noted, there were exceptions. To be sure, the exceptions were devoid of any racial restrictions.

THE BIG BAND ERA

We are clearer on the era's finale than we are on its commencement. For some, the beginning was marked when Duke
Ellington issued his manifesto "It Don't Mean a Thing If It
Ain't Got That Swing" in 1932, by which time the size of his
band had increased from ten to fourteen (five brasses, five
reeds and four rhythm instruments). Others mark the era's
birth with the success of Benny Goodman's band in California
in the fall of 1935. Still others mark the beginning with the
mid-1920s' collaborative efforts of pianist/arranger/band
leader Fletcher Henderson, reedman/arranger Don Redman,
and trumpet soloist Louis Armstrong.

An irrefutable fact is that following World War I, jazz
was on the move on both the domestic and international fronts.
Head arrangements were giving way to "the book," with opportunities for solo improvisation at designated points in the
score. "Bristling brass, pungent saxes, rollicking rhythm
sections"--these ensembles within the total unit allowed for
antiphonal writing and playing between reeds (often increased
to seven) and brasses, as a lightened rhythm section (led by
the string bass) kept a regular accentuation on the beat. The
sound was refined, often sophisticated, but very danceable.
The more skilled the arranger, the better a group sounded
and the more appeal it had for audiences across the country.

There were several other indisputable facts: It was
Fletcher Henderson who

> set the classic pattern for jazz orchestral arranging,
> pitting reeds against brass for "call-and-response"
> effects, fusing them for block-voiced ensembles,
> and always placing a firm accent on a sense of
> swing, in which the use of syncopation played a
> dominant part. [43]

Also, it is generally agreed that swing

> rocked and leaped from coast to coast; it grabbed
> hold of more people, certainly than any other jazz
> style before or since; it turned bandleaders into
> celebrities as fan-worshipped as any movie star,
> and it turned jazz, for once, into a happily success-
> ful big business. [44]

As "big band" historian George T. Simon summarized, "The
big bands were like big league ball teams, and the kids knew
all the players--even without a scorecard." The big swing
bands lifted their public high in the air and gave them a sense
of friendly well-being. The era of one-nighters witnessed
"one of the happiest most thrilling rapports ever established
between givers and takers of music." [45]

Big swing band territory was all of America. Radio
stations enhanced the bands' audiences with their "live" broadcasts, often from the dance halls and ballrooms where the
bands were playing. Schooled musicians made up the band
rosters and virtuoso soloists improvised brilliantly. From
the stardom acquired in one band, many sidemen broke away
to form their own swing bands. By 1940, the big swing band
market was flooded. Jazz periodicals (Down Beat, Metronome,
Swing, Tempo, Orchestra World, Song Hits) kept the public
informed; Down Beat and Metronome conducted yearly band
polls; leading black newspapers kept a separate readership
informed and conducted separate polls.

Down Beat's 1939 Yearbook of Swing dealt with orchestral milestones of the first four decades, listing sixty-five
groups, beginning with Buddy Bolden's Orchestra, 1900-1910.
The listing was accompanied by a racial designation: forty-
three black groups versus twenty-two white groups. [46] In
1941, Decca released two separate anthologies: "An Anthology of White Jazz" and "An Anthology of Colored Jazz."
Down Beat dared to label the latter superior to the former
and journalist Dave Dexter wrote, "[T]his collection easily
surpasses the ofay package, not only from the angle of historical importance, but also musically." [47] But as Ralph Ellison wrote of the era in a 1959 article for Esquire,

> [T]he greatest prestige and economic returns were
> falling outside the Negro community--often to lead-
> ers whose popularity grew from the compositions
> and arrangements of Negroes--to white instrumen-
> talists whose only originality lay in the enterprise

with which they rushed to market with some Negro
musicians's hard-won style. [48]

By the mid 1940s, big swing bands had fallen on hard
times and swing music ceased to challenge the younger gener-
ation of jazz performers--trumpeter Dizzy Gillespie, pianists
Thelonius Monk and Bud Powell, drummers Kenny Clarke and
Art Blakey, saxophonists Charlie Parker and Dexter Gordon,
to name a few.   Singer Billy Eckstine's Orchestra, formed
in 1944, was the first big band to reflect the bebop impact,
but it survived for only three years.   The time was ripe for
singers and their sentimental ballads offered more appeal to
a war weary public.   The big ballrooms were gradually dis-
appearing; a 1942 recording ban imposed by the musicians'
union wrought havoc on the musicians, as the industry moved
to other commercial ventures.   Obviously the black pacesetters
ters felt the most negative effects.

Indeed, the International Sweethearts of Rhythm flour-
ished when big swing bands ruled the jazz empire, reached
competitive status when new jazz directions were clearly sur-
facing, and fell victim to the same devastating pressures as
all other large instrumental jazz ensembles (coupled with the
added pressures peculiar to the group that originated at Piney
Woods Country Life School).   The Sweethearts were measured
against black male bands led by Count Basie, Duke Ellington,
Earl Hines, Cab Calloway, Billy Eckstine, Lionel Hampton,
Chick Webb, Jimmie Lunceford, Coleman Hawkins, Andy Kirk,
and Erskine Hawkins; and white male bands led by Benny
Goodman, Tommy and Jimmie Dorsey, Charlie Barnet, Harry
James, Woody Herman, and Artie Shaw.   Naturally, they
were also measured against existing white female bands.

George Simon included one female band leader in his
"definitive volume" entitled The Big Bands, including over
four hundred big bands (both swing and sweet), with seventy-
two receiving profile coverage.   Ina Ray Hutton, one of the
seventy-two, was cited for her leadership of male bands and
criticized for her leadership of all-girl outfits.   Simon added,
"[H]er all-girl orchestra was like all all-girl orchestras.
'Only God can make a tree, ... and only men can play good
jazz.' "[49]   Very casually mentioned in Simon's chapter entitled "P.S." were the names of two other female leaders:
Ada Leonard and Blanche Calloway, the latter of whom was
black.   Leonard fronted an all-female orchestra and Calloway
fronted primarily all-male organizations, though she led a
women's orchestra for a brief period in the mid 1940s.

The exclusion of white women from male-dominated
ensembles sparked the creation of all-female instrumental
ensembles, specializing in both popular and elite art reper-
toires. Believed to be the first all-women's "elite art" instrumental ensemble was The Los Angeles Women's Orchestra, which was organized in 1893. In fact, twenty-eight
such orchestras existed during the half-century reign of
women's symphony orchestras.

In a more popular vein, the Marion Osgood Ladies
Orchestra (specializing in light classics, as well as music
for dancing) was established in 1884 at Chelsea, Massachusetts. The Boston Fadettes (specializing in the same) de-
buted in 1888. During the latter part of the teens, a
Ladies Mandolin Orchestra (specializing in "Music on the
lighter side") existed in Philadelphia. The Brick Tops, a
fourteen-member ladies' vaudeville orchestra, was organized
in 1927 at Indianapolis, Indiana. Singer/dancer Ina Ray Hutton, better known as "the Blonde Bombshell of Rhythm, "
formed her Melodears in 1934. The group played theatres,
made several movie shorts, recorded for Victor and Brunswick, and toured Europe in 1935. When this group disbanded,
Hutton formed another all-female outfit.

Male leader Phil Spitalny fronted a group of thirty
women musicians from 1934 to the mid 1950s. Spitalny dared
to suggest that "[d]ance music should earn consideration as
a part of good music, if only for the reason that the majority of people enjoy it.... " He added that the music should
be melodically agreeable, well arranged, and artistically
performed. In an interview with prestigious Etude music
magazine's journalist Rose Heylbut, Spitalny insisted that he
held "no brief for the inartistic combination of overheavy
brasses and unrestrained drums, that I think of as 'cannibal
music'. "50

Under the sponsorship of General Electric, Spitalny's
musical unit went on a weekly coast-to-coast NBC radio
broadcast in 1936, under the program title "The Hour of
Charm. " But big band historian Simon said of Spitalny:

> [O]nce the leader of a very good dance and radio
> orchestra, [Spitalny] lowered his musical and raised
> his visual appeal in the thirties when he surrounded
> himself with a bevy of girl musicians ... who, as
> a group, didn't play very well--and didn't always
> look so great either. 51

As the Sweethearts were nearing the end of their
reign, the male-fronted Hormel Girls' Caravan came into
existence (1947) as an advertising gimmick for a canned
meat manufacturing company. The original idea was to hire
ex-servicewomen. It started out with six recent dischargees
from the military, was soon expanded to twenty-six, and by
1951, a sixty-piece orchestra was advertised and the ex-GI
restriction dropped. The group's regular broadcasts over a
national network of 227 radio stations justified the label
"Darlings of the Airwaves. "

Jazz historian Frank Driggs raised this question in
1977:

> Were the "all-girl" bands just a novelty from an
> era now long past or did they contribute meaning-
> fully to the development of American music?

He responded in the affirmative: They were certainly more
than a passing fad and they made a valuable contribution.
Driggs added,

> Despite the fact that women have been active and
> outstanding since the start of pop music and jazz
> seventy-odd years ago, the music business has re-
> warded them very rarely. [52]

Recognition notwithstanding, the black International
Sweethearts of Rhythm had little competition from their white
counterparts. Though Spitalny boasted the fact that many of
his group's members were conservatory graduates and veterans of symphony orchestras, borrowing from Duke Ellington,
it didn't mean a thing because they lacked the swing. The
Blonde Bombshell of Rhythm and Her Melodears got the
breaks, but could not maintain a prominent position. The
"girl music makers" from Piney Woods Country Life School
outdid them all. Between the years 1939 and 1949, the International Sweethearts of Rhythm earned a reputation that was
still standing in March 1980 as the "best all-women swing
band ever to perform. "

NOTES

1.   Booker T. Washington, "The National Negro Business
     League, " An Era of Progress and Promise, 1863-1910,
     ed. by W. N. Hartshorn. Boston: Priscilla, 1910,
     p. 414.

2. W. E. B. DuBois, The Souls of Black Folk. Greenwich,
    Conn. : Fawcett, 1961 (originally, Chicago: A. C.
    McClurg and Co. , 1903), p. 48.

3. Washington, "The Bible in Negro Education," An Era
    of Progress and Promise, loc. cit. , p. 554.

4. Washington, "The Kind of Education the Negro Needs,"
    An Era of Progress and Promise, loc. cit. , pp. 383-
    384.

5. George Sale, "Our Part in the Solution of a Great
    Problem," An Era of Progress and Promise, loc.
    cit. , p. 68.

6. "How the Public Received the Journal of Negro History,"
    Vol. I, No. 2, April, 1916, The Journal of Negro
    History, pp. 230-231.

7. W. E. B. DuBois, "Close Ranks," The Crisis, July 1918,
    p. 111.

8. Benjamin Quarles, The Negro in the Making of Amer-
    ica. New York: Macmillan, 1964, p. 203.

9. James Weldon Johnson, Black Manhattan. New York:
    Alfred A. Knopf, 1930, p. 255.

10. Charles S. Johnson, The Negro in American Civiliza-
    tion. New York: Henry Holt, 1930.

11. Theodore G. Bilbo, "An African Home for Our Negroes,"
    The Living Age, June 1940, p. 330.

12. Negro Education: A Study of the Private and Higher
    Schools for Colored People in the United States,
    Bureau of Education, Department of Interior, Washing-
    ton, D. C. , 1917, pp. 338-339.

13. Ibid. , pp. 367-368.

14. W. E. B. DuBois, "Negro Education," The Crisis, Febru-
    ary 1918, pp. 173-175.

15. James Weldon Johnson, op. cit. , p. 87.

16. Ibid. , p. 93.

17. Henry T. Sampson, Blacks in Blackface: A Source Book on Early Musical Shows. Metuchen, N.J.: Scarecrow Press, 1980, p. vii.

18. Black Theater USA: 45 Plays by Black Americans, 1847-1974, ed. by James V. Hatch. New York: The Free Press, 1974.

19. Langston Hughes, "The Negro and American Entertainment," The American Negro Reference Book, ed. by John P. Davis. Englewood Cliffs, N.J.: Prentice-Hall, 1966, p. 833.

20. James Weldon Johnson, op. cit., p. 263.

21. Arna Bontemps, "The Negro Contribution to American Letters," The American Negro Reference Book, loc. cit., p. 859.

22. George Schuyler, "The Negro-Art Hokum," The Nation, June 16, 1926, p. 662.

23. Ibid., p. 663.

24. Langston Hughes, "The Negro Artist and the Racial Mountain," The Nation, June 23, 1926, p. 694.

25. "The Jubilee of Jubilees at Fisk University," Southern Workman, February 1922, pp. 73-80.

26. James Dugan and John Hammond, "In Retrospect ... An Early Black-Music Concert, From Spirituals to Swing," The Black Perspective in Music, Fall 1974, pp. 191-208.

27. The Negro Handbook, compiled and edited by Florence Murray. New York: Wendell Malliet, 1942, pp. 217-229.

28. Recall that this was still the era in which the industry's handling of blacks settled into two categories: "films in which colored people were the butt-end of crude and insulting jokes, and films in which colored people were portrayed as devoted slaves who 'knew their place'." (Carlton Moss, "The Negro in American Films," Freedomways, Spring 1963, p. 136.)

29.   "Editor's Study," Harper's Monthly Magazine, January
      1910, p. 313.

30.   Henry Allen, "End of an ERA," The Washington Post,
      July 8, 1982, D1.

31.   Eunice Fuller Barnard, "Home--Job--or Both?   The
      Woman's Problem," The Nation, June 2, 1926,
      pp. 601-602.

32.   Note: Spelman College (Atlanta, Georgia) celebrated a
      "Century of Service to [Black] Women Who Achieve"
      in 1981, having grown from an institution fostering
      reading, writing, religion, basketry, and sewing to
      a competitive liberal arts college.   Celebrated Spel-
      man alumnae include actress Esther Rolle, author
      Alice Walker, opera star Mattiwilda Dobbs, and civil
      rights lawyer Marian Wright Edelman.   See Aminah
      Montgomery's "Spelman College, A Century of Ser-
      vice to Women Who Achieve," The Black Collegian,
      April/May 1981, pp. 90-93.

33.   Life, Special Report, 1976.

34.   Lerone Bennett, "No Crystal Stair: The Black Woman
      in History," Ebony, August 1977, pp. 164-170.

35.   Marjorie McKenzie, 50 Years of Progress for Negro
      Women.   Pittsburgh, Pa. :   Pittsburgh Courier Re-
      print, 1950, p. 2.

36.   Elizabeth Ross Haynes, "Two Million Negro Women at
      Work," Southern Workman, February 1922, p. 65.

37.   Ibid. , p. 66.

38.   Ibid. , p. 64.

39.   Ibid. , pp. 67-68.

40.   Eileen Southern, "In Retrospect: Black Prima Donnas
      of the Nineteenth Century," The Black Perspective
      in Music, Spring 1979, p. 95.

41.   Perry Bradford, Born with the Blues. New York: Oak
      Publications, 1965, p. 13.

42. Jack Maher, "Leave It to the Girls!" Metronome,
     December 1956, pp. 18-19.

43. Leonard Feather, The Book of Jazz. New York:
     Bonanza Books, 1965, p. 176.

44. Orrin Keepnews and Bill Grauer, Jr., A Pictorial His-
     tory of Jazz. New York: Crown Publishers. 2nd
     ed., 1971, p. 155.

45. George T. Simon, The Big Bands. Rev. ed. New
     York: Collier, 1974, pp. 11-13.

46. Paul Eduard Miller, Yearbook of Swing. Chicago:
     Down Beat, 1939, pp. 18-19.

47. Dave Dexter, "12 Great Negro Bands in New Jazz
     Anthology Album," Down Beat, April 1, 1941, p. 14.

48. Ralph Ellison, Shadow and Act. New York: Random
     House, 1964, pp. 211-212.

49. Simon, op. cit., p. 261.

50. Rose Heylbut, "The Hour of Charm," The Etude,
     October 1938, p. 639.

51. Simon, op. cit., p. 511.

52. Frank Driggs, Women in Jazz: A Survey. Brooklyn,
     N.Y.: Stash Records, 1977, p. 3.

CHAPTER III

PINEY WOODS COUNTRY LIFE SCHOOL

To tell the story of the Sweethearts is to tell the story of Piney Woods Country Life School, the bands' birthplace; to tell the story of Piney Woods Country Life School is to tell the story of Laurence Clifton Jones, the school's founder/president and the bands' organizer, promoter, and director-general.

The "Miracle in Mississippi" has long been a popular stop for curiosity seekers drawn to the campus by a highly visible, attention-attracting sign on Highway 49, thirty miles south of Jackson, the state's capital. The sign reads as follows:

THE PINEY WOODS

COUNTRY LIFE SCHOOL

Founded by Dr. Laurence C. Jones in 1909
Visitors are welcome to drop in for
a visit and have a cool drink of water
Turn Right - - - - James S. Wade, President

Others have learned of the school from its many impressive graduates scattered throughout the country; the school's quarterly news release; articles in such national publications as Sunshine Magazine, Reader's Digest, Southern Observer, Liberty, and the Iowa Alumni Review; or the popular television program "This Is Your Life" (1954). Thousands of visitors tour the campus yearly. They are received and directed by well-informed student guides who tell the Piney Woods story and give "literature which breathes the

75

spirit of goodwill." State officials regularly visit the campus.
Many foreign educators are directed to the school by the
American Council on Education.

Current publicity includes the following:

> Piney Woods School continues the commitment of
> its founder.... We are educating students for
> careers and daily living.... Piney Woods School
> believes in spiritual and religious growth. We
> provide religious experiences based in Christianity,
> but with a form which is non-sectarian and ecumen-
> ical in spirit.... Piney Woods School remains
> committed, as when we began, to serving the stu-
> dent who does not have the financial resources,
> home environment, educational opportunity or com-
> munity situation necessary to meaningful learning
> and real development of individual potential.

All students must earn while they learn; attend all
classes, meals, school functions, and church services; do
homework and related class work; keep rooms, buildings,
and grounds neat; respect the rights and property of others;
be well groomed, courteous, and well behaved; and be where
they are supposed to be. The school's program is designed
to develop each student's "head--mental capacities; heart--
spiritual, social and psychological growth; and hands--working
skills for making a living. Upon graduation, students receive
a diploma and a vocational certificate. [1]

Piney Woods Country Life School has often been referred to as the school that faith built, the school that ante-
dated the war on poverty. Its founder has been referred to
as John the Baptist of Negro Education and a one-man VISTA
corps. With $1.65, a meager bit of clothing, a Bible, and
copies of Wallace's Farmer and Successful Farming, Jones
cast his lot among "those whose life started at a discount" in
the piney woods section (noted for its longleaf pine) of South
Mississippi--the state's first hills to be settled by whites.
Braxton, on the border of Rankin and Simpson Counties, was
the specific post office for that bit of land that became Piney
Woods Country Life School.

In the fall of 1909, Jones started teaching a young
black under a cedar tree, one that today is listed among the
nation's "Famous and Historic Trees" by the American Forestry Association. In the sight of Jones, a teacher on one

end of a log and a student on the other was sufficient beginning for a school. For a quarter of a century, the district
Sunday School Convention had been trying to create a high
school in the area for black youths, with little to show in
1909 for its efforts. "High school" at that time meant teaching and learning through the sixth and seventh grades.

        Soon three young blacks sat with Jones under the cedar
tree. The three soon became twelve--five boys and seven
men. Before long there were fifty students, both male and
female, ranging in age from seven to sixty--all seeking to
know and to know how.

        Jones's analysis of his people's needs was like that
expressed by the American Baptist Home Missionary Society's
Superintendent of Education in 1908:

> It is a sort of well-worn adage ... that knowledge
> is power. And it is one of those half truths that
> are sometimes very dangerous. Knowledge is not
> power. A man may know a great many things, and
> be able to do a very few things. We should re-
> member that knowing is one thing and knowing how
> is another. [2]

        By New Year's Day, 1910, Piney Woods Country Life
School was in full operation in a shed, formerly occupied by
sheep, as well as "lizards, snakes, owls and a full crop of
weeds."[3] The shed was donated to Jones by a local farmer,
"the only colored man in the section at that time who had anything ahead."[4] Along with the shed the donor gave forty acres
of land and fifty dollars. Students and the "little professor"
(as Jones was known) cleared the grounds, improved the
shed's roof, built a chimney and whitewashed the building.
This building still stands and beneath the nearby cedar tree
rest the remains of the school's founder and his wife.

        By the close of the first school year, Piney Woods
had enrolled eighty-five students, secured the services of
five teachers, and laid the foundation for the erection of its
first real building. Simpson County's Superintendent of
Schools persuaded Rankin County's Superintendent of Schools
to join him in giving to Piney Woods the small monthly ap-
propriation (eighteen dollars) previously given to a one-teacher
school, located midway between the two counties, which had
been operating only four months. During the school's second
academic year (1910-11), the Jeanes Fund launched its work

Piney Woods' first building, first faculty, and first group of
students.

of rural Negro education aid in Mississippi.   The first
Jeanes teacher in Mississippi was assigned to Piney Woods.

        Also during the school's second year of operation,
someone donated a hand press, making possible the printing
of a campus news release.   Called The Pine Torch, the
paper was published monthly, "in the interest of primitive
Christianity and Education."   In later years, the fifty cents
per year subscription rate was discontinued and the monthly
publication became a "free" quarterly, "dedicated to SERVICE
and EDUCATION of the HEAD, HAND and HEART."   The
Pine Torch was and still is Piney Woods' manner of keeping
the school's name before a national public; keeping friends
informed of improvements, activities, and projections; reporting on campus visitors; and sharing names of friends and do-
nors who "keep in touch."

        Enrollment continued to increase.   Wrote Beth Day,
one of several chroniclers of the school's history,

        They carried their children dusty miles to deliver

> them to the "little 'Fesser"; they trailed him when
> he walked, and they spoke with hushed awe about
> this strange young man who so obviously "had a
> han'." Just as the "conjuhs" were influenced for
> the devil, they decided that the "little 'Fesser" and
> his "mo' dan a mystery" school were powers for
> good. 5

Commented historian George Alexander Sewell,

> Piney Woods struggled and grew on a "hand to
> mouth" basis with gifts of clothing, seeds, equip-
> ment and money from donors throughout the United
> States. 6

As an example of their shoestring budget, the school
has preserved the list of contributions and contributors (rela-
tives and friends) toward the education of the first female
boarding student, Georgia Lee Myers, who was an orphan
who found her way to the opportunity school.

> Aunt Hester Robins, a pound of butter and a dime
> Grandma Willis, a chicken
> Aunt Lucy McConnell, four bits
> Sarah Pernell, a chicken
> Effie McCoy, five cents
> James Buckner, two bits
> Mrs. Church, seven cents
> Meal Kyle, two bits
> Mollie Pernell, a few things
> Bessie Harvey, one of her dresses
> Chlora Pernell, a dime
> Washington Lincoln Johnson, two pecks of meal
> Mandy Willis, a dozen eggs

Following graduation (1919), Georgia Lee Myers worked as
Industrial Supervisor for Simpson County. She later founded
several schools--all based on the Piney Woods Country Life
School model--in other educationally deprived areas of Mississippi. Dr. Jones's teaching techniques merited emulation.

Born in St. Joseph, Missouri in 1882, Jones was the
son of a hotel porter and the eldest of four children. His
mother was a homemaker and a part-time seamstress. According to Jones, his mother

> possessed that intense practical industry so often

demonstrated by the women of her race, who dream
more splendid dreams and bravely strive, through
the humble mediums within their reach, to make
their dreams come true. [7]

Jones's maternal grandfather, Prior Foster, founded
Woodstock Manual Labor Institute at Addison, Lenawee County,
Michigan in 1846.

[B]elieved to be the first integrated educational institution, founded and incorporated [1848] by an Afro-
American, in the United States ... [t]his early
awakening of the basic need for education of "both
hand and head," ... was the dominate [sic] factor
which led to the founding of "Republican" Michigan
Agricultural College (now Michigan State University)
near Lansing ten years later.... [8]

Designed to serve "colored people and others," Woodstock
operated on a work-your-way-through basis, securing additional support from founder Foster's regular fund-soliciting
and friend-making journeys in the East.   Foster was often
accompanied by singing students from the Institute.

Jones went out on his first fund-raising mission during the summer of 1911.   As he later explained, "On my
frequent pilgrimages upon a similar mission, I have to remember that after all, I have come by my inheritance justly;
I am simply 'taking after' my grandfather."[9]

Jones recalled an experience from his sophomore year
at the University of Iowa when the school's president used the
expression "noblesse oblige" during one of his speeches.   Said
Jones, "I realized that because of the superior advantages for
schooling that had been mine, I was morally obligated to pass
the opportunity on to those less fortunate than myself."[10]   He
valued the opportunity that had been his to work his way
through the college course, "tending furnaces and waiting
tables."   He also valued earlier work experiences that included bootblacking, newspaper delivering, and janitorial
duties.

The idea of "noblesse oblige" was reinforced during
the seminar phase of an industrial arts class in his junior
year, when he was given the task of developing a theme on
the work of Booker T. Washington and Tuskegee Institute.
Jones was impressed by the fact that Washington devoted his

Laurence Clifton Jones.

life to helping his people believe in the dignity of working
with the hands and had gone to the "black belt" of Alabama
to start a school.

Other students were given an hour each for their reports, but Jones was given six hours. A review of each of
his presentations was carried in the local newspapers. Jones
also discussed the philosophy of sociologist/civil rights activist W. E. B. DuBois and wrote in 1922:

> From industrial training [per Booker T. Washington]
> to the scholarship of Dr. DuBois seemed a long step,
> but it showed the possibilities of the Negro....   Dr.
> DuBois was not opposing industrial education....
> [H]is great contention was that there was not so
> much a "Negro Problem" as a "Human Problem"
> ... and that industrial education was no more a
> means for the complete development of the Negro
> than any other kind of education. [11]

Completing his college work in 1907, Ph. B. recipient
Laurence Jones headed South. He explained his desire to go
South as a "modern version of 'Go West, young man,' ...."
"To become acclimated," he went first to Hot Springs, Arkansas, where he worked in a planter's home, caring for a
horse and carriage and milking a cow. After a short while,
he accepted a position at Utica Institute in Hinds County,
Mississippi, though he had received an offer from Booker T.
Washington to join in the work at Tuskegee Institute. Over
the Christmas holidays in 1908, Jones visited with one of his
students whose home was Piney Woods, Mississippi. He
recognized immediately that his ambitions could best be realized there. Resigning from Utica Institute, Jones returned
to Piney Woods the following May and remained there until
his death in 1975.

On the occasion of Piney Woods Country Life School's
celebration of seven decades of existence (1979), The Pine
Torch reported:

> In the glaring sun of that 1909 lazy spring day, a
> young Negro stepping from the Jim Crow section of
> the Gulf & Ship Island train in Braxton, Mississippi,
> was to set the stage for one of the most unusual,
> dramatic beginnings of any school.
>   A Missouri native, ... Laurence C. Jones took
> on the self-imposed task of educating the "forgotten

children" of his race in the Black Belt of Mississippi. [12]

Upon his arrival, Jones visited homes, churches,
neighborhood meetings, and "under the trees at noontime"--
wherever he could gather an audience. As he explained,

> I saw that the future of the majority of the people
> must be as country-folk, and that to make them a
> better country-folk was the task of their helper.
> It was clear that the base of operation must be in
> the kitchen, the household, the garden, and the
> farm. [13]

Jones also recognized the unreliability of the area's one-crop
(cotton) economy and the disadvantages of the credit system
for small black farmers.

Piney Woods Country Life School came into existence
legally and formally in 1913, with the granting of a charter
by the State of Mississippi. As stated in the Charter of In-
corporation,

> [T]he purpose for which it is created is to establish,
> maintain and develop a country life school in which
> to train the head, heart and hands of boys and girls
> for a life of Christianity, character and service. [14]

According to the By-Laws, the school's "objectives, purposes
and functions" were

> far over and beyond the mill run idea of a school.
> Piney Woods is not only a school in the usual sense
> of the word, but it is a spirit, a home, a way of
> life. It's an opportunity school for boys and girls
> who have no money or financial backing, but who
> are willing to work for an education. That, to-
> gether with its being first of all a Christian school,
> is the only excuse for its existence. Change or
> dissipate the above and Piney Woods becomes a
> "mill run" of a school. [15]

Following more than seven decades of development,
Piney Woods Country Life School is by no means a "mill
run" school. Dr. Jones's successor, James S. Wade, reported at the beginning of academic year 1981-82 the following Student Program:

1. Regular classes (academic, vocational, occupational)
2. Meaningful work (related to a particular class)
3. Regular work (routine jobs) [all students are required to work a minimum of fifteen hours]
4. Supervised study
5. Electives (art, music, tailoring, food service, painting, automotives, printing, etc.)
6. Christian Education
7. Recreation (swimming, basketball, tennis, baseball, etc.)
8. Special events (assembly, musical programs, state competitions, intramurals, etc.)[16]

The honoree and guest speaker for Founder's Day, 1982, was Mississippi's United States Senator John C. Stennis, a donor and influential supporter of the beginning of Piney Woods School's highly successful forestry program. The 1982 Commencement Address was delivered by the world-renowned author of Roots, Alex Haley.

From a handful of original students, the enrollment grew to five hundred in the late 1930s and today prospers with an enrollment of over three hundred. Laurence Jones traveled continuously throughout America in pursuit of operating funds. When he asked for money to construct a new building, he was always able to add, "If our supporters will provide the material, our boys will make the brick and do most of the construction work." This offer still holds true today.

Throughout the school's history, the only requirement for enrollment has been a desire to learn. The school would develop the mind and make idle hands productive. As one former student recalled, "Piney Woods taught us how to do ordinary things in an extraordinary way." All students worked, even when they were able to pay. Classes were held at night for those who worked their way in full. Jones accepted some students just short of reform school, but few were ever expelled.

All was carefully spelled out in the school's catalogue. For female enrollees in 1938, the following applied:

GIRLS WORKING THEIR WAY THROUGH SCHOOL

We have room for a limited number of full time

A typical Piney Woods Commencement Exercise (1922) in which graduates demonstrate their skills.

work girls.... [Those] who are physically unable to do laundry work, canning, scrubbing, etc., should not apply for admission as full work students. Full time work girls cannot choose the work they would like to do but must work wherever the school needs them. It is necessary to work one year as a full time work student before entering school. The amount of credit work students receive will depend upon the way they do their work. All work students will begin school in the fall after having been here one year.

GIRLS WORKING A PART OF THEIR WAY

You will be given work to do immediately after registration and at the end of the month cash credits earned will be applied on your board and room[,] leaving the difference to be paid in cash. If you earn $2.00 during the month you will have to pay $10.00 in cash. If you earn $4.00 you will only

have to pay $8.00.   What you pay in cash will de-
pend upon the kind of work you have been doing and
the way you did your work. [17]

Keep in mind these stipulations as we later consider the work
assignments of several girls to a touring jazz band.

Through the years, no school ceremony was more
breath-taking than Piney Woods's commencement exercises.
According to a program from the Twenty-Fifth Annual Commencement (1946), the high school graduates demonstrated
for the visitors their skills in some vocations.   The morning
program's theme was "Better Homes--Better Americans."
Students displayed their skill at the following: chairing a
meeting, fixing a truck, preparing a well-balanced meal,
cleaning a room, covering a chair, making pillow cases,
making a chenille bedspread, converting feed sacks into a
table cloth and a pair of curtains, making a dress that fits,
laundering, repairing electrical appliances, crocheting a rag
rug, caring and testing seed for planting, and serving a meal.

The afternoon theme was "Better Teaching--Better
Americans," which was exemplified by the following demonstrations: points to emphasize in group singing, inspiring
the use of the dictionary, encouraging physical education for
every student, correcting the false impression that public
speaking is oratory, showing the value of the rhythm band as
creative expression, making instruments for the rhythm band,
the rhythm band in action, operating a store, starting a
varied educational program, setting-up a visual-education
program, and threading a motion picture projector.   Three
of the four graduating presenters were members of the Junior
International Sweethearts of Rhythm (Leaster Bethea, Ora
Dean Clark, and Nina de La Cruz).

Dr. Jones began telling the Piney Woods story for
posterity in 1910 with his first book, Up Through Difficulties.
There followed his Piney Woods and Its Story (1922), wherein
he tells

the story of the lighting of a torch--a torch indeed,
but one blazing like the sun, one which shall fur-
nish a new and compelling inspiration to the children of many generations, each striving to perform
his or her part in making brighter the home, the
race, the community, the nation, and the world. [18]

There followed two additional books by Jones (The Spirit of
Piney Woods, 1930, and The Bottom Rail, 1934) and numerous articles.

Until 1945, Mississippi had a school for crippled black
children but no facilities for the blind. With help from a
blind State Senator, Jones succeeded in securing enough funds
to pay a meager salary for one trained teacher and to supply
lodging for ten students. Housing, lodging, and instruction
for black visually disabled Mississippians took place at Piney
Woods Country Life School. When after three years state
funds were discontinued, Piney Woods did not dismiss a student. Instead, it continued to make every enrollee self-
supporting by the time he or she completed the designed program. Finally, Dr. Jones succeeded in getting the celebrated
Helen Keller to visit the campus (1945) and appear before the
state legislature. The result was the provision of adequate
state aid for Mississippi's black blind youth and a building
and staff in nearby Jackson.

Just as telling the story of Piney Woods requires re-
lating the story of Laurence Jones, so telling his story requires mention of his helpmate Grace Morris Allen, who
married Jones in 1912. They met during his junior year in
college when he spoke at a Missionary Society meeting. In
the audience was Grace M. Allen, who was in town in the
interest of Eckstein-Norton School in Kentucky (a school very
similar to Piney Woods), which later merged with Berea College.

Like her husband, Grace Allen was the only black
member of her high school graduating class (Burlington, Iowa).
She studied further at a business college (also like her husband) and at the Chicago Conservatory of Music, mastering
dramatics and public speaking. Her mission in life paralleled
that of her husband. She founded the Grace Allen Industrial
School in Burlington and continued as the school's director
until the city's public schools included industrial arts in the
curricula.

Now Laurence Jones's fund-raising efforts (and results)
were doubled, since both traveled on behalf of Piney Woods.
Even if some people opposed solicitation they "gave Mrs.
Jones checks because it was such a pleasure to have her
call.... Her ability to raise money for Piney Woods was
almost an art and it was one which few people can hope to
emulate." It was she who conceived the idea of sending out

The story of Laurence C. Jones and his school reaches a
national audience by way of Ralph Edwards' program "This
Is Your Life" (NBC--December 15, 1954).

singing groups, later known as the Cotton Blossoms, and
managed them. "She was mother, instructor, school-teacher,
and as often cook and laundress for the crowded groups who
went out in ... house cars."[19]

    When not on the road, Grace Allen Jones agitated for
prison reforms in the state, organized the school's mothers'
club, reorganized the Mississippi State Federation of Colored
Women's Clubs, headed the school's extension program, directed the handicrafts department, and supervised English
classes. School historian Leslie Harper Purcell wrote that
a common theme of Mrs. Jones's speeches was that "women
must arouse themselves to a sense of their responsibilities
in doing something tangible to build up the welfare of their
race...."[20] Purcell gave attention also to Mrs. Jones's
success in getting the Mississippi Board of Education to inte-

grate Negro History into the teaching of Mississippi and
United States history.   Also through her efforts, the State
began providing libraries in all Negro public schools.

The greatest support for the school came by way of
an NBC coast-to-coast television program, December 15,
1954.   The story of Laurence Clifton Jones and his school
was the subject of television personality Ralph Edwards' program "This Is Your Life," a program known for honoring
"citizens who have traveled the rugged road to success and
fame."   Lured under the disguise of a trip to Hollywood to
address the Rotary Club (strong supporters of Piney Woods),
Jones, after two days of Rotarian hospitality, was carried to
the television studio, totally unsuspecting that he was the
evening's honoree.   There Jones found his former students,
friends, and school supporters, all singing the praises of the
"little 'Fesser" who lived his life "praying as if it was all up
to God, and working as if it was all up to him."   Included
were Jones's high school principal; a high school classmate
(Past President of the Mother Church Christian Scientist of
Boston); a college classmate; school trustees; Piney Woods's
academic department head; former students--one a college
president, another a county school supervisor, and still another a successful contractor; and the donor of a girls' dormitory at Piney Woods, given in memory of his "Black Mammy."
Dr. Jones once wrote of the latter, "I have heard many,
many Southern white people tell how much they loved their
old Mammies; but this is the first instance I have known of
a real true worthwhile monument to her memory."[21]

Jones's school had grown from a class of one (held
under a cedar tree) to an institution offering instruction from
kindergarten through junior college, with an enrollment of
over five hundred students. [22]   The impressive story caused
Edwards at the conclusion of his program to request that each
of his several million viewers place one dollar in an envelope
and mail it to Dr. Jones.

By the end of the first week, $150,000 had been re-
ceived.   At the end of two weeks, over $600,000 had been
received.   Deposit Guaranty Bank and Trust Co. had to en-
list extra help in order to keep up with the heavy flow of
money.   By the time The Rotarian magazine gave its report
in March 1955, $776,000 had been received.   This amount,
added to the school's already existing small endowment, established the Dr. Laurence C. Jones Foundation.

Always "more than a full" day of work for Dr. Jones (until his death in 1975).

Dr. Jones sits "on a log, under a cedar tree" where Piney Woods School began. Soon his remains would rest near those of his wife, Grace Morris Allen.

In addition to providing national recognition, the show won lifetime friends for Jones and his school. The January-March 1980 issue of The Pine Torch included letters from friends in Pennsylvania, Louisiana, Illinois, Minnesota, Alaska, Vermont, Nebraska, Oklahoma, Mississippi, and Ohio, most including a donation and many indicating that they became acquainted with Piney Woods and Dr. Jones through the program "This Is Your Life." The new Administration Building is named in Ralph Edwards' honor. On hand for the dedication in 1964, Edwards returned to be the Founder's Day speaker in March 1980, at which time he was awarded the Laurence C. Jones Distinguished Service Award.

Through the years, there were other honors bestowed upon the "little 'Fesser." Ten years following the school's founding, Jones had won enough respect to be invited by the State Superintendent of Education to work with a committee establishing standardization of the State's educational program for Negro high schools and a few years later, to supervise the State's Normal School for Teachers, held during the summer.

In 1947, Jones was cited by the University of Iowa for "Outstanding Achievement." Another alumnus so honored that year was the pollster George Gallup. Jones received the Distinguished Service Award from the same institution in 1967 and was the recipient of honorary degrees from Albertine College, Cornell College, Tuskegee Institute, and Bucknell University. The short, soft-spoken, gentle-mannered but determined Laurence Clifton Jones was given the Civic Award from the Mississippi Society of Civic Awards in 1954 and in 1981 was inducted posthumously into the Mississippi Hall of Fame, the first black to be so honored.

The Laurence Jones/Piney Woods Country Life School story was recalled and updated in the Negro History Bulletin's Special Bicentennial Issue devoted to "Distinguished Black Americans." According to reporter Tommy W. Rogers, music was an integral feature of Piney Woods Country Life School. Let us consider the extent to which this is true in terms of both the school and its founder/principal.

Laurence Jones completed grammar school in St. Joseph, Missouri, but had to drift to Marshalltown, Iowa before he could settle into the rigors of high school. There he served as editor of the school's paper for grammar grades and participated in most school musical productions. Marshall-

Top: On Highway 49, 30 miles south of Jackson.
Center: Today's entrance to the campus.
Bottom: A campus dotted with epigrammatic truths.

town High School's "first colored graduate" was also composer
and lyricist of the class song.

Discovered at Piney Woods was a published copy of a
composition for voice and piano entitled, "Sweet Memories of
Dixie," which according to one source "brought in enough
money to provide for 40 penniless boys and girls." Only the
following was indicated on the sheet music: Laurence C.
Jones, Publisher; Piney Woods School, Piney Woods (Near
Braxton), Mississippi; Copyright, 1924 by Laurence C. Jones.
The back page included "Results of Fifteen Years Struggle--
Piney Woods Country Life School--Material Development,
1910-1921," with photographs and impressive captions. The
question arose, Was Dr. Jones the composer, the lyricist,
or possibly both? Contact was made with Nellie E. Bass,
Jones's younger sister. According to Mrs. Bass, Laurence
Jones was both lyricist and composer. From her it was
also learned that Laurence and his three sisters all studied
music, that the older sister was a piano teacher, and that
Laurence played the violin while in college. [23]

Even before the school had moved beyond the sheep
shed, a piano was secured. Jones found the acquisition important enough to write about it in his book Piney Woods and
Its Story. There was a piano available in nearby Jackson
for $30--more than the school had. "But we needed music
and this piano was just the kind and price for us. Finally
one of our enthusiastic farmers ... came to our rescue."[24]
That piano is on view in the preserved shed today, though
unplayable and beyond repair.

An undated Piney Woods Catalogue (probably from the
early 1930s) lists seven School Divisions: "Business, Religious, Academic, Boys Trade, Agricultural, Disciplinary and
Musical." The Academic Department included an instructor
of Piano and Voice and an instructor of Public School Music
and Piano. Listed as personnel under the "Musical" Department were four persons: a Director of Band and Orchestra,
an Assistant Director of Band and Orchestra, an Instructor
of Piano, and an Instructor of Voice. This represented a
music faculty of six. The following descriptive paragraph
appeared:

> We have a very splendid musical department con-
> sisting of band, orchestra, piano and voice, quar-
> tette, glee club, choruses, etc. The cost of piano
> lessons is $2.00 per month which includes the use
> of a piano for practice. The cost of voice training

is $4.00 per month (two lessons per week). Train-
ing in quartette and chorus work, etc. free.[25]

In the early years, Piney Woods was consistently
plagued by fire. An October 1933 issue of The Pine Torch
reported a fire that brought damage to a building that housed
the dining hall, girls' dormitory, apartments for teachers,
sewing department, food supplies store room, ice house, and
the band/orchestra department. "Fortunately the band had a
date at our Capital City--Jackson, thus most of the band instruments were saved."[26] Showing the extent of the band/
orchestral program, the same paper carried a request for
replacement of those instruments lost in the fire:[27]

1 ...	Bass Drum	$ 35.00
1 ...	Bass Horn	60.00
3 ...	Pairs of Drum Sticks	1.15
3 ...	Cornets, $30 each	90.00
1 ...	Cornet	90.00
6 ...	Violins, $40 each	240.00
1 ...	Violin	150.00
1 ...	Violin	50.00
1 ...	Clarinet	35.00
1 ...	Clarinet	75.00
	Band & Orchestra Music	100.00
2 ...	Tenor Horns, $10 each	20.00
1 ...	Tenor Saxophone	50.00
	Drum Traps	10.00
7 ...	Tambourines	10.00
	Costumes	75.00
	Music Racks	5.00
	Victrola and 50 Records	

Writing in the Special Bicentennial issue of the Negro
History Bulletin, Tommy Rogers provided this update of recent music activities at the school:

> A ... male quartet is reviving the spirit of the
> old "Cotton Blossom Singers" through appearances
> on radio, television, and organizational programs....
> The Piney Woods Singers, a contemporary choir
> group ... appear regularly on over a dozen radio
> stations in Mississippi and neighboring states.
> Mrs. Mary Thomas, who heads the elementary de-
> partment and whose beautiful voice made her a
> member of the Cotton Blossoms during her student
> days, trains the little folk in singing.[28]

Rogers' musical updating referred to things vocal, but obviously an instrumental program continues. Note the following appeal from President Wade in 1978:

> HELP!
> The Music Department at Piney Woods is growing and we need your help. Won't you send us the musical instrument which is in your closet or basement gathering dust? We have a particular need for cornets, flutes, saxophones, baritone horns, and all other orchestra instruments (violins, violas, cellos and string basses). [29]

The above is sufficient evidence that music was essential in the life of Laurence C. Jones and was essential throughout the history of Piney Woods Country Life School. Let us consider now the events that led up to Dr. Jones's most ambitious idea, namely, creating and sending out a women's jazz band.

As the school's money problems increased at the start of the 1920s, Mrs. Jones came forth with an idea: utilizing the innate ability of Piney Woods students. There would be no problem putting together a singing group, since nearly every Piney Woods student could sing, "simply, effortlessly and with remarkable beauty." Grace Allen Jones firmly believed that there were additional merits: "It will be a wonderful experience for [the students] to get out and see the country and meet people in different places, and if it proves out, we might keep groups of them out all year round."[30]

She accompanied the first touring group during the summer of 1921, taking along her two little sons and twelve-year-old Eula Kelly to assist with the boys. Principal Jones saw these singers as school "witnesses," capable of spreading the word throughout the country--making known school needs, school philosophies and school success stories, in addition to being providers of wholesome entertainment. The performances were free, and the singing was followed by the telling of the Piney Woods story by Laurence C. or Grace Allen Jones and the students, who then collected any donations. Securing funds for the present was not the only concern however; securing friends for the future was equally important.

The first Cotton Blossoms toured Iowa, where the school's president and his wife had many admirers and personal friends. The success of this adventure guaranteed

many more tours and the creation of many more Cotton Blossom singing groups--male, female, and mixed.   When funds
for blind students were denied by the state, groups of blind
singers were sent out to keep the program solvent.

Performing in churches, for private parties, before
civic clubs, in court house squares, at garden clubs, and on
radio, the various small singing groups attracted thousands
for present and future support.   Persons who visited the
campus were so impressed that they arranged appearances
in their hometowns.   The Daughters of the American Revolution at Rock Rapids, Iowa once arranged a splendid schedule
of programs.   At that time, the D.A.R. came to stand for
"Do All Right" to the folks from Piney Woods.   Other sponsors included the Rotary and Kiwanis clubs, civic improvement associations, church groups, voters' leagues, lodges,
and various fraternal orders.

The first tours were made in a donated open Ford
automobile that carried passengers and camping equipment.
Occasionally the hosts housed and fed the singers, but for
the most part, they ate picnic style camped by the roadside
or in public parks.   In 1927 a house car was given to the
school by Mentholatum's A.A. Hyde.   It had "bunk beds that
pulled down like pullman berths, cooking facilities, and even
a rug on the floor."[31]   A group led by Mrs. Jones instantly
headed out for an eighteen-month tour that took them from
California to New England, raising thousands of dollars.
The group returned to campus with a seriously ill Mrs.
Jones, who passed away shortly thereafter.   But the tours
continued.

By the early 1930s, there were as many as twelve
troupes appearing throughout the country, now under the
supervision of Eula Kelly, Mrs. Jones's original helper.
Since the groups were out for long periods at a time, a
spare teenage boy was often carried along, because a tenor
might well have become a baritone before returning to Piney
Woods.   Also, having some students away from campus re-
duced housing problems as enrollment increased.

The Cotton Blossom Singers gave the public what it
wanted--plantation songs in their purest form.   Favorites included "Old Black Joe," "Carry Me Back to Old Virginny,"
"Sweet Kentucky Babe," "Swing Low, Sweet Chariot," and
"Keep A-Inchin' Along."   President Jones often preceded the
singing with the explanation that "in trouble and under op-

pression the negro [sic], instead of putting dynamite under
buildings and voicing his protest by violence, looked to God
for comfort and help and poured out his feelings in song."[32]
Sometimes the girls and boys included a reading from a black
poet. The sincerity of their mission rang forth loud and
clear.

In the summer of 1933, a female quartet spent six
weeks touring St. Louis, Chicago, and Milwaukee. Their
earnings totaled $1,200. In Chicago the group made four ap-
pearances at the Century of Progress, singing at the Mississippi exhibit in the Hall of States. As one Mississippi official "high in the affairs of the state" remarked: "Mississippi
... through the Cotton Blossom Singers of Piney Woods Country Life School received more favorable publicity than in any
other way."[33]

In the mid-sixties, stories from the early years were
compiled in a booklet, generally included in the packet given
to all campus visitors. Entitled Happy Hours in the Tour of
the Cotton Blossom Singers, the booklet was dedicated

> To the stars under whose glimmers we slept,
> To the flies with whom we quarreled over our food,
> To the fireflies that lighted our myriad camps, and
> To the thousand nameless passers-by of whom we
>   inquired the way.

Following numerous recollections of a tour made in
the early 1920s (selling Piney Woods School to thousands of
people), the booklet continued with a typical week's itinerary:

Saturday: An 8:00 p.m. concert in Hubbard, Iowa;

Sunday: Sang for the morning service at Honey Creek
Church, followed by a seventy-mile drive to
Conant's Park for an afternoon concert, fol-
lowed by an evening concert in Traer;

Monday: A seventy-mile drive in long, cold and hard
rain to Cedar Rapids for a noon appearance
before the Rotary Club. Then back to
Genesco (near Traer);

Tuesday: A morning trek of seventy-miles to Marshalltown to appear before the Marshalltown Rotary Club at noon. Then over to Edgeworth

to the home of loyal supporters for an informal concert and to Iowa Soldiers' Home
to sing for Civil War veterans in their chap-
el.   Then another home visit followed by an
evening engagement at the First Congrega-
tional Church.

Wednesday: Early morning arrival at Cedar Rapids for a
noon day concert before the Kiwanis Club.
Then the group added musical surprise to a
surprise birthday party for one of the school's
supporters.   Finally, an evening engagement
at St. Paul's M. E. Church.

Thursday: A drive to Anamosa, following another informal concert for still another school supporter.

Friday: From Anamosa they traveled to Maquoketa
for an evening engagement, adding an extra
twenty-four miles en route to entertain another supporter at his bank in Springville.

Saturday: The journey from Maquoketa to Evanston,
Illinois.

Sunday: Appearance at First Baptist Church in Evanston.   In the afternoon, an informal concert
for still another school supporter.

Then the writers posed the questions "When do we eat?
ınd "Where do we sleep?" and answered thus:

We eat when we can--sometimes by the roadside
while Jasper [the driver] is cleaning a spark plug
or changing a tire; sometimes as we ride along we
munch the crackers and bologna left from yester-
day's lunch, and sometimes, to be honest, we just
don't eat because engagements crowd so fast that
there is no time to prepare our meals.   Usually
our nights are spent out under the open sky with
our camp outfit for equipment.   This is conveniently
(or inconveniently) swung to our travelling car.   The
nights it rains are the biggest problems.   Sometimes
a kindly minister will let us go into the basement of
his church; sometimes we can find a shed to keep
off the downpour; and sometimes, God bless them!

someone opens their door wide and says, "Come in,
everyone of you and stay with us tonight. [34]

One Cotton Blossom singer is especially important to
the history of the International Sweethearts of Rhythm. Her
name is Consuella Carter. She was born into poverty, the
youngest of nine children, in Haynesville, Alabama. Her
mother died while Consuella was quite young and though she
remained for a while with her father, the early years were
basically itinerant ones. Work for her was essential, and
though she possessed a natural yearning for knowledge and
formal training, the opportunity to fulfill that yearning was
slow in presenting itself.

Though Carter was far behind in academic development,
she managed to leave Pensacola, Florida (her home at that
time) with a group of youngsters to study at Snow Hill Institute in Snow Hill, Alabama. "[T]his lady who was in the
Church was telling about getting the children off the street. . . .
I just got in the bunch and went," she later wrote. [35] The
curriculum at Snow Hill included farming, carpentry, wheel-
wrighting, blacksmithing, painting, brickmaking, printing,
sewing, and housekeeping. Like Piney Woods, it was a
"work-your-way-through" program for blacks.

Snow Hill also provided an outlet for the talented. It
was there that Miss Carter's interests in acrobatics and dancing were cultivated. One of Piney Woods' early graduates
was a secretary at Snow Hill and it was this secretary who
made contact with Laurence Jones in Miss Carter's behalf.
Consuella Carter and another young lady from Florida were
Piney Woods' first out-of-state students.

Miss Carter commented on her new school:

> Orphans, the lame, blind and underprivileged found
> a home at the school. They also developed their
> own talents at Piney Woods. They let you develop
> your talent. Groups of girls would get together to
> sing. We went down to the auditorium on Sunday's
> to put on a program. Someone discovered I had a
> voice so, they put me in a quartet. [36]

Dr. Jones's love for music and realization of the advantages of such exposure for his students continued to grow.
Charles Unash, a white band director "from the North," was
brought in to form a boys' band. Miss Carter was so im-

Nellie Jones Bass on
Founder's Day, 1982.

pressed that though she was
near the age of twenty (a bit
late for beginning preparation
for a career in music), she
secured permission from Dr.
Jones to study with Mr. Unash.
"Because she would have no
one to look after her after
graduation, Dr. Jones made
it possible for her to practice
day and night so she could
learn a 'trade'."

Consuella Carter's first
instrument was the violin
(probably upon Dr. Jones's
recommendation) and then
she learned all the instruments in the band. The
trumpet, however, emerged
as her principal interest.
She recalled a program that
Mr. Unash put together featuring her on all the instruments:

> We put on a tramp act. The public was invited
> and people came from miles around to see a black
> girl and a white man give a program.... After
> the program the white people came on stage to
> see where this white man came from and why he
> was teaching a black all this music. They refused
> to shake his hand....[37]

In time, Carter became Unash's assistant and then
took over as Piney Woods' band director during a year of
Unash's absence. The fact that Unash found the program
running smoothly upon his return encouraged further musical
collaboration between them, even though Carter had completed
only the twelfth grade and all her music instruction had come
from this one source.

Because she was eager to learn still more, Carter
accompanied Unash (and his sister) to Oregon a few years
later and remained there for three years, all with the bless-
ings of Dr. Jones.

Advertising for the Syncollegians (1935), Piney Woods' Male
Jazz Band.

I stayed there until
I got where I could
handle everything.
My whole thing was
music. I was doing
that for Piney Woods.
I knew I had to go
back to teach the
children what I
knew. 38

She returned to Piney Woods
to become the school's first
full-fledged band director,
teaching anyone, male or fe-
male, who wanted to learn.   Claude Phifer, 1982

Several jazz bands be-
gan to develop among the male
students around 1936.   The
best known was the Syncollegians (Syncopating Kollegians) led
by Laurence Clifton Jones, Jr., who assumed the name Don
Clifton.   The Syncollegians played mainly for CCC camp
dances, with players earning little more than expenses.   When
Dr. Jones discovered the existence of several all-white female jazz bands on the national scene, the idea of pulling together Piney Woods' female instrumental resources and chan-
neling them in a syncopated direction for the benefit of the
school began to seem possible.   It is highly commendable
that Laurence Jones dared to consider, develop, and foster
the idea of creating and promoting jazz--something at the
time totally rejected by music orthodoxy, the upward bound
black community, and religious leaders--at this "Christianity
based" country life school.

By now the country was familiar with the Fisk Jubilee
Singers' extraordinary accomplishments on behalf of Fisk University.   And surely Dr. Jones was also acquainted with the
undertakings of Rev. Daniel Joseph Jenkins of the Jenkins
Orphanage Institute in Charleston, South Carolina, who, to
supplement the school's income, took his trained bands and
choirs on the road throughout the North, giving free concerts
on the streets, in churches, clubs, and hotels.   The plate
was always passed following these musical offerings.

The bands of Jenkins Orphanage Institute had a diverse
repertoire, but their specialty was syncopated music.   Their

fund-raising efforts were sufficient to keep the doors of the orphanage open and the quality of the bands' performances led to several trips abroad, including an appearance at the Anglo-American Exhibition in London in 1914. The same year, the boys' band from Jenkins Orphanage marched in the Taft Inaugural Parade.

As Mrs. Jones had recognized the innate vocal abilities of the Piney Woods students, Dr. Jones recognized their innate instrumental abilities. For a decade and a half the Cotton Blossom Singers had been one of the school's main sources of income. Expansion was now in order. There was no endowment, so gamble he would.

Annie B. White ("Baby White"), a pianist and guitarist, offered what assistance she could to the girls and director Carter. Because she was from Memphis, Tennessee, Miss White had grown up surrounded by syncopated music and had received some coaching from jazz bandsman Jimmie Lunceford. Consuella Carter's instruction on every instrument in the band and her knowledge of both good bandsmanship and good showmanship insured that a Piney Woods ensemble would be both competent and competitive. A flair for the theatrical was clearly evident among the girls. From the forty-five-piece girls' marching and concert bands would be pulled those players possessing the greatest potential for further development along the syncopated instrumental line.

Piney Woods graduate, former Cotton Blossom singer, clerical instructor, audiovisual specialist, and assistant postmaster Claude Phifer spotted the name "Swinghearts of Rhythm" while driving through the state. He returned to the campus and gave Dr. Jones the idea of calling the girls "The Sweethearts of Rhythm." Dr. Jones, most skilled in public relations matters, added the word "International," since many of those selected were of mixed parentage and visually reflected more of the foreign than the native. Phifer had been pianist with the Syncollegians and was now working as its front man. This experience would prove beneficial to the success of the International Sweethearts of Rhythm.

During the school year 1938-39, the fifteen-piece girls' dance band took to the road, touring Mississippi and attracting a following as they played at county fairs and after sports activities at neighboring educational institutions. Their touring began to attract other musically talented students to the school. [39]

Claude Phifer and Dr. Jones's sister Nellie Bass
served as managers and booking agents under the supervision
of Dr. Jones.   Thus began the extraordinary saga of the
International Sweethearts of Rhythm.   One can only speculate
as to what Laurence C. Jones's reaction might have been to
the 1980 Salute in Kansas City.   Without a doubt he would
have been very pleased, for he was a man in love with life,
music, and people; capable of forgiving and forgetting; and
committed to the preparation of young people of his race to
take their rightful place in society.   His young women had
taken their place and had left their mark.

NOTES

1. Brochures/Fliers--Piney Woods School (1982).

2. George Sale, "The Present Needs of the Negro," An
    Era of Progress and Promise, 1863-1910, ed. by
    W. N. Hartshorn.   Boston: Priscilla, 1910, p. 53.

3. George Alexander Sewell, Mississippi Black History
    Makers.   Jackson: University Press of Mississippi,
    1977, p. 171.

4. A Pictorial History of the Piney Woods Country Life
    School.   (Fortieth Anniversary, 1910-11--1950-51),
    n. d. , p. 1.

5. Beth Day, The Little Professor of Piney Woods.   New
    York: Julian Messner, 1955, p. 97.

6. Sewell, op. cit. , p. 174.

7. Laurence C. Jones, Piney Woods and Its Story.   New
    York: Fleming H. Revell, 1922, p. 27.

8. Blanche Coggan, et al. , Prior Foster: Pioneer Afro-
    American Educator.   Lansing, Mich. : no publisher,
    1969.

9. Jones, op. cit. , pp. 31-32.

10. Ibid. , p. 49.

11. Ibid. , p. 52.

12. "Piney Woods School Celebrates Seven Decades of Student Service in '79," The Pine Torch, January-March 1979, p. 1.

13. Jones, op. cit., p. 56.

14. Important Facts About Piney Woods Country Life School. Piney Woods, Miss.: no publisher, no date (booklet), p. 3.

15. Ibid., p. 13.

16. James S. Wade, "A Holiday Message from the President," The Pine Torch, October-December 1981, p. 2.

17. Piney Woods Catalogue, 1938, pp. 7, 9.

18. Jones, op. cit., p. 8.

19. "Managing the Cotton Blossom Singers," The Pine Torch, April 1928, p. 2.

20. Leslie Harper Purcell, Miracle in Mississippi: Laurence C. Jones of Piney Woods. New York: Carlton Press, 1956, p. 66.

21. A Pictorial History ..., op. cit., p. 11.

22. Piney Woods became a junior college sometime in the 1930s. It has since returned to a K-12 institution. As President James S. Wade explained: "It is not a college or university. It is not a junior college. It is simply a K-12 school doing its part to help young people cast their lot in our great society." (The Pine Torch, Fall 1980, p. 3).

23. Correspondence with Nellie E. Bass, March 21, 1981.

24. Jones, op. cit., p. 83.

25. Piney Woods Catalogue, 193?, p. 10.

26. Claude Phifer, "Four Fatal Fires," The Pine Torch, October 1933, p. 3.

27. The Pine Torch, October 1933, p. 3.

28. Tommy W. Rogers, "The Piney Woods Country Life
     School: A Successful Heritage of Education of Black
     Children in Mississippi," Negro History Bulletin,
     September/October 1976, p. 614.

29. The Pine Torch, July-September 1978, p. 1.

30. Day, op. cit., pp. 141-142.

31. Ibid., p. 15.

32. Happy Hours in the Tour of the Cotton Blossom Singers.
     Piney Woods, Miss.: no publisher, no date (booklet),
     p. 8.

33. The Pine Torch, October 1933, p. 1.

34. Happy Hours ..., loc. cit., pp. 26-27.

35. Consuella Carter, A Pictorial History of the Tiger
     Band. 1976, no publisher, p. 5.

36. Ibid.

37. Ibid., p. 6.

38. Ibid.

39. Conversation with Claude Phifer, August 9, 1978,
     Mendenhall, Mississippi.

CHAPTER IV

THE SWEETHEARTS' EARLY YEARS

Versions of the International Sweethearts of Rhythm's creation
and rise to national prominence (as well as its severance of
ties with Piney Woods Country Life School) are almost as
numerous as the persons involved. Unfortunately, the key
witnesses (Laurence C. Jones and the unrelated Rae Lee
Jones) are deceased.

        Historian Beth Day reveals nothing about the group
in her book The Little Professor of Piney Woods (1955), published with the school's endorsement. [1] Chapter seventeen is
devoted entirely to the Cotton Blossoms singing groups and
references are made to the groups in all subsequent chapters,
but nowhere does she mention the International Sweethearts
of Rhythm or any other of the school's instrumental ensembles.

        Leslie Purcell's 252-page history Miracle in Missis-
sippi: Laurence C. Jones of Piney Woods (1956), another
school endorsed publication, includes the following:

            The year 1939 was outstanding for the number of
            groups on the road. "The Sweethearts of Rhythm"
            were making successful appearances in different
            parts of the United States....

            . . .

            In addition to "The Sweethearts of Rhythm," there
            was a junior band on campus called "The Junior
            Sweethearts." Yvonne Plummer ... was director

of the band. Mrs. Bertha Dishman ... was pianist
for the groups. There were special assistants:
James C. Polite, teaching saxophone, trumpet and
other instruments; and Thomas Crisp, instructing
in the trumpet and bass viol. All the students
seem[ed] to be reveling in music at this period,
when only a few years back many of them had
never known of saxophones or trumpets or trombones. Many students were actually singing and
playing their way through high school and college....

...

This group was dubbed "The International Sweethearts of Rhythm" by Dr. Jones, because there
were a Chinese saxophonist, a Hawaiian trumpet
player, and a Mexican clarinet player in addition
to the Negro members. [2]

The preceding quotations begin a chapter entitled "A
Liberal Governor Befriends Colored Folk." In a chapter entitled "Creative Outlets for All," Purcell wrote:

In 1939-40 there were several swing bands on the
campus, the girls and boys in separate groups,
with more girls in the band than boys. [3]

It could be assumed that Day and Purcell were simply
negligent in their research, though press coverage (Chicago
Defender, Afro-American, and Pittsburgh Courier) of April-
May 1941 strongly suggested that there were reasons to support the omission and neglect.

*   *   *

My visit to Piney Woods Country Life School in July
1977 was preceded by a telephone call to President James S.
Wade, at the helm since 1974 (one year prior to the death of
Dr. Jones). Wade assured me that I would be graciously received by "the Piney Woods family," though chances were
that he would not be available. His assistants (most of whom
were new at the institution) offered what information they
could, the most valuable of which were the names of Claude
Phifer, Consuella Carter, and Eula Kelly Moman, all of
whom, they believed, "were at Piney Woods during those
years and had a lot of association with the International
Sweethearts of Rhythm, as well as good memories."[4]

Piney Woods' Female Band in 1937, with leader Consuella
Carter in the center.

        Claude Phifer, a graduate of Piney Woods' high school
and junior college, had been associated with the school for
fifty-three years and had been co-manager/booking agent for
the International Sweethearts of Rhythm.   Only recently retired, Phifer had become a full-time volunteer with the Mendenhall Ministry at nearby Mendenhall, Mississippi.

        My informants pointed out that Consuella Carter, a
Piney Woods graduate (high school) had only recently retired
from the position of band director at Coahoma Junior College
in Clarksdale, Mississippi.   If they recalled correctly, she
was one of the early teachers and leaders of the International
Sweethearts of Rhythm.   Reading a copy of her retirement
booklet, A Pictorial History of the Tiger Band, Under the
Direction of Consuella Carter, assured us that she was important to my research efforts.   Carter was living in the
Clarksdale/Lyons, Mississippi area.

        Eula Kelly Moman had been an administrator at the
school for fifty-two years.   Her school assignments included

supervising the Community House, serving as school treasurer,
and functioning as dean of women students. She traveled with
the Cotton Blossoms, mainly assisting Mrs. Laurence C.
Jones and taking over full responsibilities when Mrs. Jones
died in 1928. The extent of her involvement with the Sweethearts was probably only financial. She was believed to be
in the area of Hattiesburg, Mississippi. [5]

Since Claude Phifer was still in the Piney Woods area,
I immediately set out to locate "the man and his trailer." I
suspected that he was one of the seventeen faculty, staff and
volunteer members retired by the new administration and
forced to move from the school grounds, "despite assurances
from Dr. Jones [that] they could remain."[6] Included in this
group of dispossessed persons were Eula Kelly Moman and
Nellie Jones Bass, sister of the late Laurence C. Jones,
longtime school postmistress, and co-manager/booking agent
for the International Sweethearts of Rhythm. Phifer later informed me that he was not one of the seventeen, since he
retired before Dr. Jones's death. As for his moving away
from the campus, events of 1976-1977 suggested that shelter
elsewhere was advisable.

On this first visit of mine to Piney Woods, I located
the trailer but not Claude Phifer. I spent the time exploring
the campus library and touring the beautiful 2, 000-plus acres
of farm campus. Now comprised of more than forty buildings
and accommodating three hundred students, the school had
only recently received complete certification for its elementary and secondary schools from the Southern Association of
Colleges and Schools (SACS), the highest accreditation that
the school had ever received. Pride in this accomplishment
was apparent.

The spirit of Laurence C. Jones was alive and well.
As I talked with various students, I recalled statements made
by one Jackson State University student in the mid 1960s:

> There's something uniquely different about those
> Piney Woods students enrolled here at Jackson
> State. They all seem to have a sense of direction.
> They're hard workers, willing to accept any work
> assignment. Their minds seem to be set on aca-
> demic achievement, becoming worthy contributors to
> society. They're just different, in a special kind
> of way. [7]

The tour guides were very articulate senior students, most familiar with the school's history and its mission. Though the school's founder and his wife lay buried under the nearby cedar tree, such expressions as "Work Is a Blessing," "Devote Yourself to a Worthy Task--You Can't Fail to Have a Worthy Life," and "Those Who Think They Can't Are Usually Right," posted throughout the campus, were constant reminders of his presence.

The library search for information was extremely discouraging. Library staff explained that a wealth of material had been removed from the files upon the retirement and death of Dr. Jones. A review of school scrapbooks contained an abundance of information about the Cotton Blossoms, but essentially nothing about the International Sweethearts of Rhythm, who probably achieved far more national recognition for the school than did the Cotton Blossoms, and in a shorter period of time. Particularly curious was the absence of Pine Torch issues from the years 1937 to 1942.

Back home, only a few days passed before I wrote to Claude Phifer:

July 20, 1977

Dear Mr. Phifer:

Perhaps you were informed of a person visiting on the Piney Woods campus recently, seeking information on the International Sweethearts of Rhythm. My day there coincided with a day that you were away from the area. Hence this correspondence.

I am currently completing research on the general subject "Black Women and American Orchestras" [for what became my book Black Women in American Bands and Orchestras].... Please accept this letter as my personal request for any and all possible assistance. The enclosed check is to assist with the cost of xeroxing....

I was totally unaware at the time that only a few years later I would be completing research on the specific subject "The International Sweethearts of Rhythm."

Phifer responded without delay (returning my check). He confirmed the absence of memorabilia at the school, but offered no explanation.

Band leader Consuella Carter, still providing musical leadership in 1979 (Lyons, Mississippi).

July 24, 1977

Unfortunately posters, letterheads, pictures, etc.
are no longer available. However, some of [the]
members of the band may have some information.
I will give you their names and addresses, some
several with whom I still have contact.

Included in his list were the names and addresses of two people who would be crucial to my research, namely Nellie Jones
Bass, now a Jackson, Mississippi resident and Pauline Braddy
(Williams), a Washington, D.C. resident. He indicated that
these two persons could put me in touch with others. Phifer
continued:

Dr. Jones' sister and I served as booking agents
for the Sweethearts of Rhythm and the Rays of
Rhythm. They were booked in clubs, dance halls,
schools, theaters, etc., in practically every state

Jazz band assistant Annie ("Baby") White.

in the Union. Some of these dates were made by
mail, but we did lots of travel as advance agents,
making personal contact with the various managers
of halls.

I would later learn that the [Swinging] Rays of Rhythm was
the group that school historian Leslie Purcell referred to as
the Junior Sweethearts.

Curiously, Phifer's absence from the immediate area
was the result of his trip to Jackson for a meeting with visiting Myrtle Young (a Jackson, Mississippi native),

one of the saxophone players, both for the Sweethearts and the Rays of Rhythm. She still plays
and has her union card up-to-date. She was the
one I went to see in Jackson the day you were in
Piney Woods. I did bring her down to see the
school that day. I am of the opinion that we were
on campus while you were there.

Despite several unsuccessful efforts at reaching alto/
tenor saxophonist Myrtle Young at her Philadelphia, Pennsylvania address, I did learn that she was one of the few who
continued in music by touring South America with trumpeter/
leader Flo Dreyer, holding membership in the Darlings of
Rhythm in the early 1950s, and leading her own combo in the
mid 1950s (Myrtle Young and Her Rays of Rhythm). Young
was featured (along with Winburn, Burnside, and Davis) in a
Jet story ("Why Girl Bands Don't Click"), February 1954,
and her five-piece combo received attention in an April 1954
Our World article titled, "They Make Music in Baltimore."
According to Phifer, she continued as a professional musician well into the 1970s, but out of the limelight.

Though others suggested that the popularity of white
Ina Ray Hutton's Melodears was the motivating factor behind
Laurence Jones's idea to send out an all-female swing band,
Phifer wrote that Jones "got the idea of the all-girl dance
orchestra from Phil Spitalny's all-girls' orchestra." Most
likely, Dr. Jones had noted the popularity of both groups and
the existence of others, including several all-girl, all-black
ensembles.

Phifer concluded his correspondence:

I am returning your check, because at present,

I do not have any material that I can send you.
However, if in the future I can get some, I will
forward it to you. I feel that an interview with
you would be more fruitful, because you know the
information that you want.

Two days later "a batch of pictures" of the Swinging Rays of
Rhythm arrived with an assurance that as others (of the Sweethearts) were duplicated, copies would be forwarded.

My letter to Pauline Braddy, dated August 23, 1977,
also brought an early response (September 2, 1977), as well
as many photographs of the Sweethearts. Pauline was a native of nearby Mendenhall, Mississippi, though the family had
moved to Jackson by the time she entered Piney Woods. All
members of the Braddy family attended the school and a sister sang with the Cotton Blossoms. Piney Woods was the
source of all of Braddy's education--first through eleventh
grade. Consuella Carter, teacher of all instruments in the
band, was her music instructor. As she recalled, "Piney
Woods was my life, the only part that I want to remember."

Pauline Braddy was indeed an "original" Sweetheart,
beginning "somewhere around 1938 or 1939" and remaining
with the group until the late 1940s. Most memorable of the
experiences for her were the 1940 World's Fair competition
with more than a hundred other school bands and the 1945
USO tour of France and Germany. A few months later, I
was sitting with the Sweethearts' own "Queen of the Drums"
in Washington, D.C. and by late summer (1978), I was to
have my first formal meeting with Claude Phifer.

Claude Phifer had indicated that a visit would be welcomed, but that I should precede it with a telephone call.
Soon after arriving at the Mendenhall Ministries' Thrift Shop
(as I had been instructed) on August 9, 1978, I found the
ever-busy volunteer Phifer and together we went over to the
little blue trailer. An extremely organized man, Phifer ran
through his note cards in search of Sweethearts' (and Rays')
addresses and telephone numbers. Fortunately for me, he
had located his boxes of photographs.

One photograph was that of a young woman playing
bagpipes, dressed in complete Scottish attire. "What have
we here?" I inquired. An amused Mr. Phifer responded:

That is Yvonne Plummer (Terrelongue), daughter

Corine ("Tom Cat") Posey in 1939.

of the artistically multi-talented James Plummer,
the one who laid out the beautiful rock garden at
Piney Woods and assisted with the school's land-
scaping. Yvonne had little contact with the Sweethearts, but was certainly involved with the Rays--
more in a coaching/teaching capacity. Yvonne
traveled with the Major Bowes Amateur Program.
I can't let you have this photograph unless she
agrees. Here's her address and telephone number;
try contacting her. [8]

The memory of "the girl with the bagpipes" lingered
on. I wanted that picture; I wanted to understand the connection between a bagpipe player and a swing band at Piney
Woods. Contact with Yvonne Plummer's daughter was made
during a late August trip to New York City. Yvonne Plummer (Terrelongue) was in England, but would return to Jamaica, Long Island (her place of residence since the late
1940s) in about three weeks. My introductory letter followed;
telephone contact was made in mid October and on October
28, 1978, Plummer and I met at Virginia Beach, Virginia.

Born in Brighton, England to a British mother and a
black American father, the bagpipe player arrived in America
on New Year's Day, 1936, at age sixteen. She was met at
the pier by a corps of newspaper reporters and photographers,
the ship's captain having cabled ahead, alerting New York
City to the arrival of a one-girl orchestra--performing on
bagpipes, Hungarian and Spanish guitar, trumpet, trombone,
banjo, mandolin, saxophone, drums, musical saw, violin,
accordion, and several other instruments. Her black American father had insisted that she "learn more than anyone else
and do everything better than anyone else, because she was
different." Within a period of less than one week following
her American arrival, Plummer had appeared on the Major
[Edward] Bowes Amateur Hour at Radio City, scored a first
place win and acquired a contract for work with one of Bowes'
amateur units traveling the Midwest circuit.

Illness soon forced Plummer's return to New York
City and eventual departure for Tuskegee Institute. From
there she went to Piney Woods, where she worked as "teacher of crafts, employee in the campus print shop, music instructor and ladies swing band chaperon."

Almost four decades had passed since Plummer was
at Piney Woods. As best as she could recall, her years of

residence were 1939 to 1942.   Only occasionally did she play
with the Swinging Rays of Rhythm and when she did, the instruments were saxophone and guitar--"never bagpipes."

> The girls were mainly coached by male student
> saxophonist James Polite.   My duties were those
> of chaperon.   [From the press and school historian
> Purcell we know that she also served from time to
> time as director.] The thing that stands out most
> in my mind about those Piney Woods years was
> what Laurence C. Jones and his staff were able to
> do for children who came from such impoverished
> backgrounds.   It was miraculous what that school
> was able to do.   It re-made those children's lives.[9]

Following the Piney Woods years, Plummer returned
to Tuskegee Institute, married, mothered three children and
abandoned the idea of a career in music.   The years passed;
the memory faded, but the preserved boxes still included
Swinging Rays of Rhythm photographs which Plummer was
willing to share.

The first letter to Dr. Jones's sister Nellie Bass was
sent August 24, 1977.   Once more, there was an early response.   Mrs. Bass's comments were useful from the stand-
point of confirmation rather than new information.   In her
opinion, the most reliable sources were Claude Phifer and
Pauline Braddy, with both of whom personal contact had been
made.

Since Black Women in American Bands & Orchestras
was completed, additional research was necessary for the
current writing.   The summer of 1980 turned up the article
"Piney Woods School, Death of a Dream?" written at the end
of 1977, only a few months following the Handy/Bass communication exchange.   Journalist Bill Minor remarked therein,

> In the last year, 17 of the old faculty and staff
> members who had been part of the school have
> been retired by the new administration, and forced
> to move from the school grounds.
> Among them is Mrs. Nellie Jones Bass, sister
> of Dr. Jones, ... who was forced out of the house
> she occupied 52 years, even though she had a letter
> from her brother authorizing her to use the house
> as long as she lived.

President Wade indicated that "it was all part of a necessary reorganization of the affairs of the school, and that every person either retired or asked to move was amply taken care of. "[10]

The reporter indicated that the death of Dr. Jones (and naming of a new president) "brought on an era of hard feelings, suspicion and disillusionment among those who had long been a part of the 'family' of Piney Woods Country Life School. " Mrs. Bass believed that the initial purpose of the school was fading, whereas President Wade believed that it was his obligation to "move the program along consistent with 1977 style, ... "[11] Strangely enough, no bitterness or hard feelings were detected in Bass's letter of September 1977, (a second correspondence received three years later) or during our first meeting at Piney Woods on the occasion of Founder's Day, 1982.

It was Mrs. Bass who put me in touch with Sweetheart trombonist Helen Jones (Woods), Laurence and Grace's adopted daughter. The opportunity to serve as evaluator for the First National African/Afro-American Crafts Conference in Memphis, Tennessee (May 29--June 3, 1979) afforded the occasion to visit with Consuella Carter in Lyons, Mississippi. Before settling down to a conversation, Carter handed me notes secured from Helen Jones on the occasion of Founder's Day at Piney Woods, only a few months prior. These notes further confirmed data previously acquired and added:

> The first arranger was a lady from Mississippi who played guitar. She arranged mostly chords for the girls to play and she played all the solos. Later the girls were trained to play stock arrangements and we traveled around Mississippi for six months playing small dance halls. Then we started playing all over the South. [12]

This "lady from Mississippi" was Annie White from Tennessee. The year was probably 1937. I was informed that Annie White was married to a minister, was currently residing in Memphis, and would prefer not to be disturbed.

It is still difficult for me to understand how it was that the name Consuella Carter was never once mentioned at the Kansas City Salute, since it was certainly she who gave most of "the originals" their musical start. Carter's name

(and that of Annie "Baby" White) was recalled, however, in
private conversations and on completed "Personal Data
Forms." Those who mentioned White's name indicated that
she shared what she knew, lent support to the effort, and
performed with the girls in the formative stages, but each
one emphasized that she was certainly not in the same league
as Carter.

Correspondence with Consuella Carter began July 19,
1977. In this letter I stated:

> Unfortunately the books reveal nothing, with the
> exception of a photograph [and accompanying label]
> that appears in Gene Fernett's Swing Out (Great
> Negro Dance Bands), 1970.... According to your
> A Pictorial History of the Tiger Band, "you taught
> all the members of the famous Sweethearts of
> Rhythm Band at Piney Woods." With this informa-
> tion, I am certain that you can be of great assist-
> ance to me.

In short order, her response came, followed by other
letter exchanges and telephone conversations. She had only
recently retired from Coahoma Junior College and Agricultural High School in Clarksdale, Mississippi, following forty-
five years in the education profession--the last twenty-nine
spent at Coahoma.

Upon the occasion of her retirement, Coahoma's president wrote: "Your bands have been a reflection of your dynamic personality, your versatility and your love of excel-
lence." The Coahoma County Teachers Association presented
a plaque that read: "To Miss Consuella Carter who has been
a Golden Ray of Light through the dark and lonely days in
the birth of education in Mississippi." As trumpet player,
band leader, and now university music administrator Dollye
Robinson recently recalled:

> I saw Consuella Carter when I was a junior high
> school student. It was at one of those Mississippi
> Music Teacher's meetings in Jackson. That was
> my first exposure to a female trumpet player and
> a female band leader. Then too, she was a black
> woman. Her band was certainly the pride of the
> State--perhaps even all of the South. Her bands
> were always so disciplined, so musically solid.
> When I encountered this lady, I knew what I would

do with my life.   Consuella Carter was absolutely
fantastic. [13]

Consuella Carter graduated from Piney Woods (high
school) in 1927 and remained in service to the institution until 1942, with only three years away for purposes of "growing
musically" in Oregon.   As Piney Woods' first full-fledged
band director, it was Carter's teaching skills and ability to
make even the weakest players feel strong that produced a
twenty-plus-piece concert band and a forty-five-piece marching band.   She supplemented the girls' instrumental bandsmanship with vocal and dancing techniques.   As she wrote:

> All of the girls I had in the band could dance and
> play well.   At the final concert every year, we
> had band music, floor shows and jokes.   It was
> just like what you see in the movies. [14]

My visit in May 1979 allowed for elaboration on all
that Carter had previously written and provided an opportunity
to personally observe this senior citizen in action--still playing and teaching (privately) and leading a rhythm band of senior citizens.   Since leaving Piney Woods (1942), she had organized and directed many other bands (in Missouri and Mississippi) and completed her bachelor's and master's degrees
at Rust College (Holly Springs, Mississippi) and Vandercook
College of Music (Chicago) respectively.

Claude Phifer recalled that Dr. Jones sent him and
three others to Fairfield, Iowa to "learn all they could" over
a period of several months from the musical Armstead family
in the early 1930s.   The boys lived with the family, absorbed
all that they could and fully impressed the Armstead family
with the Country Life School's human development capabilities,
using techniques initiated by Laurence C. Jones.   Several
years later, this family was persuaded to relocate at Piney
Woods and daughter Edna, now well into her teens, was to
take over as leader of the fifteen-piece girl's dance band.
Always when Jones advertised and negotiated for a teacher,
he stressed "mastery of one's profession" rather than degrees.   Obviously age was also of no significance.

A 1937 photograph acquired from Miss Carter certified
that Piney Woods' females were instrumentally involved quite
sometime before the midwestern coaches were brought in.
On campus musical extravaganzas were routine; participation
in the Memphis Cotton Festival had become an annual event.

Twins Ione and Irene Grisham.

With a nationally competitive outfit clearly evident, Dr. Jones was convinced that this group should join the ranks of other "traveling school messengers and fund raisers." The only missing element now was a chaperon, an absolute necessity since the girls' ages (including that of leader Edna Armstead) ranged between fourteen and nineteen. And, one of eight stipulations of "requirements for Graduation" was

> good general conduct. Students receiving demerits for improper conduct during [their] senior year will not be permitted to graduate. Students whose general deportment for four years is of questionable character will not be permitted to graduate. 15

The conduct of "traveling school messengers" would of necessity be above reproach.

Jones soon secured the services of Rae Lee Jones from Omaha, Nebraska, a woman with a proven record of leadership among youth and one who could assist the girls in the vocal department. No one could recall the exact date of her arrival on the Piney Woods scene, but a Rae Lee Jones/International Sweethearts of Rhythm association was apparently first noted in the press [Chicago Defender] in August 1939. My personal curiosity about Mrs. Jones (née Rae Lee Middleton) produced the following: She was born in 1899; spent much of her life in Omaha, Nebraska; was a WPA worker; and immediately prior to her Piney Woods/International Sweethearts of Rhythm affiliation, was director of the Long Recreation Center in Omaha. I could not confirm that she was a social worker, as the press (and various Sweetheart members) often indicated.

Mrs. Jones attended Fisk University (high school department) for one semester during the academic year 1917-18 and enrolled in the following courses: Sightseeing (?), German, English, and Music. Records at the university list Dallas, Texas as her hometown.

Actress/concert singer Etta Moten (Barnett) recalled that Rae Lee Jones was for one year a member of the Western University Chorus at Quindaro, Kansas, under the leadership of Professor R. G. Jackson. (From the Western University Chorus emerged the popular early 1920s Jackson Jubilee Singers.) Moten thought the year to be 1919. She further stated:

Rae Lee was a tall, slender young lady, with long
black hair.   She possessed a dynamic personality,
showed leadership capabilities and was always well
dressed and stylish.   She had a beautiful soprano
voice and gave evidence of solid musical training.[16]

Her activities in the 1920s could not be determined,
though it was certainly during this time that she married.
The 1931 Omaha City Directory listed Rae Lee Jones as a
coal dealer, no doubt the area in which her now deceased
husband worked.   The 1937 City Directory listed her area
of employment as that of laborer with the WPA.   The 1939
City Directory listed her area of employment as that of
recreation supervisor.   Announcements of various illnesses
were frequent in the local black newspaper Omaha Star during the mid and late 1930s.

The Omaha Star carried the following information September 9, 1949:

Mrs. Rae Lee Jones, 49 years, ... died Saturday,
September 3rd [in Omaha].... Mrs. Jones was
prominent in the musical world as she was the
promoter and manager of an all-girl orchestra,
"The Sweet Hearts [sic] of Rhythm" which was
known from coast to coast and internationally. [17]

Elsewhere in the same edition, Rae Lee Jones was described
as one of Omaha's best known citizens.   The non-black
Omaha Evening World Herald carried details about the funeral
arrangements.

A somewhat contradicting report of her death was
carried in the Afro-American:

Mrs. Rae Lee Jones, founder, leader and co-owner
of the International Sweethearts of Rhythm, famous
all-girl orchestra, succumbed after a lingering illness, last Friday, at her home in Denver, Colorado
[!] ... Mrs. Jones, herself a musician and teacher
of music [?], was responsible for the "discovery"
of the original Sweethearts of Rhythm band, then
an obscure, unknown all-girl group in Piney Woods,
Miss. [18]

Events of the intervening years (1939-1949) will be apparent
in all that follows.

Individual and group photographs of the swing band
from Piney Woods began appearing almost weekly in the
Chicago Defender by mid 1939. Indicative of Dr. Jones's
prestige, any activity with which he was involved was news-
worthy and merited coverage. The inscriptions read:

> Here are the Sweethearts of Rhythm ... In Texar-
> kana, Arkansas ... as the headline attraction at
> the Ambassador Ballroom.

> A bevy of beautiful girls--who can also play.

> An assortment of feminine talent seldom seen in
> the musical world.

> Here are the Snyder sisters, Lucy and Ernestine,
> who are attractions in the International Sweethearts
> of Rhythm Orchestra, now on a nation-wide tour.

> Swing fans who have heard the International Sweet-
> hearts of Rhythm play during their recent tour of
> the States have given Miss Nova Lee McGee the
> title of Hawaiian Sunshine girl.

> A better pen name for Edna Williams would be that
> of "Miss Satchmo," for she plays a trumpet in a
> manner that resembles that of Louis Armstrong.

> Willie Mae Wong ... One of the most attractive
> members of the International Sweethearts of Rhythm
> Orchestra ... The swingsters are now in Florida.

> Helen Elizabeth Jones ... One of the youngest trom-
> bone players in the country is one of the star sen-
> sations.

> Pauline Braddy ... This young swing drummer is
> one of the reasons why the International Sweethearts
> of Rhythm is by far the most popular girls' orches-
> tra in the country today.

> Meet the "Sweethearts of Rhythm" ... talk of the
> musical world.

The Sweethearts were traveling extensively by August
1939, at which time the girls were "bringing a swing type of
music, ... both hot and sweet" to jitterbugs in Texas, Louisiana, Arkansas, Alabama, and Tennessee. The group then
headed for Wisconsin, beginning a three-month tour of the
Midwest. Discriminating journalists proclaimed the International Sweethearts of Rhythm to be "one of America's finest
coming [emphasis added] dance bands," traveling in a "unique,

Helen ("T.D.") Jones.

palatial and altogether suited-to-the-purpose semi-trailer."
The vehicle included pullman beds for the Sweethearts and
their chaperon, lavatory facilities, dressing and make-up
rooms, kitchenette, three clothes closets, and cabinet drawers
for each girl.   There was space for all of the instruments
as well as a practice piano.   There were studio couches and
boudoir chairs such as those found in railroad observation
cars.

> To keep a group of girls comfortable and controlled
> for long weeks and months on the road and to over-
> come the "camping out" feeling ... [was] the aim
> in arranging the big Hi-Way Home and the planners
> ... achieved the ideal in an artistic and satisfying
> way with the big bus.   In dimension it [was] thirty
> feet long and eight feet wide.   Every detail [had
> been] worked out to give a maximum of efficiency
> in a minimum of space and weight. [19]

Mr. and Mrs. Jack Williams, the orchestra's directors,
were accommodated in one of five inside compartments.   Mrs.
Jack Williams was none other than Edna Armstead and subsequent notices--well into 1941--carried the name Edna Williams
as musical director.   Trumpet stylist Williams was also a
respected vocalist and accordian player and was fully capable
of filling-in on any instrument in the band.

Mid October 1939 found the Sweethearts in Chicago,
following engagements in Des Moines, Iowa; Omaha, Nebraska; and Kansas City, Missouri.   Public relations strategist
Laurence C. Jones managed to include a photographing session at the office of the Chicago Defender, guaranteeing still
wider recognition in the black community.   Listed as leader/
vocalist was trumpet and accordian player Edna Williams.
Rae Lee Jones was now designated chaperon/voice director.
The roster included saxophonists Willie Mae Wong, twins
Irene and Ione Grisham, and sisters Lucy and Ernestine Sny-
der; trumpeters Sadie Pankey and Nova Lee McGee; trombonists Helen Jones and Ina Belle Byrd; pianist Johnnie Mae
Rice; bassist Bernice Rothchild; drummer Pauline Braddy;
vocalist Virginia Audley; and entertainer Nina de La Cruz.
Lena and Corine Posey were soon to join the trombone sec-
tion.

Fourteen-year-old Helen Saine was so impressed with
the band when she heard it in Bolivar, Tennessee (following

a basketball game) that she persuaded her parents to permit
her to enroll at Piney Woods. With no musical background,
Saine's first months on the school grounds were spent learning the fundamentals of music and the saxophone. In time,
she was able to join the group on the road, adding immensely
to its physical attractiveness and contributing mildly to its
artistry.

On one of Dr. Jones's trips to New York City, he
spotted an attractive young woman en route home from her
lesson carrying a saxophone case. Dr. Jones, who was always on the alert for new talent, followed the young lady
home, identified himself and the school that he represented,
and proposed to the Puerto Rican family the idea of all moving to Piney Woods--the father to teach Spanish and saxophone
student Grace Bayron to play with the Sweethearts. Though
Grace's sister Judy had little to contribute musically at the
time, Dr. Jones assured Mr. and Mrs. Bayron that the master teachers at Piney Woods could soon have Judy ready to
join the troupe.

Dr. Jones's offer was refused, but when both parents
died a year later, Grace called Dr. Jones to plead for acceptance. Soon both teenagers arrived at the country life
school and by the next tour, added their "internationalism"
to the Sweethearts' roster. [20]

Christmas time in 1939 found the band playing at the
Pythian Temple Auditorium in Dallas, Texas. Greeted by
"a thousand and 49 dance fans and those who came to 'look',"
the dance started one hour earlier than scheduled because of
the early arrival of an overflow crowd. Of their Texarkana,
Texas appearance (while on the same tour), one journalist
wrote:

> [T]he "glorified girls of the brown races" played
> at the beautiful Ambassador nite club, where they
> were wildly applauded.... A local newspaper man
> came out with 26 other white men and women from
> a dinner party. The group stayed two hours to
> listen to the swing orchestra that created a new,
> distinctive style in music, a product of a mixture
> of several nationalities--Mexican, Negro, Chinese
> and Indian--as represented by members of the
> band. [21]

Continuing through the Lone Star State, the band stopped at
Wiley College in Marshal.

The musicians then headed for Los Angeles, where
they scored hits in dance, concert, and radio engagements.
Heading back for Piney Woods, the girls were treated to a
surprise nine-course dinner party at the Palm Tavern in
Dallas, hosted by Laurence C. Jones himself.   On this occasion Dr. Jones introduced to the group saxophonist Jennie
Lee Morse of Dallas,

> [a] student of Professor Jackson, head of the music
> department of the Dallas high school [Booker T.
> Washington] ... [and] the first girl outside of the
> Piney Woods school to be allowed to become a
> member of the unit. [22]

Shortly thereafter vocalist Evelyn McGee from Anderson,
South Carolina, a second non-Piney Woods School enrollee,
was welcomed into the group.

The group's itinerary for January 1940 was announced
in the Pittsburgh Courier: Eustis, Florida (16th); St. Simon
Island, Georgia (17th); Jacksonville, Florida (19th); Brunswick,
Georgia (20th); Waycross, Georgia (21st); Valdosta, Georgia
(22nd); Gainesville, Florida (23rd); Bainbridge, Georgia (24th);
Melbourne, Florida (28th); Hobe Sound, Florida (29th); Ft.
Lauderdale, Florida (30th); and Miami, Florida (31st)--twelve
engagements in sixteen days.

Dr. Jones's enthusiasm over the events of recent
months was clearly evident in an article that he wrote for
the Chicago Defender in late February 1940:

> Piney Woods, Miss., February 23--(Special)--
> Shivering "stay-at-homes" may well envy the hun-
> dreds of swing-lovers who have found that a per-
> fect recipe for combating the cold wave is to dance
> to the music of the "International Sweethearts of
> Rhythm."
>   In night spots throughout the south the torrid
> rhythms of the sensational all-girl orchestra proved
> the perfect remedy for frostbitten toes and chilled
> bodies.   Despite the south's recent cold wave, the
> "International Sweethearts of Rhythm" have played
> to large crowds and have not had to cancel a date.
>   The Chinese, Indian, Mexican and Race girls
> who give the band its "International" character have
> stirred up enough heat in the last several engage-
> ments to bring on summer again.   The music maids

Johnnie Mae Rice.

> are now starting their southland tour at Gaines-
> ville, Ga. , Feb. 21. [23]

Fifteen black girls, between the ages of fourteen and
nineteen, had officially begun their ascent to national recognition. With their new type of dance music, described by one
writer as "combined savage rhythm of ancient African tom
toms, the weird beat of the Indian war dance and the quaint-
ness and charm of the Orient," Laurence Jones's brainchild
was gradually reaching the age of maturation. Local journalists in cities where the girls played offered such descrip-
tions as "A wheel of talent, beauty and charm--topflight entertainment in anybody's language"; "The best playing, finest
looking bunch ever to grace the stage or a cafe bandstand";
"A package of music wrapped in the cellophane of loveliness";
"No hotter bunch ever tooted a horn or beat a drum. " One
journalist dared to label the group "The female Duke Ellington troupe. "

Chaperon Rae Lee Jones demanded that the young
ladies exhibit polish, refinement, and culture both on and
off the bandstand. Little intermingling with audiences was
permitted. Break-time generally found the girls relaxing in
their highway home, rather than fraternizing with the crowds.
Mrs. Jones heeded the warning expressed by one of Billboard's editors to the Women in Music editor. Paul Denis
wrote:

> Many are the problems confronting girl musicians
> in the popular music field.... Girl dance band
> musicians must not smile at patrons, because they
> may be misunderstood. They must not engage in
> friendly banter with male patrons near the band-
> stand because the women patrons may suspect that
> the girl musicians are trying to steal their men.
> The girl musicians must be dressed attractively
> but not flashily--so that they will impress as mu-
> sicians and not as flirts. The leader of the girl
> band must be careful, too. She must be genial,
> and more attractive than the rest of the orchestra--
> but she, too, must be careful not to be flirting
> with male patrons. [24]

March 1940 found the girls capturing fans in Florida,
offering "internationally flavoured swing" at black-owned winter resorts and entertainment centers. Still on the road, the

swing aggregation made a return visit to Florida in mid May, drawing still larger crowds than on their first engagements.

By mid June it was reported that the band had been "on the road for a solid year" and was now back at Piney Woods. A two-week vacation was in the offering for the girls, and the press was notified how each would spend her holiday. Keeping the "International" idea before the public, it was announced that Willie Mae Wong would vacation with her family in San Francisco's Chinatown; Bernice Rothchild would be in a Creole colony in New Orleans; Alma Cortez would enjoy bull fights with her family "South of the Border Down Mexico Way"; and Nova Lee McGee, having decided that Hawaii was too far for the limited vacation time, would spend her two weeks in Kansas City, Missouri.[25]

By early July the girls were back at Piney Woods preparing for another year on the road. The July 10-27 itinerary included playing engagements in Virginia Beach, Fredericksburg, Alexandria, Winchester, Harrisonburg and Charlottesville, Virginia; Washington, D.C.; White Sulphur Springs, Beckley, Logan, Bluefield, and Charleston, West Virginia.

On July 26, 1940, the band played at the City Auditorium in Bluefield, West Virginia for the "Miss West Virginia Digest" contest, preliminary to the "Miss Bronze America" finals at the American Negro Exposition in Chicago. A dance followed. It was announced that whites would be admitted as spectators for fifty cents per person and all others for seventy-five cents in advance and one dollar at the door.[26]

The performance at the Howard Theatre in the nation's capital was a return visit "by popular demand," causing one journalist to write: "Just why gay New York has overlooked signing the bunch remains a mystery."[27] On August 28, 1940, the International Sweethearts of Rhythm did appear in New York City, though not yet at the famous Apollo Theatre or at any of the city's first-rate ballrooms. The Sweethearts was one of thirty bands participating in the large-band division contest sponsored by Swing magazine and staged at the New York City World's Fair. The Piney Woods group was the only all-female entry in the contest and they placed third.

Whereas September for most school age youth meant a return to the classroom, it meant more one-nighters for the Sweethearts, more exposure of bright lights to the mem-

bership, more money for the Piney Wood coffers, and more
publicity for the school (some of which was now negative).
Distance seemingly presented no problems--from Atlantic
City, New Jersey to Des Moines, Iowa in early September.
By mid September, their itinerary included nine engagements
in eleven days: from Fredericksburg, Virginia to Frederick,
Maryland and back to Virginia for engagements in Alexandria,
Emporia, Petersburg, and Martinsville; from there to States-
ville and Charlotte, North Carolina and then to Columbia,
South Carolina. By mid December, the group was back in
Des Moines for a pre-Christmas holiday show.

Further indication of the group's rapid rise to national
musical prominence is the following: On October 12, 1940,
the Sweethearts rated thirty-seventh in the Chicago Defender's
"Number One Band" Poll. Only one month later, the Sweethearts rated twentieth in a ranking of forty bands, preceding
those led by such jazz luminaries as Horace Henderson,
Benny Carter, Harlan Leonard, Lionel Hampton, and Hot
Lips Paige. By the contest's end (December 2, 1940), the
Sweethearts had moved up to eleventh in a ranking of thirty-
seven bands, still in advance of the previously mentioned,
as well as above those led by Claude Hopkins, Coleman Hawkins, and Earl Hines. On radio and at all-day frolics, con-
ventions, college dances, beach clubs, dance halls, ballrooms,
theatres, night clubs, armories, and warehouses, the new
band rage was becoming truly competitive in all of swingland,
scaling a notch higher than mere "sweethearts" in this exclusive musical province.

Well into a new school year, it was announced that a
new Sweetheart feature would be a portable school, with Vivian Crawford, a graduate of the University of Akron (Ohio),
serving as instructor of academic subjects (and filling in on
tenor saxophone). Earlier, tutoring in academic subjects
was in the hands of chaperon/manager/vocal coach Rae Lee
Jones. But as one "original" Sweetheart pointed out, the
girls' academic needs were still not being met. Wrote another:

> We were only supposed to play in the Summer and
> come back to school in the winter. After the first
> year, we stayed on the road doing one-nighters.
> When we spoke about it, they sent a tutor out.
> But this wasn't enough, because she could only
> teach music. [28]

Stressing the "International" in advertising the Sweethearts:
(left to right) Nina de La Cruz, Indian; Willie Mae Wong,
Chinese; Nova Lee McGee, Hawaiian; Alma Cortez, Mexican;
and Sadie Desmon Pankey, Afro-American.

The following regulations from the school's catalogue illus-
trate its academic policy:

> Students in Piney Woods School who have an oppor-
> tunity to travel with some organization of the
> school [do] not receive literary credit or promo-
> tion from one grade to another on the basis of
> travel. While there is education in travel a stu-
> dent must complete every course offered by the
> school before he can be promoted. Travel broad-
> ens his knowledge along different lines and gives
> much needed experience but the school subjects
> must be mastered. [29]

Nevertheless, it must be remembered that the Sweethearts
were traveling under auspices of Piney Woods School and
that band members were not the booking agents.

By late December 1940, it was announced that the
sensational trumpet player Jean Starr would give up her position with the New York World's Fair production of "Gay
New Orleans" and join the band.   Also noted for her singing
and dancing in Harlem as well as on Broadway, Starr was
the first "big name" artist to become affiliated.   It was rumored that other established female "instrumentalists of
color" were contacting the school to inquire about the pos-
sibility of signing-up.   Discussion was underway for the
Sweethearts to make two movie shorts "with one of the industries' largest companies" and one of the nation's best
known managers of race bands "stood ready to sign the
troupe. "   The name Ray Barrow of Arkansas was mentioned
as an addition to the arranging staff and William Francis of
California was added to the "school on wheels" staff.   Bookings and the establishment of itineraries were still handled
by the forces back home, but now with the additional assistance of D. C. agent Daniel M. Gary, who possessed both
business savvy and big-business vision.

An International Sweethearts of Rhythm engagement
was an attraction with considerable built-in gimmickry.   The
object was to entertain an audience--put on a show.   And as
vocalist Evelyn McGee recalled, "one cannot imagine the
thrill of seeing the long lines of people waiting to get into
the theatres--just to hear and see the Sweethearts, " knowing
that they would get more than their money's worth.   The
girls were charming, attractive, classy, and very person-
able.   But as one anonymous "trained" member (who joined
the group at a later date) stated the case, "oftentimes personality was stressed over musicianship. "

Rae Lee Jones was now offering not only individual
vocalists, but duets, trios, quartets, and a playing-singing
glee club.   The ever-supportive press began to compare the
Sweethearts' vocal renditions to those offered by the artistically polished Fred Waring's Pennsylvanians (a group well-
established in the white world), as it earlier compared them
instrumentally to Phil Spitalny and Ina Ray Hutton's all-white
female outfits.

By January 1941, the band was rated as "one of the
nation's best draws--a sweetheart for the box offices. "   They
had broken all attendance records at such places as Cincinnati's Cotton Club, D. C. 's Howard Theatre, Atlantic City's
Rosedale Beach Club, Chicago's Regal Theatre, Los Angeles'
Plantation Club, Miami's Rockland Palace, Ft. Lauderdale's

Windsor Club, and Detroit's Greystone Ballroom, to name a
few.   Before one engagement was completed, the girls were
being committed to a return visit.   These "original" Sweethearts had proven that they could live, travel, and work together.   Laurence C. Jones guaranteed that as one Sweetheart fell out, she could be replaced with another.   Members of the Junior Sweethearts stayed in readiness.   The
girls had also proven that they could survive the road as
well as the grind of long tours and one-night stands and
sergeant-general Rae Lee Jones saw that they avoided any
temptations.   One journalist wrote that "they were above reproach in conduct and void of bickering, petty jealousies and
hostility toward one another. "

     This group of youngsters who enrolled at Piney Woods
Country Life School only a few years earlier, with no more
than the desire to get a basic education and learn a trade
such as cooking, sewing, laundry work, bookkeeping or ste-
nography, were now participating in popularity contests with
such jazz stalwarts as Duke Ellington and Count Basie.   Certainly these young women had no illusions of artistic gran-
deur when they enrolled.   Most entered "the school that educated the head, heart and hands" with no musical background
and as school historian Purcell wrote, many weren't even
aware of such objects as trumpets, trombones and saxophones.

     None were musical genuises, but all were teachable
and many were fast learners.   The predominantly black dis-
taff group nevertheless affirmed its right to exist.   At the
time, there were successful male jazz bands on the road
from other black institutions--Alabama State, Wiley (Texas),
Kentucky State, and Wilberforce (Ohio), and there had been
black female jazz trailblazers.   However, none had behind
them the management skill of Rae Lee Jones, the contacts
of Laurence C. Jones, or the backing of Piney Woods Country Life School.   The fact that the group was from Mississippi made the idea all the more novel.

     More questions were being asked about the girls'
academic development, particularly about the obligation of
the institution to its charges.   The girls themselves were
questioning the administration about their academic development, mainly with a concern for when--or if--they would
receive their high school diplomas.   There was apprehension
expressed about the places the girls were performing.   School
supporters were questioning the group's mission: To what
extent were the philosophies and needs of the school still

being fostered? And according to Dave Clark, one of the
nation's first black promoters, strong disagreements between
Rae Lee Jones and Laurence C. Jones over operating pro-
cedures were now evident.

From Pensacola, Florida in early March 1941 came
the following: "[N]ot in many moons has the band met with
such success as has been recorded in this section ... [The]
girls are swinging out as never before. " One week later,
it was announced that the Sweethearts, "saddened by the
death of one of their members, Mrs. Lucy [Snyder] Adams,
[were] taking a much-needed rest prior to another long tour. "

After another week, it was announced that the girls
were back in Florida, "with standing room at a premium" at
all engagements--Ft. Pierce, Lakeland, Avon Park, and
Pensacola. The plan was for them to move on to Waycross,
Georgia and Andalucia and Dotham, Alabama then to Chicago,
New York, Washington, and other points East. Bookings
were "pouring into the offices at Piney Woods. " But one
month later, the following headline hit the press: "17-Girl
Band Which Quit School at Piney Woods, Rehearses For Big
Time. " The article indicated that there had been a "parting
of ways"; the girls followed their manager and tutor to Washington, D. C. When Laurence C. Jones issued an "indefinite
furlough" to their chaperon/manager and tutor, the girls
broke with Dr. Jones and the school.

> The girls held a tete-a-tete with their manager
> and tutor and all agreed that the organization
> should not be broken up. They reasoned that what
> had been done for Piney Woods could be done for
> themselves, and at the same time building an in-
> stitution of the seventeen-girl orchestra. 30

Another paper covered "the happening" this way:
"Girls' Band Flees Dixie After Tiff With School. "

> Washington--The girls who had been traveling for
> three years under the sponsorship of the Piney
> Woods School of Mississippi, playing dance dates
> and sending the funds back for the support of the
> school, severed their ties....
>   The girls, most of whom are orphans, played
> the dance dates in exchange for their tuition....
>   The young women were allowed only $2 a week
> wages and fifty cents a day traveling expenses, they

charge, and returned thousands of dollars to the
school....
     Upon arrival in Washington, the girls secured,
through Daniel Gary and Al Dade, local realtors,
an option on a house in Arlington, Va. , which they
have named "Sweetheart House," and which is to
be their permanent home.   They will pay off the
obligations from funds realized from dance and
theatre engagements.   The house has been furnished
throughout like a dormitory with recreation rooms
and a culinary department.
     Rehearsals are going on daily, with Banjo
Bernie instructing the girls. [31]

It was left to journalist Jim McCarthy to write the
most thought provoking article, bringing to print what many
had been thinking and verbalizing.

[W]hen announcement was made that an all-girl
jazz band from Piney Woods (Mississippi) School
was touring the nation's dance halls to raise money
for that institution, we envisaged two problems.
First: Whether the chaperonage was adequate and
whether dance halls were the proper locale for a
girl's activity which would aid a school.   Second:
How much those tours would interfere with studies....
[O]ur queries were justified.   Eighteen girls* of
Piney Woods School band quit the school, took the
school bus and, pursued by highway police, fled
through seven States to Washington and freedom....
     Playing dance dates and sending funds back to
the school had not taken the place of studying lessons....   Piney Woods School learns too late that
jazz bands and studies do not mix.   It is an experiment experienced educators do not make. [32]

NOTES

1.   Beth Day, The Little Professor of Piney Woods.   New
     York: Julian Messner, 1955.

---

*The number in the group consistently varied from fourteen
to eighteen, as did the girls' reported ages.

2. Leslie Purcell, Miracle in Mississippi: Laurence C.
   Jones of Piney Woods. New York: Carlton Press,
   1956, pp. 88-89.

3. Ibid. , p. 191.

4. President Wade's assistants: Director of Business Affairs, Director of Educational Services, and Assistant
   to the President for Development.

5. Contact was made with Eula Kelly Moman in early July
   1982. She stated that her involvement with the Sweethearts was only in the capacity of school treasurer.
   She could add nothing to what the other contacted
   sources had already provided.

6. Bill Minor, "Piney Woods School, Death of a Dream?"
   The Capital Reporter, December 15, 1977, pp. 1, 6.

7. Observation made by Dr. Jeanette Jennings, a Hattiesburg, Mississippi native, then enrolled as an under-
   graduate student at Jackson State University, where
   the author was a member of the faculty.

8. Conversation with Phifer, Mendenhall, Mississippi,
   August 9, 1978.

9. Conversation with Plummer (Terrelongue), Virginia
   Beach, Virginia, October 28, 1978.

10. Minor, op. cit. , p. 1.

11. Ibid. , p. 6.

12. Memo from Helen Jones (Woods), via Consuella Carter,
    received at Lyons, Mississippi, May 28, 1979.

13. Conversation with Robinson, Jackson, Mississippi,
    March 15, 1982. Dr. Dollye Robinson is Chairper-
    son, Department of Music, Jackson State University.

14. Correspondence with Carter, August 31, 1977.

15. Piney Woods Catalogue, 1938, pp. 21-22.

16. Telephone conversation with Moten (Barnett), October
    25, 1982.

140 Sweethearts of Rhythm

17. "Death of Rae Lee Jones," The Omaha Star, September 9, 1949, p. 2.

18. "Hearts' Founder Dies in Denver," Afro-American, September 17, 1949, p. 8.

19. "Orchestra Hi-Way Pullman," Chicago Defender, September 16, 1939, p. 19.

20. Conversation with Judy Bayron, Lobby--Crown Center (Third Women's Jazz Festival), Kansas City, Missouri, March 23, 1980.

21. "Sweethearts of Rhythm Click in South and West," Chicago Defender, January 20, 1940, p. 20.

22. "Sweethearts of Rhythm Get Welcome in Dallas," Chicago Defender, January 27, 1940, p. 20. Coincidentally, Professor A. Stephen Jackson III was my trumpet teacher and band director at Booker T. Washington High School (Dallas) and is the deceased uncle of former Mayor of Atlanta, Maynard Jackson.

23. Laurence C. Jones, "Dixie Music Lovers Like All Girls Band," Chicago Defender, February 24, 1940, p. 20.

24. Paul Denis, published in Women in Music, Vol. IV, No. 7, April 15, 1939.

25. "This Girl Band Is Much Too Much with Swing and Jitter," Chicago Defender, June 15, 1940, p. 20.

26. "All-Girls Band in W. Virginia," Chicago Defender, July 20, 1940, p. 20.

27. "A Vote for D.C.," Chicago Defender, July 13, 1940, p. 21.

28. Correspondence with Braddy, September 2, 1977.

29. Piney Woods Catalogue, op. cit., p. 26.

30. "17-Girl Band Which Quit School at Piney Woods, Rehearses for Big Time," Pittsburgh Courier, April 19, 1941, p. 21.

31. "Girls' Band Flees Dixie After Tiff with School," <u>Afro-American</u>, April 26, 1941, p. 13.

32. Jim McCarthy, "A Jazz Band Flees," <u>Afro-American</u>, May 3, 1941, p. 13.

CHAPTER V

IN THE BIG TIME

Without a doubt, Laurence Clifton Jones and Piney Woods Country Life School had birthed and nurtured a musical winner. Though it has since been proven that jazz bands and studies can mix, in the late thirties and early forties a Country Life School/ladies' jazz band mixture was almost unholy. Consider the following: 1) Jazz had not yet been accepted as a legitimate art form and consequently was totally unacceptable as a part of the curriculum in institutions of learning, be they higher, lower or a combination of both; 2) In the sight of many, where jazz was, there the Holy Spirit could not possibly be; and 3) Release of women from their traditional roles had not even reached the discussion stage. So despite the odds against them, in early April 1941 seventeen attractive, talented, and enthusiastic black females, an economically astute chaperon/manager, and a musically talented academic tutor headed for brighter lights and professionalism.

In discussing the Sweethearts' break from Piney Woods, one must remember that the principal characters (Laurence C. Jones and Rae Lee Jones) are now deceased; nothing remains on file at the creation site; and memories often fit personal convenience. According to an April 19, 1941, entry in the Pittsburgh Courier, the break occurred

> when it became known that [Laurence C. Jones] allegedly refused to keep a promise to graduate several of them in June....
> The supposition was that he refused to graduate the girls in order to have them remain students and just pay them no more than a dole. [1]

The <u>Afro-American</u> allegedly based its April 26, 1941,
report on an exclusive interview given by the girls themselves in Arlington, Virginia, their new place of residence.
Supposedly eight of the members were scheduled for graduation. The girls believed that they were entitled to more respectable salaries and they resented the fact that "all insurance policies were payable to the school." One member,
who shall remain anonymous, remembers distinctly signing
her policy with the understanding that her mother was the
beneficiary.

The girls threatened a strike, at which time

> President Jones ... sent a wire, firing both Miss
> Crawford and Mrs. Jones and ... sent officials to
> return the girls to the school.

In order to reach Washington, D.C., the girls eluded an
army of highway patrolmen in seven southern states.

> Word was flashed throughout the South that the bus
> in which the girls were traveling had been stolen
> and that both bus and passengers were to be held
> wherever captured.... [T]hey fled as far as Mont-
> gomery, Ala., where they abandoned the school
> bus and sent it back to the Piney Woods School by
> the driver.
> Through contacts in Washington they were able
> to have their fares guaranteed to the Greyhound
> Company and took another bus into Washington. [2]

The girls were pursued as far as Memphis, Tennessee where they were halted by a roadblock. Once the au-
thorities were assured that the Piney Woods bus had been
sent back to the school, the girls were permitted to continue
on their "journey to musical paradise."

The seventeen "escapees" were Alma Cortez, Willie
Mae Wong, Grace Bayron, Helen Saine, and twins Ione and
Irene Grisham--saxophonists; Nova Lee McGee and Sadie
Pankey--trumpeters; Helen Jones, Ina Belle Byrd, and Corine
Posey--trombinists; Johnnie Mae Rice--pianist; Bernice Roth-
child--bassist; Pauline Braddy--drummer; Judy Bayron--
guitarist; Edna Williams--leader/arranger; and Evelyn
McGee--vocalist. The Grisham twins were soon delivered
back to Piney Woods by their older sister, along with Helen
Saine, who was returned by the Virginia Welfare Department
and had to remain until reaching age sixteen. Then for

Saine it was back to Arlington, Virginia to continue her participation in the extraordinary saga of the International Sweethearts of Rhythm.   Sadie Pankey and Corine Posey's names
soon disappeared from newspaper listings of band personnel.
It seems that both were taken seriously ill, thus bringing
closure to their musical careers.   "Teacher" Vivian Crawford's name also disappeared from Sweetheart publicity.

Al Dade, prominent D. C. businessman, became the
group's sponsor.   Bookings were handled exclusively by the
Amusement Corporation, represented by Daniel Gary, another
local businessman.   Through Dade and Gary, the group secured an option on a house at 908 S. Quinn Street in Arlington.   The girls' obligations were to be met with funds realized from playing engagements.

In an exclusive interview to the Pittsburgh Courier's
staff correspondent Anselm J. Finch, published May 3, 1941,
Laurence Jones aired his views.   He stated that "the band
girls had no reason to leave."   Elaborating, Jones pointed
out that many of the girls had been taken in with absolutely
no resources; many were orphans; one was his adopted
daughter.   Few had had any musical training prior to entering the Piney Woods School.   He and Piney Woods faculty
and staff had done everything to make life pleasant for the
girls, covering their room and board, use of books, and
music lessons.

According to Jones, there were two objectives when
the band was organized:

> to prove that it could be done, the living together
> of the darker races in harmony, regardless of
> race or creed and the other, the finding of a new
> outlet for our girls other than teaching or entering
> domestic service. [3]

Jones indicated that only a few months ago the school had
sent publicity material to colleges, high schools, and promotion agencies from coast to coast, "seeking a higher field"
for the girls.   "We wanted to get the Sweethearts out of the
dance halls to as high a [plane] as that held by the Phil
Spitalny Girls on the 'Hour of Charm'."

Fiscal accountability and maximum return on funds
invested were always priorities at Piney Woods.   Jones
claimed that the school had spent $28,391.12 developing the

group and that $27,768.30 had been earned. Therefore, the group's deficit was $622.82. In response to charges that the girls scheduled to graduate would not receive diplomas, Jones added:

> [This is] as untrue as all the other things published, as any student enrolled at Piney Woods entitled to graduation surely will, regardless of what work they are engaged in. It's a regrettable situation, one that should never have happened.

Jones accused Al Dade of waving the magic wand before the girls, "sending powder and paint" and allowing them to call him daddy. 4

Several weeks later, the Pittsburgh Courier issued a disclaimer to the story above and published Al Dade's denial of Jones's charges. According to Dade, he personally was

> not the cause of the bolt taken by the all-girl orchestra.... [T]he band has no feeling whatsoever against its former home grounds, but acted because of the opportunity offered in its present field. 5

Preparing for the "big time" in Arlington, Virginia (1941) are several members gathered around Rae Lee Jones (left), manager and chaperon, and Vivian Crawford, instructor.

In the school's defense were the "stipulations for graduation" quoted in the previous chapter and the following:

> It must be understood and agreed upon by parents and students that when students enter Piney Woods School as work students that such students are to work any where the school might see fit to place them. They might go singing with a quartet or travel with a baseball team [or a jazz band], as the school needs them. As this is work for their board and room under the school's supervision it is the same as working here at the school.
> It must be further understood by parents and students that any work done at the school, or traveling ... performed by students working their way through school IS NOT FOR WAGES or PECUNIARY PROFIT and DOES NOT HAVE MONEY value but is IN EXCHANGE for EDUCATION here in Piney Woods only. [6]

Obviously, there were many controversies.

For the survival strategies of historically black institutions it was traditional (and absolutely necessary) for student musical groups to tour the country in search of funds. Benefits to the participants were experience, travel, and exposure. But it is probably safe to say that fundraising efforts by students, both fostered and sanctioned by school administration, had never before reached the magnitude attained by the Sweethearts.

My own father, Rev. William Talbot Handy, Sr., was a member of one of two traveling Tuskegee Institute Quintets for a period of two years (1916-18). As he wrote in his autobiography:

> Having come out of the Gallatin community [Hazlehurst, Mississippi] and now to be invited to sing and travel with the Tuskegee Singers, I felt a great sense of personal pride.
> As I remember, one year the group went to the Central West. Another year we went out through New England.... The plan was for the Quintet to render a program and Mr. Wood [leader/chaperon] would make the address and take up an offering.... [The second year] I was selected to be in charge of the group. The pay was $30.00

> a month--the [student] leader receiving $35.00.
> An allowance of $2.00 was given each day for
> meals. If one wanted to fast a day or any part
> of it, he could save something for himself. [7]

Compare these figures with those given by Sweethearts
saxophonist/treasurer Willie Mae Wong for the years 1938
to 1941:

> The original members ... received $1 a day for
> food plus $1 a week allowance, for a grand total
> of $8 a week. [8]

Rev. Handy further stated that he and other members
of the quintet demanded more money after the first successful year of touring, but Tuskegee Institute President Robert
R. Moton flatly refused and threatened to cancel the scheduled tour. Quintet members reconsidered and more than
sixty years later, the student leader wrote:

> I have often reflected on this situation. Tuskegee
> Institute had taken me in with all of $9.00 and
> very little preparedness. When I reached the
> point where I could make a contribution to the
> school, I rose above myself and the situation at
> hand. Fortunately, I got the message before it
> was too late. Tuskegee had managed well prior
> to my coming and could get along very well with-
> out my presence and my services. [9]

Negotiations for improved conditions in the case of
the Sweethearts were not in the hands of the girls, other-
wise they, too, might have reconsidered. Nevertheless, as
Piney Woods managed well prior to the Sweetheart members'
arrival and the band's creation, so would it manage without
them. And because of the foresightedness of Dr. Jones, it
would still have as one of its messengers a ladies' jazz
band--existing for approximately the same period as the
International Sweethearts of Rhythm. The Sweethearts would
also survive.

So what was once a beautiful (perhaps exemplary)
relationship--among a Mississippi country life school, teenage black female jazz music-makers, and a visionary prin-
cipal--had ended. In order to offset negative publicity and
keep the funds flowing in, Jones scheduled a musical extrav-
aganza at the city auditorium in nearby Jackson for early

May 1941 and released the announcement to a national press.
The program included several small vocal ensembles (the
Orange Blossoms, Magnolia Blossoms, and Cotton Blossoms),
a hundred-voice chorus (all from Piney Woods School),
Jones's son Don Clifton's Syncopating Kollegians, and as a
special guest, the local singing group "Songs of Soul." The
evening's feature was the Swinging Rays of Rhythm (formerly
the Junior Sweethearts of Rhythm), "America's newest all-
girl orchestra from the school recently deserted by the
Sweethearts of Rhythm."[10]   Laurence Jones was well prepared for the inevitable.

As saxophonist with the new group and occasional
leader, Lou Holloway pointed out in a 1980 interview with
historian Alferdteen Harrison, the Swinging Rays of Rhythm
were understudies for the Sweethearts.

> [T]he Rays of Rhythm, they'll practice at home
> while the Sweethearts are out.... Because if a
> girl gets sick on the road that plays saxophone,
> you take a girl out of the Rays and take her out
> there to replace that girl. The understudy group
> had to always practice, and they practiced the
> same book, ... So all those dates that had been
> booked when the Sweethearts cut away from the
> school couldn't be filled [;] ... the Rays of Rhythm
> were sent out to fill those dates. And they became
> the traveling group for Piney Woods. [11]

The name change was understandable. As new approaches
and strategies were warranted, so was a new name.

The Swinging Rays began filling the Sweethearts' dates
immediately. Before the performance at the city auditorium,
the Rays traveled to Louisiana, scoring a tremendous success at a fraternity ball at black Southern University in
Baton Rouge. Following the procedure that had so effectively
promoted the Sweethearts, Jones and his booking assistants
used the black press to introduce the girls, individually and
by sections.

An action photograph appeared of Eleanor Moore, with
the caption "captivating and talented pianist, ... little dynamo

[Opposite:] The Swinging Rays of Rhythm with Earl "Fatha"
Hines in 1942.

of swing and rhythm"; Lillian Carter, "one of the finest
basso pluckers on the rialto's main stem.... one who can
challenge any girl in the good ole U.S.A."; Robiedell Webb,
"twelve-year-old miniature edition of Mary Lou Williams";
Myrtle Young, "one of the best girl tenor players of the
day"; The Rhythm Quartet--Thelma Perkins (drums), Eleanor
Moore (piano), Chela Vegas (guitar), and Lillian Carter
(bass)--"Wowing 'em in the South."

The public relations strategies kept the engagements
flowing in. Laurence Jones, Claude Phifer, and Nellie Bass
were once again selling a girls' jazz band from Piney Woods,
largely to raise desperately needed operational funds for the
school. Holloway estimated that the Rays, like the Sweethearts, were capable of bringing in two or three thousand
dollars a month.

Not all the "international" flavor of the school de-
parted when the Sweethearts took flight to Arlington, Virginia. There was still "the little Spanish Señorita Chela
Vegas" and the "two Indian Maidens Phoebe and Nina de
La Cruz." President Jones now stressed the girls' youth,
innocence, and linkage with Piney Woods School. In an exclusive interview with a Chicago Defender representative,
Jones indicated that the girls "are still happy little sepia
junior debs, growing and developing in a school atmos-
phere...."[12]

Following the great escape, there was criticism both
outside and within, but Jones managed to endure. According
to Holloway, the girls were often told, "You going out there
on that band, ain't goin to be nothin but street women."
Jones always told the young swingsters:

> [S]ometimes people can't see so far, but you go
> on and do this because you're doing this to get
> through school, so you can go out there and do
> something. The other girls are doing something
> else.[13]

Today Lou Holloway is a distinguished historian and university professor, but can pick up her horn and still make a
living.

When criticism arose over the school's image, Jones
always retaliated with a financial report, hopefully an improvement over the one given shortly following the Sweet-

Still stressing "international" (though now in The Swinging Rays of Rhythm) are advertising poses by Phoebe de La Cruz, Chela Vegas, and Nina de La Cruz. (Note: spellings consistently varied.)

hearts' departure. Sure there were other groups bringing
in money, but the biggest money-maker was the girls' jazz
band.

By July 1941, the Swinging Rays of Rhythm was
headed for Nebraska, Ohio, Kansas, and Illinois. Supposedly
the band was scheduled to perform in the nation's capital,
"but inability to break previous dates blocked the plan."
Soon Piney Woods was reporting that the Rays were in the
strange position of having more engagements than they could
fill and "the bookies unwilling to accept a substitute."

Always with a concern for the proper associations,
arrangements were made for the girls to hear the "First
Lady of Swing," Ella Fitzgerald, when she appeared at the
Rhythm Club in New Orleans in June 1941. Fitzgerald kindly
consented to chat with the girls during her intermission. It
was curious that no photographer was present for the historic event.

With the "proper contacts" still in hand, the band ap-
peared as guest artists at the National Association of Colored
Women's meeting in Oklahoma City during the following month.
In November, the group appeared at the Dallas State Fair.
The Earl Hines Band was touring the same area and Dr.
Jones managed to have the group photographed with Earl
"Fatha" Hines himself. The following September (1942),
Hines visited the school and reportedly rehearsed the Swing-
ing Rays of Rhythm, as well as "The Junior Swinging Rays
of Rhythm."

In late December 1941, there appeared in the Chicago
Defender a photograph of the saxophone section with pianist
Mary Lou Williams. The caption read "Andy Kirk's Pianist
Hears Greatest Femme Sax Section."[14] When Williams was
asked to recall the meeting, she emphatically denied such an
event, adding that perhaps some clever publicity agent dubbed
her in. A second viewing of the microfilm verified Williams'
speculation. More false advertising was evident when the
Chicago Defender announced that trombonist Helen Jones
(Laurence Jones' adopted daughter, who was now fully occupied with the International Sweethearts of Rhythm) "was
making the band even hotter than it was."[15]

The Rays filled many USO assignments, entertaining
soldiers at various military bases. Jones's Swinging Rays
of Rhythm was ranked sixteenth in the No. 1 Band Contest

sponsored by the Chicago Defender, ending January 31, 1942.
Based of course on popularity, the Rays was the only all-
female band included in the twenty-seven band listing.   Duke
Ellington's band placed first, with 76, 897 votes against the
Rays' 52, 532--well in advance of those bands led by Tiny
Bradshaw, Coleman Hawkins, Earl Hines, Lucky Millinder,
and Claude Hopkins.

    From Piney Woods came this conciliatory report in
late August 1942:

> A few years ago President Jones decided to give
> the world something new, a band of beautiful girls
> who would represent various nationalities and could
> be known as an international band.... [H]e gave
> us a band of beautiful girls in whose veins ran the
> blood of five different races....
>   In all it was about the highest class organiza-
> tion that ever traveled among our people, both in
> appearance and ideals.   The general comment was
> that "No one but L. C. Jones could get together
> such a group, keep them together and maintain a
> high standard of conduct. "
>   ... [Then] Professor Jones brought out a sec-
> ond band composed of some of the members of this
> first group and others whom he had in training at
> ... Piney Woods School.
>   This band had a lilting swing to their music
> that earned for them the title "Swinging Rays of
> Rhythm.... "
>   The third band created by this genius in build-
> ing all-girl bands carries the name "The Junior
> Swinging Rays of Rhythm. "[16]

Laurence Jones, who gave the Chicago Defender interview,
had decided himself to ensure that the connection of the International Sweethearts of Rhythm with the Piney Woods Country Life School was remembered.   Piney Woods would no
longer attempt to eradicate the fact that the International
Sweethearts of Rhythm swing band was once theirs.   At the
same time, they would assure recognition of other similarly
inspired Piney Woods Country Life School ladies' bands.

    Several members of the Rays were selected to tour
with the Silas Green Show, a popular black entertainment
unit traveling continuously throughout the South for several
decades (c. 1904 to late 1940s).   Silas Green was to the

southland what Ringling Brothers and Barnum and Bailey
were to the nation. Replacements for the girls touring with
the tent show came from the Junior Swinging Rays, a group
that Holloway recalled as the "Flashers."[17] Earnings from
the affiliation were sent to the school; the girls received
their customary allowance.

From its inception, the chief coach and arranger was
James Polite, a member of the school's male jazz band.
When Polite was called to the military, those band members
whom he had trained took over the leadership, with additional
coaching from Yvonne Plummer, Mr. Strand (who was
brought in from Jackson three times a week), Willie Rice,
and whoever else was available. The band coasted along
for several years, though by the mid forties extensive traveling and accompanying publicity began to decrease. By the
end of the decade, Laurence C. Jones and Piney Woods
Country Life School had abandoned the ladies' jazz band idea.
As informant Claude Phifer wrote:

> The Rays of Rhythm Orchestra was disbanded when
> the school went all out for religious emphasis,
> upon the recommendation of the head of the reli-
> gious department. [18]

Lillian Carter poses for a Swinging Rays of Rhythm ad.

*   *   *

I was able to make personal contact with only three
former members of the Swinging Rays of Rhythm: trombonist/
bassist Juanita Clark (Williams), a resident of Jackson, Mississippi; clarinetist/saxophonist Marion Estella Simmons
(Scruggs), a resident of Detroit, Michigan; and mellophonist/
trumpeter/drummer/trombonist Yvonne Busch, a resident of
New Orleans, Louisiana.

A native of Jackson, Clark was enrolled at Piney
Woods from 1943 to 1949, completing the seventh through
the twelfth grades.   Her enrollment resulted from a personal and family desire to have Juanita benefit from the
"quality" music program at the country life school.   She
recalled the names of Doris Nicholson and Lou E. Holloway
as leaders/coaches; Emma Myers as chaperone; and as
Piney Woods music teachers, Doris Nicholson, Alice Latti-
more, and Don Kzary.

Clark (they called her "Skeeter") saw as the group's
strength "the young ladies' determination and knowledge of
their goals."   The opportunity for "travel throughout the
United States, presenting an all-girls' orchestra from Piney
Woods School, was a memorable experience."   Of the six
years spent at Piney Woods School, the thing that impressed
Clark most was "the wonderful President Jones and how he
cared for others and saw that each enrollee received a full
education."

Clark's four years of membership in the Junior
Sweethearts/Swinging Rays of Rhythm band (which she joined
in 1944) prepared her to make the necessary accommodations
required for a successful marriage to a jazz musician.
When asked how she benefited most from the experience,
"Skeeter" jokingly responded:

> Being able to marry a musician and deal with the
> life of a musician's wife.   I don't think I would
> still be married to the same man [after 31 years]
> if I had not had such an experience. [19]

Juanita "Skeeter" Clark was one of the few who continued in
the profession, becoming a member of various pick-up groups
playing around Mississippi and taking part in her husband's
sextet.

Saxophonist Marion Simmons, a native of Kosciusko,
Mississippi, had two sisters enrolled at Piney Woods. She
recalled,

> Dr. Jones persuaded my parents to allow me to
> attend. I was there from 1940 until 1946, grades
> 4 through 10. My first engagement with the Rays
> was on an Easter Sunday, 1941. I was ten years
> old. I went back to Kosciusko in October, 1946
> because my mother was in poor health and wanted
> me to come home.

Simmons' most cherished memory about the Piney
Woods' years was the meetings with novelist Sinclair Lewis
and author/lecturer Helen Keller. In terms of her female
jazz band affiliation, Simmons pointed out that she was af-
fectionately referred to as

> little Johnny Hodges; but I never considered my-
> self anything other than a student at Piney Woods,
> helping to pay for my education. Being very
> young, we were supervised very closely. Dr.
> Jones was determined not to make the same mis-
> takes with us that were made with the Sweethearts.
> No one person had complete control over the Rays.

Unlike Juanita Clark, Simmons never really wanted
to be a professional musician, believing that "a career in
music was not a fitting lifestyle for a woman. If I had a
chance to make a choice now, I might consider it."[20] Instead she entered the field of life insurance.

Native New Orleanian Yvonne Busch entered Piney
Woods upon the suggestion of her cousin James Clifton Polite,
also a native of The Crescent City. Polite convinced Busch's
parents that Piney Woods could offer the proper training and
environment for the musically thirsty Yvonne. At age eleven she had heard the band when it appeared in New Orleans
and was overwhelmed with enthusiasm.

When interviewed in early November 1982, Busch
stated,

> I was at Piney Woods for about three years--I
> believe it was 1941 to 1944. My mother never
> knew that I spent the first year working rather
> than attending classes. But it didn't matter; I

The International Sweethearts of Rhythm in the "big time"
(1942). Bottom row (left to right): Edna Williams, trumpet;
Ina Belle Byrd, trombone; Anna Mae Winburn, leader/
vocalist; Grace Bayron, saxophone; Willie Mae Wong, saxophone. Middle row: Helen Jones, trombone; Evelyn McGee,
vocalist; Helen Saine, saxophone. Top row: Marian Carter,
trumpet; Margie Pettiford, saxophone; Pauline Braddy, drums;
Johnnie Mae Stansbury, trumpet; Amy Garrison, saxophone;
Judy Bayron, trombone; Lucille Dixon, bass; Roxanna Lucas,
guitar; Johnnie Mae Rice, piano.

just wanted that music. I was just a youngster
and I would get so tired. Once I fell asleep in
the bathroom. Then I remember that the doctor
ordered me home to get plenty of rest and drink
a lot of milk. But I returned. The band practiced all day long. It wasn't as much musicianship as it was the drilling. I loved the idea of
playing and traveling--Louisiana, Mississippi,
Arkansas, Florida, Texas, Tennessee, Alabama,
North and South Carolina. We played clubs, army

camps, dance halls and big theatres. We were on
the bill with some of the big named bands. The
only name that I can recall is that of Ted Lewis.

After high school graduation from Gilbert Academy
(New Orleans), a college degree in music from Southern
University (Baton Rouge), several summers at Vandercook
School of Music (Chicago), a two-year stint with the William
Houston band (New Orleans), twelve years of private teach-
ing, and thirty-two years as band director in the Orleans
Parish Schools, Busch still gave credit to James Polite,
Willie Rice, Yvonne Plummer, and Piney Woods School.

I got my musical start at Piney Woods. They
started me on mellophone; then I played trumpet
and when the drummer got sick I had to fill in
for her. It was after Piney Woods that I was
converted to trombone. At Piney Woods I acquired
something that you can't touch, i. e. feeling. Jazz,
you know, is feeling. I also learned the importance of timing--being at places and doing things
at a given time. I gained confidence in myself.
I learned to meet the public, unafraid. You were
up at five. There was a time for breakfast, a
time to wash up and even a time to pray. If they
said pick up the paper on the campus, you got a
stick and picked it up--right then. Everything was
on schedule. I certainly learned musical and personal discipline at that school. [21]

That discipline is reflected in Busch's "hard-working, intelli-
gent planning and musically solid" students, performing and
leading bands throughout the U. S. A.

Though contact was made with only Clark, Simmons,
and Busch, the names of additional members of the Junior
Sweethearts ensemble are known: Virginia Audley, Leaster
Bethea, Estelle Bluitt, Marion Bridges, Leora "Zoom"
Bryant, Ora Dean Clark, Deon Deshab, Ione and Irene
Grisham, Dora Henderson, Sammie Lee Jett, Mrytle Polite,
Corine and Lena Posey, Sarah Scott, Delores Smith, J.
Stagg, and Mary Stuart. Doris Nicholson and Leora Bryant
continued in the profession as music instructors and band
directors.

*   *   *

Despite the swing craze nationally, times were not
easy for black big band musicians "making it" on the road.
Associated Negro Press journalist Nell Dodson filed this report in March 1941:

> After the dances they quick for the nearest hash
> joint open and find the proprietor has raised the
> price on beef stew from two-bits to 50 cents.
>   They are going to stay overnight, so they head
> for home and a bed, only to find beds are as
> scarce as hen's teeth, so it means every man for
> himself.
>   It ends up with 14 men trying to get some
> shuteye in three beds, ... This goes on indefin-
> itely when the towns are small and colored fami-
> lies few.
>   Other band lads will tell you about towns where
> they had a pocketful of money, but couldn't even
> buy a sandwich, or where they had pepper slipped
> into their food as a warning not to come back on
> the next trip.... It's picking the hard way to
> earn a living, and don't let anyone tell you dif-
> ferently. 22

Regardless, Rae Lee Jones and The International Sweethearts
of Rhythm would challenge the system as well as some pre-
dictions that the very nature of their departure from Piney
Woods Country Life School insured the band's failure.

In late May 1941, the Pittsburgh Courier gave extensive coverage to the ladies' jazz band, as theatrical editor
Billy Rowe brought the nation--certainly its black populace--
up-to-date on "America's No. 1 all-female orchestra." One
week following the second Louis-Baer fight, a photograph of
the Sweethearts was taken with champion Joe Louis, whose
training camp was next door to Sweetheart House. One
photograph portrayed a member of the band in a practice
session and another, captioned "more work and less play,"
showed band members gathered around their chaperon/
manager and tutor for instruction.

A contemporary headline read: "$30,000 Spent on
Sweethearts of Rhythm." "Money is no object," said Rae
Lee Jones, "since the backers of the band have implicit
faith in [the girls'] ideals."

The article continued,

> [D]espite the reams and reams of pro and con
> controversy which have arisen in their cause,
> these sixteen maids without a male are happy
> children ready to stand or fall, but together.

The band was now supposedly incorporated, with each
member a co-owner. However, the girls were later told
that "the government" did not allow bands to be incorporated.
They were successful in joining Local 710 of the American
Federation of Musicians, D. C.'s black musicians' union.

Of the $30,000, close to $10,000 was spent on the
house, $4,300 to purchase a bus (with sleeping accommoda-
tions for twenty-two), and an unspecified amount on new
stock arrangements. The house on Virginia's Columbia Pike
was a ten-room brick building, two stories high, allowing
ample space for practice, recreation, group lodging, entertainment, and business operations.

William Francis, Piney Woods' bus driver and "school
on wheels" staff member, was now the official driver of the
Sweethearts' newly acquired "big time" bus setting out from
Arlington, Virginia. Francis had avoided prosecution for
his role in the "great escape" when he argued that he was
merely following orders given by the teachers, who in his
opinion were officials of the school.

The girls were now practicing six hours a day, sending out "sweet notes and sour ones, too." As stated by the
enthusiastic reporter Rowe:

> With the exception of a few vicinity dances ...
> the band remains inactive ... awaiting the "ready"
> note from each instrument before stepping in
> higher circles. [23]

Testing its newly self-declared independence, the band
traveled to Tidewater Virginia in mid July. Local reporters
noted that the girls "seem[ed] none the worse for the recent
experience." Though not yet ready to move "in higher circles," by late July the Sweethearts of Rhythm was listed in
the Pittsburgh Courier's "Parade of Coming Bands," along
with those led by Jeter-Pillars and Les Hite. Tour arrangements were now being handled by Lee Matthews of Pittsburgh's New Artist Service, with the girls remaining under
the personal supervision of Amusement Enterprise (Gary and
Dade).

The Sweethearts' leader, Anna Mae Winburn.

All was falling in place; the only missing ingredient now was musical refinement. The current membership consisted of the same young women whose musical exposure and subsequent training had only been initiated a few years prior. Established composer/arranger/guitarist/trombonist Eddie Durham took over the reigns, with plans of "setting the jazz world on fire." The new musical director was particularly impressed by the musicians' discipline, musical ability, and eagerness to learn.

A veteran of such well respected bands as those fronted by Benny Moton, Jimmie Lunceford, Count Basie, Glenn Miller, Artie Shaw, and Ina Ray Hutton's all-girl band, Durham offered this explanation of his association with female instrumental aggregations (his own and the International Sweethearts of Rhythm) to jazz historian Stanley Dance:

> Then I got the girls' band together. That was the only way I could stay out of the army. I met an old West Indian guy, a politician, who got me with the Treasury Department's bond drives. So long as I kept the girls' band, I'd be deferred from the army every six months for the duration. And so long as I gave some service to the USO, the Treasury Department cooperated with whatever agency I was with.... That's how I got involved with the International Sweethearts of Rhythm![24]

According to one source, Durham's own all-female band came into existence during the same period that Durham was working with the Sweethearts. Changes in the latter's roster were often warranted by the desertion of some Sweethearts to the new musical director's own personal outfit.

In late August 1941, the "feminine musical dynamos of rhythm" made their initial theatrical debut (since terminating their affiliation with Piney Woods School) at the Howard Theatre in the nation's capital.

> Truly amazing was the anxious throngs of rabid jitterbugs and staid oldtimers who waited for hours before show time, forming long lines extending for more than a block, in all kinds of weather and at every performance....
> [T]he entire Show Schedule had to be changed from five to six shows daily, after the first day in an effort to accommodate the huge crowds.

> ...[O]nce inside, things began to rock! The
> "Hep Cats" began to jump and the Jitterbugs began
> to "Jitter" as the Sweethearts began to romp!

By the end of the week, attendance had reached 35,000 persons, establishing an all-time record. [25]

The all-female revue included dancing and comedy acts, harpist Lavella Tullas, trumpeter Dolly Armendra (Jones), and recording star Billie Holiday, obviously the show's headliner. A few band members recalled that "Lady Day" Holiday resented appearing on the same bill, as a result of band songbird Evelyn McGee's receiving audience acclaim that rivaled her own. One critic wrote of McGee's ability to deliver a song:

> [She] is one of the few singers in the world who
> has learned the secret of literally pouring herself
> into the mike. She sings so intimately to the audi-
> ence that she has the crowd won over, as individ-
> uals, from the very opening strains of her [pre-
> sentation]. [26]

Two weeks later, the Sweethearts made their debut at the famous Apollo Theatre in New York City, this time headlining the all-female revue, which included on the bill comedians, a tap dancer, comedy dancers, and acrobats. A week's run at the Apollo, a Harlem landmark, confirmed that the girls were approaching the ultimate. They were now presenting themselves to what many believe was the toughest audience in American show business. Thousands of curious patrons were on hand to greet the band, thereby assuring a return engagement.

Later in the same month, the band appeared at the celebrated Savoy Ballroom, "Home of the Happy Feet," sharing honors with the extremely popular Lucky Millinder. Pittsburgh Courier's staff correspondent Isadora Smith was on hand and filed the following report:

> Unlike the various groups of all-girls bands that
> come upon the musical horizon from time to time,
> the Sweethearts possess the basic talent that when
> fully developed will move them into the circles of
> the great bands of today.... To say that they are
> great musicians would be an infringement upon the
> standout ability of Don Redman, Lionel Hampton,

The Saxophone Choir, left to right: (bottom) Grace Bayron and Willie Mae Wong; (top) Marge Pettiford, Helen Saine, and Amy Garrison.

The Trombone Choir, left to right: Ina Belle Byrd, Judy Bayron, and Helen Jones.

Erskine Hawkins and Roy Eldridge, but to say that
they have the stuff that makes champions would be
a statement not disputed by the efforts of others
more seasoned in the profession....

...

The crew itself has a punch and tonal quality with
it that's rare in female organizations and seemingly
backed by determination of purpose and a high
spirit that goes beyond the understanding of their
youth and the glamour and glitter of the spotlighted
glare of their chosen profession. [27]

The Big Apple's Apollo Theatre announced another all-
woman revue for mid January 1942, again headlined by the
International Sweethearts of Rhythm.   On the same bill appeared the singing Three Brown Sisters, the sensational
acrobats Six Abdulla Girls and the remarkable comedienne
Jackie "Moms" Mabley.

In an exclusive interview with journalist Nell Dodson
following the opening show of this Apollo Theatre appearance,
members expressed a desire "to be recognized as musicians."
According to Dodson,

The thing that impresses one most, both on and
offstage, is their lack of so-called glamour trap-
pings, and their femininity.   Too many girl musicians make the mistake of trying to dress and act
like men, and as a result they appear both hard
and unnatural. [28]

Dodson pointed out that three (?) of them were married.   As
for the others, one member told Dodson:

If it came to a toss-up between marriage and our
career, everyone would take a career....   We
meet loads of nice fellows and have a lot of chances
to go out, but nobody is head over heels in love--
so far!

Dodson concluded that all of them

want to be appreciated for their musical ability,
and not just because they're girls with musical
ability....   With the war and draft threatening to

deplete the ranks of men musicians, the International Sweethearts of Rhythm may find themselves
in the big money class very soon, and so in anti-
cipation they are preparing themselves to blow as
long, loud and fine as any of the others. [29]

Gradually more new members, all well experienced
in the music business and devoid of Piney Woods connections,
were brought in. It was announced in Down Beat that
guitarist/trombonist Judy Bayron was now fronting the band
and that Anna Mae Winburn had been added as vocalist.
One month later, the same publication stated that Bayron
had been "returned to her trombone chair" and that vocalist
Winburn was "now handling the baton."[30]

Winburn, a seasoned performer, joined the group in
January 1942. She joined the band from Omaha, Nebraska
upon the recommendation of Jimmie Jewel, owner of the
Dreamland Ball Room in Omaha. [31] Winburn had sung with
the Hoosier Hot Shots, had fronted bands directed by Lloyd
Hunter and Red Perkins, and for brief periods led the famous Blue Devils and her own Cotton Club Boys. Of her
performance at Iowa Centennial in September 1938, the
Omaha Star reported:

> Anna Mae Winburn ... led her Cotton Club Boys
> through four hours of red-hot swing rhythm at the
> Negro Day Celebration....
>
> ...
>
> So entrancing was the music of Miss Winburn and
> her band, that the midway of the Centennial was
> all but deserted as the crowd ... chose to either
> enter the dance or remain in close proximity to
> the hall. [32]

Once in front of the Sweethearts, Winburn remained
for the band's duration. Pictures of "the girl with the win-
ning personality" appeared regularly in the press, with such
captions as "Shapely, Talented Queen of Leaders" and
"Bronze Venus."

It was announced in early March 1942 that the Frederick Brothers booking agency would promote a musical
"battle of the sexes," in a series of one nighters, beginning
Easter Sunday, April 5. Fletcher Henderson's band would

represent the males and the International Sweethearts of
Rhythm, the females.

> The two bands will play alternate sets on these
> double-header events, winding up with a concert
> "finale" for which Smack [Henderson] will conduct
> the combined bands in a 35-piece arrangement of
> his own. 33

Henderson's band was composed of virtually all new players,
since he had placed most band members "on notice" only a
few weeks prior. Recalling the fact that Fletcher Henderson's wife, Leora Meoux, was an outstanding trumpet player,
one is not surprised that he would consent to participate in
perhaps the first orchestral "battle of the sexes. "34

Former members recalled other "battles," but could
remember no specific names. However, the New York Age
reported the following in early 1944:

> In a recent "Swing Battle of Music" before a crowd
> of ten thousand, [the Sweethearts] actually received
> a larger vote than was given to Erskine Hawkins
> and his band! They have participated in similar
> swing battles with Earl Hines and others of the
> great "name" bands. 35

When drummer Pauline Braddy was asked about the
"battles," she could remember only one with the band that
had as its vocalists Bob Eberly and Helen O'Connell. "It
was one of the Dorsey Brothers' bands I think. One of the
band's big hits I remember was 'Green Eyes.' As for any
other 'battles,' I can't remember specifically. "36 From
this information it was determined that the band indeed had
been Jimmy Dorsey's.

As musical refinement efforts continued, so did the
personnel changes. Though an announcement had been made
much earlier that trumpet sensation Jean Starr was considering joining the band as the replacement for Ann Cooper,
Down Beat noted in April 1942 that she had only recently
been added. One month later, Down Beat announced the replacement of Jean Starr with young Philadelphia trumpet
player Florence Jones, a name that Sweethearts' historian
Braddy could not remember. But Braddy made certain I
realized that Starr joined, left, and re-joined the band on
two or three different occasions. Another member recalled

The Rhythm Section: Lucille Dixon, bass; Johnnie Mae
Rice, piano; Pauline Braddy, drums; and Roxanna Lucas,
guitar.

Rae Lee Jones auditioning pianist Dorothy Donegan, then hot
on the musical scene. She quickly added, "But she was too
much of a soloist."

Following a record-breaking tour of the nation's major cities in the Sweethearts' own $15,000 pullman bus, the
band returned to the Apollo in late May as part of a sexu-
ally integrated show. The Sweethearts were co-featured
with The Five Charioteers, popular singing stars of the
Broadway show "Hellzapoppin."

More new skilled performers were added to the band:
Marian Carter and Johnnie Mae ("Tex") Stansbury, trumpet;
Marjorie Pettiford and Amy Garrison, saxophone; Roxanna
Lucas, guitar; and Lucille Dixon, bass. Pettiford (sister
of the fabulous jazz bassist Oscar Pettiford) gained her

experience in her father's Minneapolis-based family band.
Theoretical matters for all eleven children were in the hands
of her mother.   "Strangely--and she admits it--[Marge] was
forced to practice by her Ma, who found it necessary to
have a broomstick handy 'just in case'."[37]

Lucille Dixon had been a member of New York City's
All-City High School Orchestra and was one of two black females admitted to the WPA sponsored National Youth Association's Orchestra.   In 1942 she was "one of three recognized girl bass players in the city."   A pupil of New York
Philharmonic's Fred Zimmerman, Dixon had sought auditions
with other women's orchestras composed of white members,
but was always rejected because of her race.   Her stay with
the Sweethearts lasted only from June through August 1942.[38]

Since Eddie Durham had terminated his tenure as musical director and arranger, these crucial assignments were
now filled by master musician Jesse Stone, former music
store proprietor, talent scout, pianist, band leader, composer, and arranger.   Any band with which Stone was affiliated was known to be a polished, thoroughly rehearsed
outfit.   Stone, a well-schooled musician, knew exactly how
to display the girls at their best musical advantage.   "It
was during Stone's tenure that the band obtained its most
outstanding recognition," wrote short-term member Lorraine
Brown (Guilford), tenor saxophonist.

The band shattered all existing records at Chicago's
Regal Theatre in October 1942.   Previous records were held
by Count Basie and Louis Armstrong--most auspicious competitors.   One critic commented,

> The group plays a soft melody of swing and sweet
> numbers that are far less harmful to the ear than
> the run of bands we've listened to on the stage of
> the Regal....   You'll like the darlings of music;
> you'll leave the theatre sans the usual search for
> cotton with which to stuff a pair of ears.[39]

The Chicago visit was but a stop-off on the band's second
coast-to-coast tour of the year.

But all problems were not behind the band, nor was
Laurence C. Jones content to call the April 1941 case closed.
The band's touring was abruptly halted in Jackson, Tennes-
see on October 9, just prior to the Regal Theatre engage-

ment, when representatives of Dr. Jones swore out warrants
for the arrest of manager Rae Lee Jones, booking representative Dan Gary, and all members of the band. Only
Mrs. Jones was detained. As reported in the Jackson (Mississippi) Advocate,

> The warrants charged theft of the band and instru-
> ments and were the outgrowth of the band leaving
> the employ of the school.... Piney Woods School
> originated and sponsored the band which it used
> for money raising purposes. The girls were pre-
> sumed to pursue their studies between concerts
> and dances in a "school on wheels...."
>   Mrs. Jones was freed and the band moved on
> to its next engagement....
>   President Jones, who was represented by the
> secretary of Piney Woods, ... contends that he
> still owns the orchestra and instruments. The
> girls insist that they earned the instruments through
> years of unrequited toil but that they have bought
> all new instruments anyway. [40]

Apparently Piney Woods lost the case; the band proceeded on
its course--thus ending the legal conflict between Laurence
Jones/Piney Woods School and Rae Lee Jones, Dan Gary,
and members of the International Sweethearts of Rhythm.

By late 1942, the national band slogan was "the
smaller the better." Gas and rubber rationings suggested
that one-nighters would be a thing of the past. Many black
bands (and a few white ones) were forced to disband. But
Rae Lee Jones's outfit seemed not have been affected. The
Sweethearts' itinerary, now included in Down Beat's regular
listing of band routes ("Where the Bands Are Playing"), reflected "big time" movement across the U.S.A.

The Sweethearts helped New Yorkers bring in 1943
with a return visit to the Apollo Theatre. Now dubbed the
"Musical Novelty of the Century," early 1943 had the Sweethearts booked solid with one-nighters over a period of sixty
days in Texas, Oklahoma, Alabama, Mississippi, Louisiana,
Arkansas, and Tennessee. On opening night of a one-week
run at Memphis' Palace Theatre, more than 4,000 people
assembled; hundreds stood in line for hours awaiting entry.

As the band prepared for a return engagement to Detroit's Paradise Theatre in late April, the press reminded
the reading public of the Sweethearts'

[h]aving used 39 of the United States as a proving
ground for their rhythmical wares.... First
formed as an amateur dance band ... this outstanding talented group was long jumps ahead of
the average orchestra in discipline at the offset.
The girls had learned to live together, a prime
requisite in any orchestra, because they knew how
to cooperate and work as a unit. [41]

Continuing management's practice of hiring professionals, Rosalind ("Roz") Cron from Boston was brought in
to replace lead saxophonist Marge Pettiford sometime in
1944. Cron's being Jewish presented new problems for the
band's management. Since the band's inception, products of
mixed parentage had required explanations; now the presence
of members of other races warranted clever disguises and
ready answers, particularly in the South. Fortunately the
band's ownership of its own bus eliminated many of the obvious lodging problems.

A veteran of Ada Leonard's all-white female band,
Cron welcomed the free, swinging style of the Sweethearts.

I remember something about the difference between
working for Ada Leonard and being with the Sweethearts.... In all the theaters, when the Sweethearts started playing the audience would come in
dancing down the aisles to their seats. Black
audiences were always like that. But if you'd go
to hear Tommy or Jimmy Dorsey or Ada Leonard,
people just "walked" to their seats and sat down. [42]

A rather curious attitude toward women and jazz was expressed by Ada Leonard to Down Beat journalist Bob Fossum:

Girl bands should not play too much jazz.... People don't expect girls to play high-powered swing
all night long. It looks out of place. [43]

Roz Cron was an outstanding player and she took over
as leader of the saxophone section. When asked how she
benefited from the experience, Cron replied,

I learned lead alto phrasing. I made contacts that
have helped me throughout the years. And, I developed a closeness to black people and a deeper
understanding of the black experience, thus enrich-
ing my life for the rest of my days. [44]

Cron's reunion with the group for the Kansas City Salute
(March 1980) left little doubt about the sincerity of her
claims.

Non-black trumpeter/bassist Toby Butler, a Richmond,
Virginia native, reiterated Cron's feelings and added,

> We had love for each other. This shared love as
> sisters nurtured our personal desires to become
> better musicians. From the experience I matured
> emotionally and I learned to listen. [45]

Since Butler joined in 1943, she was the Sweethearts' first
white member. And though she did not accompany the band
on its memorable European trip in 1945, her stay with the
group was one of the longest, with the exception of "originals"
Helen Jones and Pauline Braddy.

Musical director Jesse Stone did much to improve the
women's general musicianship and carefully integrated the
more professional players with the less professional ones.
He also alerted them to the fact that they were being exploited financially, though as trombonist Helen Jones explained, "We knew we were being underpaid. But we didn't
give it much thought then; we were enjoying ourselves. "[46]

Stone's relationship with manager Rae Lee Jones was
a good one. He therefore dared to challenge the weekly pay-
roll. No satisfactory agreements were reached; thus, once
his two-year contract had been met, Stone gave his notice.

Replacing Stone as arranger/musical director was
Maurice King from Detroit. His personality won great favor
with the girls and his musical leadership capabilities resulted
in the band's continued ascendancy toward artistic perfection
and sustained popularity. As one less experienced member
recalled, "Maurice was a good teacher. "

By mid century the musical virtues of the International Sweethearts of Rhythm were being proclaimed across
the country. The girls were making short films to be used
as "fillers" in movie theaters and short clips for popular
Panorama Machines, where for ten cents one could view and
hear (for a period of two to three minutes) top artists of the
day. They were still holding their own in band polls across
the nation. The Sweethearts were riding the crest of popularity, if only in a female context. The 1944 Down Beat poll

rated the band America's #1 All-Girls' Orchestra. Engagements in California permitted a performing night in Mexico;
an engagement in Detroit permitted a similar venture into
Canada. "International" was becoming a fitting label in more
respects than the personnel.

An issue long since forgotten (certainly no longer recalled in the press) was revived in early February 1945. A
Chicago Defender article began with bits of historical information and a wealth of pseudo-historical misinformation on
the band's creation and early years. It concluded as follows:

> And so while Laurence C. Jones slept at the
> school, Mrs. Jones, following a conference with
> the girls, hit upon the idea of "running away" ...
> and took a train for Washington, D.C....
> Professionally the name "Sweethearts of
> Rhythm" has mounted to the top. Practically
> every large city in the land has raved over the
> band. Records have been set at Chicago's Regal,
> Los Angeles' Plantation Club, in Detroit's Grey-
> stone Ballroom, and in other cities.
> The Sweethearts of Rhythm organization is a
> powerful institution. An institution that has done
> much good for Womanhood. [47]

Still at the helm of this institution was Rae Lee Jones.

About this time it was rumored that the formidable
vocalist/guitarist Sister Rosetta Tharpe, who had enjoyed
tremendous success as a feature with the Lucky Millinder
band before striking out on her own, was "taking over" the
band. To this allegation Rae Lee Jones responded:

> It's ridiculous. I know nothing of Sister Tharpe
> taking over the Sweethearts. I have no intention
> of making any changes in my band. Anna Mae
> Winburn is still the director and will be as long
> as she so desires. [48]

America's involvement in World War II began only
months following the Sweethearts' movement into the world
of professionalism. In the words of former Sweethearts'
musical director Eddie Durham, because of the war, "femmes
[had] the best opportunity. " Now on the road with his own
competing all-female orchestra, Durham said:

> Since heavy induction and volunteering of orches-
> tra men into the armed forces is imminent, havoc
> is playing a major part in most name orchestras.
> Thus, it is my belief that girl orchestras possess-
> ing versatility, ability and new ideas will be ac-
> claimed tops in both name and monetary capacities. [49]

All three attributes were apparent in the Sweethearts'
development.   Management made the best of all opportunities
at hand.   The International Sweethearts of Rhythm was acclaimed tops in name if not in a monetary capacity that benefited the membership.

At the war's end, the band was at its zenith.   In the
interim, entertainers were volunteering their services to the
United Service Organization (USO) for the entertainment of
servicemen and servicewomen in army camps and naval stations throughout the country, as well as overseas.   According to a late 1945 report, "In its four years of operation,
USO Camp Shows ... sent 800 units and 4,500 entertainers
to war fronts all over the world."   A December 1944 report
gave the following statistics:

> Of the 173 units now overseas, only three are
> colored; of the 837 entertainers, only 29 colored;
> of the 383 overall units since 1941, five colored;
> of the 2,066 performers to date, 39 colored. [50]

Impresario Dick Campbell, Coordinator of Colored
Talent for USO Camp Shows, was constantly working to improve the situation for black men and women in the service
as well as for black entertainers.   Despite the signed Peace
Treaties, GIs were still stationed from Germany to Japan
and from the Philippines to Italy.   Entertainment fresh-from-
the-States was still the perfect remedy for "occupation blues"
and the craved touch of home.

The Armed Forces Radio Service, a combined operation of the War and Navy Departments, prepared broadcasts
called "Jubilee Programs" for overseas airing.   Top flight
entertainers such as Nat "King" Cole, Lena Horne, Dorothy
Donegan, Alberta Hunter, Billy Eckstine, and Ella Fitzgerald
gave of their time and talent.   The broadcasts were noted
for their diversity in programming.   Not unusual was a
broadcast of contralto Marian Anderson on the same program
with jazz trumpeter Louis Armstrong.   Recorded in the

The USO touring Sweethearts (1945). Upper left: (top) Margo Gipson and Anna Mae Winburn; (bottom) Johnnie Mae Rice and Pauline Braddy. Center: Helen Jones. Upper right: Vi Burnside and Ernestine "Tiny" Davis. Lower left: (top) Helen Saine and Ina Belle Byrd; (bottom) Evelyn McGee, Grace Bayron, and Johnnie Mae Stansbury. Lower right: (top) Ray Carter and Jean Travis; (bottom) Rosalind Cron, Willie Mae Wong, and Mim Polak.

States, the programs were transmitted by short-wave to various theaters of war and were broadcast night and day for reception at convenient listening hours.

The International Sweethearts of Rhythm also brought cheer to the GIs overseas by way of radio. To the roster had been added two stellar performers, saxophonist Viola "Vi" Burnside of Lancaster, Pennsylvania and trumpeter/vocalist Ernestine "Tiny" Davis of Memphis, Tennessee. Both were veterans of the popular mid-thirties all-black Harlem Playgirls.

The State Department was bombarded with requests from GIs for personal appearances by the Sweethearts. The result was a six-month tour of France and Germany. Attired in attractive USO uniforms, the girls sailed for Europe on July 15, 1945. Because of illness, Rae Lee Jones was unable to make the trip. Though Maurice King served as company manager, musical director, and chaperon, the official program still carried the names of Rae Lee Jones as "official operator" and Daniel M. Gary as business representative.

Though an "All-Star Cast of 19" was advertised, a program from Karlsruhe, Germany listed a cast of seventeen: Anna Mae Winburn, directress; Johnnie Mae Stansbury, Ray Carter, Mim Polak, and Ernestine "Tiny" Davis, trumpets; Rosalind Cron, Rosita Cruz, Helen Saine, Willie Mae "Rabbit" Wong, Viola "Vi" Burnside, saxophones; Helen Jones, Ina Belle Byrd, Jean Travis, trombones; Johnnie Mae Rice, piano; Pauline Braddy, drums; Margaret "Trump" Gipson, bass; and Evelyn McGee, vocals. A USO Sweetheart photograph includes saxophonist Grace Bayron, but does not show saxophonist Rosita Cruz. A clarification was unobtainable.

Bassist Bernice "Natty" Rothchild was scheduled to make the tour, but cancelled; she got married instead. Trumpeter Margaret "Trump" Gipson, showing some aptitude for the bass, began the woodshedding process during the spring and was ready to join the rhythm section on tour. The group was now totally integrated, with black, "mixed," and white members.

Thanks to Pauline Braddy (and her scrapbook), a sample program of the time can be reconstructed.

KARLSRUHE CONCERT HOUSE

Special Service, 334th Infantry Regiment
in cooperation with
USO Camp Shows
Presents

I N T E R N A T I O N A L
S W E E T H E A R T S
O F   R H Y T H M

[cont. on next page]

* Program *

1. Theme Fascination
2. LimeHouse Blues
3. Eager Beaver
4. Evelyn McGee--Vocalist
5. Vi Burnside--Tenor Solo
6. Quartette--Byrd, Braddy, McGee, Winburn
7. State Song--Can You Name It?
8. Confession--Ray Carter
9. Band Specialty
10. Drum Sticks--"A Drum Fantasy"
11. Love Will Live Forever--Rosalind Cron
12. Tiny Davis--245 lbs. of Solid Jive and Rhythm
13. Announcements
14. Theme

Wong, who was once the band's treasurer, had become
the band's reporter. In early September 1945, she directed
this information to those back home, "from somewhere in
Germany":

> We are to play for the Third Army only....
> [W]e get the best of everything. In camp we eat
> in the officers' mess and the food is fine; in the
> cities and towns we live at the finer hotels and
> the service is great.... Last week we played for
> the 99th in Paris and once again, we were a sen-
> sation....
>   We have been on two radio programs.... We
> played the Olympia Theatre in Paris and the pro-
> gram was broadcast to all servicemen who were
> unable to attend the performances. Later we
> played the University of Paris with an all GI audi-
> ence....
>   Our only regret is that more Negro soldiers
> can't attend the various performances we give....
> We have a trio of GIs assigned to us to see that
> we are well cared for and to take care of our
> jeeps and trucks. We don't have to turn a hand.[51]

One month later, journalist Melvin Patrick reported
that the band had been secured by the Seventh Army. Offering sessions twice a day at the Seventh Army's Recreation
Center Theatre in Mannheim, Germany, the band featured
the tenor saxophone wizardry of "Vi" Burnside, the remarkable singing, dancing, and trumpet playing of "Tiny" Davis,

the trumpet artistry of Ray Carter, the torch songs of Evelyn McGee, and the drum paradiddles of Pauline Braddy.

> It was too much to ask the men to sit quietly to
> listen to the songs of Directress Annie [sic] Mae
> Winburn or the musical arrangements of Maurice
> King which the orchestra featured. So, the men
> simply got up from their seats and danced to their
> hearts content in the aisle. The theatre was
> rocked in good old American fashion as it has
> never rocked before. 52

The International Sweethearts of Rhythm returned from
their extremely successful European tour in early January
1946. Shortly thereafter Leonard Feather made arrangements for the band to record for RCA Victor as part of a
disc featuring several different women's groups. The band
recorded Maurice King's "Don't Get It Twisted" and "Vi
Vigor." The Sweethearts also recorded two sides for Guild
Records, featuring "Tiny" Davis on "Stompin' the Blues" and
Anna Mae Winburn on "Do You Want to Jump, Children?"
Other opportunities were in the offing: a series of musical
shorts for foreign markets and an appearance in the short
film "That Man of Mine," starring black actress Ruby Dee.

Despite the continued successes, many members were
beginning to tire of the road; several saw this as an oppor-
tune time to abandon the idea of a career and settle into
marriage or another occupation. Trumpeter Nova Lee
McGee made her second departure when she married the
band's road manager Edward Berry. Saxophonist Helen
Saine left to begin a modeling career. Star performer
"Tiny" Davis sensed a musical shift and left to form her
own combo. But the band was to continue for a few more
years, performing at the same level and receiving the same
enthusiastic response from audiences throughout the country.

It was announced in Down Beat in early May 1946
that the Sweethearts were "on a 90-day cross-country tour,
terminating on the west coast. From there they will tour
Canada for a month and then go to the West Indies."53 No
evidence can be found that either tour materialized.

Carline Ray (Russell) was the Sweethearts' guitarist
from May 1946 until March 1947. She was occasionally featured as vocalist, always receiving plaudits from both audience and the press for the richness of her deep voice,

musicianship, and "ability to peddle a tune." As the multi-
talented Ray recalled, her involvement began during her final year at the Juilliard School of Music.

> It was 1946. Bassist Edna Smith had a trio in
> which I and pianist Jackie King were playing.
> Edna was carrying her bass (she played doghouse
> bass then). We were coming from our agent's
> office when this man approached us and introduced
> himself as Maurice King, with the Sweethearts of
> Rhythm. We of course knew of the band. Maurice
> asked if he could interview us and if he could talk
> with our agent about the possibility of us joining
> the group. Many girls were leaving and replace-
> ments were needed. He said he'd call us in a few
> weeks. He did and all three of us joined.

Ray's reasons for leaving were the same as those advanced by
many others: "Financial; problems getting paid. Then too,
the musical tides were changing."[54]

> Early in 1947, the band's management was advised of
another "schooled" musician who was close to graduation
from Virginia State College in Petersburg. Alto saxophone
player Geneva Perry had organized and played in many combos during her college years, much to the chagrin of the
"elite art" music faculty. Upon graduation, Perry joined the
Sweethearts for the summer only, replacing the "original"
Willie Mae Wong (who left to be married). "The joy was
traveling and playing with a big band--my first love," said
Perry. "It was like a paid vacation." The D.C. native
added:

> I had prepared to be an instrumental music teacher,
> but my love was always big band jazz. This ex-
> perience broadened my insights; I believe it in-
> spired me to be a better teacher. I went with the
> band again during the Summer of 1948, when the
> band was beginning to fall apart. It happened in
> Oklahoma City. I think this was the Summer that
> we participated in the Cavalcade of Jazz at Wrigley
> Field, Los Angeles. Dizzy Gillespie was on the
> same show. We got a better response than he
> did. Of course he just hadn't caught on yet.

To the question What do you think actually caused the
group's demise? she hesitated briefly and then responded:

It was understood that I was with the band for the summer only.   I had signed a contract to teach in North Carolina, beginning in September.   Mrs. Jones tried to persuade me to break the contract, saying "In this business, one knows no integrity." This was my clue.   I knew then that this wasn't for me.   "Vi" Burnside had left.   The band needed her driving tenor.   And, there were always money problems.   Mrs. Jones owed some of the girls a lot of money.   Of course I always got paid, though I found out later that I wasn't supposed to buy my uniform, which I did. [55]

Other former members also responded to inquiries about "causes of the group's demise."

[Pauline Braddy:] Old age.   The girls were getting married and having children.   Then too, the band was not the same once it lost the "original" members.

[Toby Butler:]   The death of Rae Lee Jones.

[Rosalind Cron:]   Fatigue after so many years on

Big Bertha--The Sweethearts' "home away home."

Chaperon/manager Rae Lee Jones relaxes with musical director Maurice King.

the road and the realization that the girls were grossly underpaid and exploited.

From Howard University was drawn trombonist Esther Cooke, an Atlanta, Georgia native whose tenure lasted from May 1947 until September 1948. Other "schooled" and experienced players added their names to the Sweethearts' roster, some for periods as brief as two weeks. Among these were Nancy Brown (Pratt), Norman Carson, Flo Dreyer, and Augusta Perry (Jackson) on trumpet; Ella Ritz Lucas, Pat Stulken, and Betty Rosner on saxophone; Helen Coles (formerly a member of the popular early forties Prairie View College Coeds) on bass; and Fagel Lieberman on drums. Of this group, the non-blacks were Brown, Carson, Dreyer, Lieberman, and Stulken.

As Carline Ray recalled, the musical tides were indeed changing. A music with appeal for listening was to begin replacing dance music. As jazz historian Frank Tirro summarized:

> [T]he bebop musician [Dizzy Gillespie, Charlie Parker, Thelonius Monk, Kenny Clarke, et al.] was trying to raise the quality of jazz from the level of utilitarian dance music to that of a chamber art form [3 to 6 players]. At the same time, he was trying to raise the status of the jazzman from entertainer to artist. [56]

Not all agreed or appreciated the efforts. Jazz violinist Stuff Smith called the new music "the illegitimate child of swing." Band leader/arranger/pianist (sometimes referred to as "father of the big band business") Fletcher Henderson added: "Of all the cruelties in the world, be-bop is the most phenomenal." Despite the protest, big band business was declining in popularity and bebop was taking a foothold. Popular booking agent Joe Glaser predicted in early 1947:

> Colored attractions traveling around the country, playing one nighters, getting from $650 to $1, 000 a night ... will be hit the hardest and these attractions will be forced out of business within the next six months.
> A band carrying from 18 to 23 musicians will have to cut its personnel as well as prices for jobs, since people who made big money during the war, many who were patrons of one night dances, have lost their incomes. [57]

Those gloomy forecasts notwithstanding, a determined
Rae Lee Jones announced in early May 1947 a projected second European tour for the band.   French labor permits had
been secured and the tour would begin with an appearance
at the Monte Carlo in Paris.   Musical forces would be augmented to twenty-two.   A still ailing Rae Lee Jones, now
referred to by the press as the band's guardian angel,
boasted the fact that she had been able to maintain a full
staff of musicians and added, "I think that's doing pretty
well, in view of the fact that many 'name' bands have had
to reduce personnel or fold altogether."[58]   The band was
then completing an engagement at Baltimore's Royal Theatre,
to be followed by a string of one-nighters and its fourth appearance at the June German (one of the South's largest
dances) at Rocky Mount, North Carolina in mid June.

But Jones's European projection was not to material-
ize.   When the band appeared at Baltimore's Royal Theatre
in July 1948, Maurice King was fronting the group.   Anna
Mae Winburn, only a month earlier, had left to be married.
The Baltimore appearance carried the name Betty Sheppard
as vocalist, while a September 1948 appearance at Omaha's
Dreamland featured vocalist Betty Givens, Omaha's own song
stylist.   Songbird Evelyn McGee (an "original" Sweetheart)
had terminated her involvement shortly after the band's return from Europe.

Other Rae Lee Jones visions of continued International
Sweethearts of Rhythm successes were to continue only as
dreams and these for only a short period of time.   The
powerful institution had reached its apex, as had the ener-
gies of Rae Lee Jones.   Yet she remained chief ruler of the
empire until the very end, having been stricken while on the
road with the band in Paducah, Kentucky during the summer
of 1949.

An ill and distressed Mrs. Jones was forced to bid
farewell--to Sweetheart House; Arlington, Virginia; her band;
and her few remaining friends--departing for home and the
temporary security of her parents.   As reported in the
Omaha Star, "Mrs. Helen [Jones] Woods, who learned of
Mrs. Jones' condition, came at once to Omaha to render
aid."[59]   And as Helen Jones, Laurence C. Jones's adopted
daughter, indicated in Kansas City, March 1980, only then
did she learn that all funds that she entrusted in Rae Lee
Jones's care had been spent.   As she reflected to pianist
Marian McPartland,

> I didn't realize the magnitude of it until years
> later, ... I felt so sorry for her. There she
> was, down and out, in this little old house that
> she had bought for her parents. And when she
> died she left it to me, but I didn't take it. Her
> parents were still there, and I didn't want to put
> them out. So there was nothing I could do. At
> that time I was young and I didn't know anything,
> so whatever came up, I just accepted it. That's
> life--everyone learns one way or another. [60]

Rae Lee Jones died September 3, 1949, at the age of
forty-nine. All that remained of the International Sweethearts
of Rhythm were memories--fond ones, for the most part.
Thirty-one years later in Kansas City, Missouri there was
a band reunion unlike any other in recorded history.

NOTES

1. "17-Girl Band Which Quit School at Piney Woods, Re-
    hearses for Big Time," Pittsburgh Courier, April
    19, 1941, p. 21.

2. "Girls' Band Flees Dixie After Tiff with School," Afro-
    American, April 26, 1941, p. 13.

3. Laurence C. Jones, "Piney Woods Prexy Gives School's
    Side of Bolt Taken by Sweethearts of Rhythm," Pitts-
    burgh Courier, May 3, 1941, p. 21.

4. Ibid.

5. "Did Not Cause Band to Leave," Pittsburgh Courier,
    May 24, 1941, p. 20.

6. Piney Woods Catalogue, 1938, p. 19.

7. William Talbot Handy, Sr., Up from Gallatin: An
    Autobiography. New Orleans, La.: Private Publication,
    1975, p. 9.

8. Leonard Feather, "The Memories of Sweethearts," Los
    Angeles Times, April 13, 1980, p. 64.

9. Handy, op. cit., pp. 9-10.

10. "'Rays of Rhythm' Orchestra Replaces 'Sweethearts',"
    Afro-American, May 10, 1941, p. 14.

11. Lou Holloway and Alferdteen Harrison, "We Were Professionals," Southern Exposure, Fall 1980, p. 19.

12. "Swinging Rays of Rhythm Is Newest, Hottest Band on Tour," Chicago Defender, January 21, 1942, p. 20.

13. Holloway/Harrison, op. cit., p. 21.

14. "Andy Kirk's Pianist Hears Greatest Femme Sax Section," Chicago Defender, December 20, 1941, p. 20.

15. "The Swinging Rays Triumph," Chicago Defender, December 6, 1941, p. 21.

16. "Here's an All-Girls Band That Swings Out Latest in Hot Music," Chicago Defender, August 29, 1942, p. 22.

17. No other members contacted or persons at Piney Woods could recall the name "The Flashers."

18. Correspondence with Phifer, April 5, 1982.

19. Personal Data Form from Juanita Clark (Williams).

20. Personal Data Form from Marion Estella Simmons (Scruggs).

21. Interview with Yvonne Busch, New Orleans, Louisiana, November 3, 1982.

22. Nell Dodson, "Musicians Earn Their Living by the Hard Route," Afro-American, March 15, 1941, p. 14.

23. Billy Rowe, "All Girl Orchestra Is Getting Prepared to Crash the Big Time," Pittsburgh Courier, May 31, 1941, p. 20.

24. Stanley Dance, The World of Count Basie. New York: Scribner's, 1980, p. 69.

25. " 'Sweethearts of Rhythm' Set New Box Office Record," New York Age, August 30, 1941, p. 10.

26. "International Sweethearts Big Hit in Detroit, Mich.," Jackson Advocate, May 1, 1943, p. 3.

27. Isadora Smith, "The Girls Go Swell at Savoy," Pittsburgh Courier, September 29, 1941, p. 20.

28. Nell Dodson, "Sweethearts Not Seeking Husbands," Jackson Advocate, January 31, 1942, p. 7.

29. Ibid.

30. "All-Girl Ork to 'Battle' Henderson on One-Nighters," Down Beat, March 1, 1942, p. 2; and "Sweethearts to 'Battle' Henderson Soon," Down Beat, April 1, 1942, p. 5.

31. Correspondence from Winburn, April 8, 1980.

32. "Anna Mae Winburn and Band Please Centennial and Dancing Public," Omaha Star, September 3, 1938, p. 5.

33. "All-Girl Ork to 'Battle' Henderson...," loc. cit.

34. See entry on Leora Meoux Henderson in D. Antoinette Handy's Black Women in American Bands and Orchestras. Metuchen, N.J.: Scarecrow Press, 1981, pp. 129-130.

35. "Harold Nichols and Girl Orchestra Star Acts at the Apollo," New York Age, February 5, 1944, p. 10.

36. Telephone Conversation with Braddy, May 25, 1982.

37. "International Sweethearts Big Hit in Detroit, Mich.," loc. cit.

38. See entry on Lucille Dixon (Robertson) in D. Antoinette Handy, op. cit., pp. 89-91; and Handy, "Conversation with Lucille Dixon, Manager, Symphony of the New World," The Black Perspective in Music, Fall 1975, pp. 299-311.

39. "All Girls' Band Sets Attendance Record at the Regal," Chicago Defender, October 24, 1942, p. 21.

40. "Arrest Members of All-Girl Band; School Prexy Irked," Jackson Advocate, October 17, 1942, p. 7.

41. "International Sweethearts Big Hit in Detroit, Mich.," loc. cit.

42. Marian McPartland, "The Untold Story of the International Sweethearts of Rhythm," 1980, p. 6. (To be published in Jazzwomen, Oxford University Press.)

43. Bob Fossum, "Girls Shouldn't Play Too Much Jazz, Says Ada," Down Beat, December 1, 1942, p. 14.

44. Personal Data Form from Rosalind Cron.

45. Personal Data Form from Toby Butler.

46. Conversation with Jones, Kansas City, Missouri, March 23, 1980.

47. "Sweethearts of Rhythm's Success Is Yarn of Opportunity Cashed In," Chicago Defender, February 10, 1945, p. 13.

48. E. B. Rea, "Encores and Echoes," Afro-American, March 31, 1945, p. 8.

49. Ted Watson, "War Provides 'Break' for All-Girl Bands," Jackson Advocate, May 22, 1943, p. 7.

50. E. B. Rea, "Encores and Echoes," Afro-American, December 9, 1944, p. 6.

51. Willie Mae Wong, "Nazis Gone, Germans Rave Over 'Sweethearts of Rhythm' Band," Chicago Defender, September 8, 1945, p. 14.

52. Melvin C. Patrick, "GI's Line Up Mile Long to Greet Sweethearts [of] Rhythm," Afro-American, October 6, 1945, p. 23.

53. "Sweethearts Will Do One-Reel Movie Short," Down Beat, May 6, 1946, p. 12.

54. Telephone Conversation with Ray, July 25, 1981. See entries on Carline Ray (Russell), pp. 93-94, and on Edna Marilyn Smith (Edet), p. 92, in D. Antoinette Handy, op. cit.

55. Telephone Conversation with Perry, June 2, 1982.

56. Frank Tirro, Jazz: A History, New York: W. W. Norton, 1977, p. 267.

57.   "Adjustment in Bands, Acts Ahead--Glaser," Afro-
      American, January 4, 1947, p. 7.

58.   E. B. Rea, "Sweethearts Set for Tour of Europe,"
      Afro-American, May 10, 1947, p. 8.

59.   "Mrs. Raylee [sic] Jones, Dies at Lutheran Hospital,"
      Omaha Star, September 9, 1949, p. 1.

60.   McPartland, op. cit., p. 8.

CHAPTER VI

Selected Members' Noteworthy Musical Activities
Following Their Membership in the
International Sweethearts of Rhythm

"Original" Sweetheart drummer (and blues singer) PAULINE
BRADDY (Williams) in more recent years worked as a
switchboard operator in Washington, D.C. Despite her participation in the April 1941 "Great Escape," Braddy main-
tained contact with her native Mississippi and alma mater
Piney Woods Country Life School. The pulse of the International Sweethearts of Rhythm kept her musically active until
the late 1960s, working as drummer with The Vi Burnside
All-Stars, The Edna Smith Trio (piano, bass, and drums),
and finally the trio Two Plus One (piano, bass, and drums;
two females plus one male). The latter two groups worked
primarily in and around New York City. Braddy's brief performance in Kansas City at the March 1980 Salute suggested
that she was certainly a more than adequate jazz percussion-
ist in her heyday, even though, according to Braddy, she
had not touched the skins for more than twelve years.

* * *

The exact dates and length of tenor/baritone saxophonist
LORRAINE BROWN (Guilford's) International Sweethearts of
Rhythm membership can be placed only at "sometime during
the second World War years." She wrote (in 1980) concern-
ing her departure, "I became bored. I returned twice. The
second time I had a Southern experience." Prior to joining
the Sweethearts, Brown played with Eddie Durham's all-

female orchestra. Following the Sweetheart era, Brown did "everything under the sun," including organization of another all-women's band, serving as a booking agent, managing an employment agency, selling real estate, working in politics and as a legal secretary, with all jobs centered in and around New York City. In more recent years, her musical assignments have included playing drums with various groups. Darlings of Rhythm was the name of Brown's ladies' orchestra. "From New York City," she wrote,

> I contacted and sent for girl musicians from all over the U.S. I organized the band on a shoestring--less than $5,000,000.... I went out West to negotiate--all day and night--until I got what I wanted for the band. One of the main features of the contract was a minimum pay check whenever we were not performing. I don't recall the amount, but it was adequate. Another was band outfits to be the responsibility of the agency.... I returned to New York with a good contract. Having been a member of the Sweethearts, I observed that the musicians were always broke; their health did not seem to be a major concern of management. [The band was in business].... In my over-worked condition, my mother persuaded me to take a short rest. In the interim, ... the band left New York without me ... I was invited to join the band as a musician only, not as owner/organizer. I refused. Through the years, I ran into a few of the members of the band who confided to me that they now, too late, realize what I had attempted to do for girl musicians. Of course they again were done in by having no contract to their advantage. By the way, this could be another book for you to write--"Behind the Scenes of Girl Band Business...." People will make money off and with us, but they want a 100% profit, with no responsibility. No one cares enough to invest in the musician, who gives--gives--gives, while management takes--takes--takes.

*   *   *

VIOLET ("Vi") MAY BURNSIDE is the one Sweetheart name that many remember. Jazz pianist Billy Taylor vividly recalled her command of the tenor saxophone, forceful playing, musical leadership ability, and general musicianship. Said Taylor:

Vi held her own, anywhere. She and pianist
Norma Sheppard were in competition with the best
of players in D.C. The pressure was on them to
produce. And they did.

Though possibly inaccurate, the following data from a December 15, 1964, issue of the Afro-American provide more
information than is obtainable from any other source.

VI BURNSIDE, WORLD'S GREATEST FEMALE
SAXOPHONIST, DIES HERE

Washington. . . .   A mass was said last Tuesday for
Miss Violet May Burnside, a longtime musician. . . .
The body was sent to . . . Lancaster, Penn. . . .
Miss Burnside, better known as "Vi," was born
in Lancaster, Pa. . . . [She] studied music at a
conservatory in New York City. . . . She and her
troupe toured Europe for over three years for the
USO during World War II. She was also a member of the Sweethearts of Rhythm, an all girls'
orchestra. Miss Burnside has played at the Apollo
and Small's Paradise in New York, The Academy
of Music in Philadelphia and at the Royal Theatre
in Baltimore. Recently she and her combo played
different clubs in Washington, the Howard Theatre
and the July 1964 Jazz Festival here.

The preceding obituary includes some post-International
Sweethearts of Rhythm activities. It can be stated with ac-
curacy that "Vi" led the five-piece Vi Burnside All-Stars and
the Vi Burnside Orchestra. Activities of these groups were
frequently reported in the publications Down Beat and International Musician. Also, the Burnside Orchestra cut an album
titled "Burnside Beat" (in the early fifties) on the Abbey label
(A 64, G-831, 832).

*   *   *

Trumpeter TOBY BUTLER continued in the profession primarily as a free-lancing bassist in Tacoma, Washington.
She also furthered her education by acquiring a certificate
in music supervision and an Associate degree in accounting
and business administration. Butler's activities also included
teaching.

*   *   *

Following a fifteen-month tenure with the International Sweethearts of Rhythm, trombonist (trumpeter) ESTHER LOUISE
COOKE returned to the classroom at Howard University.
Additional performance was limited to affiliation with the
Howard Swingmasters, a coeducational group sponsored by
a campus fraternity and started around 1949. The direction
shifted from this point on. Cooke wrote in 1978, "After
leaving Howard [with a B. Mus.], I began pursuing a future
in music of the classics. It could well be that I was never
really a 'jazz' artist." She then acquired the M. Mus. degree from Eastman School of Music and a certificate in composition from the Juilliard School of Music. Her strong
background in string and brass performance (string training
dated back to the pre-college years), piano, and music theory
made her an attractive prospect for the university classroom
and music studio. From 1953, Cooke taught strings and
brass and directed orchestras and bands at Tennessee State,
Grambling, and North Carolina A & T universities, and at
St. Augustine's and Edward Waters colleges. When last
heard from (1978), Cooke was Supervisor of Music for the
Wilkes County (Georgia) public school system and completing
requirements for the doctorate in musicology from Emory
University.

                          *   *   *

Following her International Sweethearts of Rhythm years as
saxophone (alto) section leader, ROSALIND CRON studied and
taught clarinet extensively and in more recent years began
studying the flute. Throughout the 1960s, Cron played with
various studio bands in Los Angeles. In 1979 she organized
a short-lived seventeen-piece all-women band and followed
this effort with another short-lived "male/female-black/white
band." But, she wrote,

> The pressures of a day job (executive secretary)
> made it impossible for me to continue with the
> added pressures of keeping a big band together.
> Also, I was completely lacking in capital and could
> not continue to finance the project.

Other activities included one year at the American Institute of Foreign Trade, marriage, and the raising of two
sons.

                          *   *   *

Trumpeter ERNESTINE "Tiny" DAVIS was one of the band's
featured soloist, both here and abroad. Additionally, the
Memphis native's blues vocals and comedy routines consistently drew the plaudits of audience and critics alike. She
left the group shortly following the USO tour abroad and
formed her own band. A September 1948 notice indicated
that "Tiny Davis and her all-girl orchestra, all formerly
with the Sweethearts of Rhythm" were playing at Baltimore's
Club Astoria, only one of many stops across the country.
She followed this activity with the formation of a six-piece
combo called The Hell Divers. Working out of Chicago for
about six years, the group was managed by the popular agent
Joe Glaser. As reported at the 1980 K.C. Salute, "Tiny"
was still performing, primarily with her own trio, which included her daughter Dorothy (Harney) on keyboard and bass.

* * *

In a letter dated May 14, 1981, former Sweetheart bassist
LUCILLE DIXON (Robertson) wrote,

> This September will be seven years that I've been
> playing at An Evening Dinner Theater in Westchester,
> New York. Also, I completed my college work last
> December.

Dixon's college matriculation began at Brooklyn College
in 1941 and ended with a degree from Iona College. During
the summer of 1981, Dixon was part of an all-female quintet
featured in a program called "Women Blow Their Own Horns"
at Carnegie Hall in New York City, followed by a jam session
with Dizzy Gillespie and Clark Terry--all a part of the Kool
Jazz Festival. International Sweethearts of Rhythm membership (1942) was Dixon's first professional experience. The
intervening years (1942-81) have been filled with numerous
musical involvements (symphony and jazz band membership,
symphony orchestra management, jazz band organization and
leadership), the selling of real estate, clerical jobs, artistic
activism, marriage, and mothering (of three children). Her
symphony orchestra affiliations included the National Orchestral
Association, National Symphony of Panama, Boston Women's
Symphony, Orchestra of America, Westchester Philharmonic,
Ridgefield and Scranton Symphony Orchestras and Symphony
of the New World. Other "elite art" affiliations included the
Radio City Music Hall and Dimitri Mitropoulos Conducting
Competitions Orchestras.

When in 1943 Dixon's desire for permanent membership in a major symphony orchestra appeared to be an un-
realistic pursuit (despite her extensive training, experience,
and receipt of numerous orchestral achievement awards), she
turned to jazz. "I decided that I had to make a living and
would just have to go into some other kind of music." There
was membership in the Earl Hines Band and then the formation of her own band--a six-piece unit featuring, among
others, Sonny Payne, Buddy Tate, Taft Jordan, and Tyree
Glenn. The Lucille Dixon Band played at New York City's
Savannah Club for twelve years. Through the years, Dixon
performed and/or recorded with such popular artists as Tony
Bennett, Ella Fitzgerald, Sarah Vaughan, Dinah Washington,
and Frank Sinatra. Efforts at assisting those blacks whose
ambitions were similar to hers never ceased. Dixon consistently fought for "equality of opportunity" in symphonic circles. She organized committees, wrote letters to and articles for the New York Times, and was one of the founding
members of the Symphony of the New World (New York City,
1964)--a fully integrated, professional orchestra. In the orchestra's final years, Dixon served as the orchestra's manager.

                          *   *   *

The lady whose voice once challenged that of "Lady Day"
Holiday for popularity left the Sweethearts shortly following
the band's return from its USO tour. "Original" Sweetheart
EVELYN McGEE (Stone) indicated that by this time, "the band
was falling apart and it was clear that money was being mis-
managed." Then came marriage and child rearing (two),
years as a telephone operator, and finally (in the early sev-
enties) singing and playing the drums at private clubs as a
part of a jazz duo with Jesse Stone. Her second marriage
was with the Sweethearts' former arranger/musical director
Stone in 1975. Then came a return to the classroom for the
high school dropout, first earning the GED certificate and
then enrolling at Kingsboro Community College. Voice lessons were also on the agenda. McGee said in a July 1981
telephone conversation,

> I'm getting an act together now [around preparing
> for a gala 80th birthday celebration for husband
> Jesse]. I know that I'm supposed to be out there
> entertaining people. The Good Lord gave me a
> talent and though I'm now 60, I've got to use it.

Audience response to her 1979 appearance at New York City's
Carlyle Hotel (with pianist Marian McPartland) and the March
1980 Kansas City Salute suggested that the public would be
very receptive.

*   *   *

Sweetheart members called her "teacher," a proper name for
the recent graduate of Virginia State University. Alto/tenor
saxophonist GENEVA FRANCES PERRY spent the school years
1947 to 1949 working as band director and social studies instructor in Warrenton, North Carolina and worked in the same
capacity from 1949 to 1953 in Kinston, North Carolina. She
began her study of the alto saxophone at the Mary Potter
Boarding School in Oxford, North Carolina. In addition to
the Bachelor of Science degree (with a major in music) received from Virginia State University, she engaged in further
study at Virginia and Howard universities, specializing in
Early Childhood Education. The third grade teacher returned
to her native Washington, D.C. in the mid-1950s. Around the
teaching activities, she continued to perform until the mid
1970s--occasionally as leader of her own combos in and
around Washington, with Anna Mae Winburn and Her Sweethearts of Rhythm, with Vi Burnside ("when she augmented
her combo to play dance halls and the theatre circuit"), and
with various groups working out of Philadelphia. In the final
playing years, Perry's activities were limited to summer
park jobs in and around the nation's capital.

*   *   *

CARLINE RAY's resume includes the following as areas of
musical expertise: bass, guitar, piano, voice, and choral
directing. When guitarist Carline Ray (Russell) joined the
Sweethearts in 1946, the daughter of musicians was already
a graduate of the Juilliard School of Music, having majored
in piano and composition. Following her May 1947 departure,
she joined the Erskine Hawkins band as guitarist/vocalist. In
the early 1950s, she joined former Sweetheart members Edna
Smith and Pauline Braddy in the Edna Smith Trio, performing
as pianist. The late pianist/band leader Luis Russell (1902-
63) hired the group as a two-week substitute at New York
City's Town Hall. The girls were so successful that they
held the date for six months. In 1956, Luis Russell and
Carline Ray were married, the same year that Carline received the M.Mus. degree from Manhattan School of Music,
with a major in voice. Their offspring Judith Catherine

Russell, a 1981 graduate of the American Academy of Dramatic Arts, continues the Russell tradition as a skilled pianist, mandolin player, singer, and dancer.

Friend Edna Smith's mastery of the fender bass encouraged Carline Ray to expand still further. In the capacity of bassist, Ray worked with such top jazz musicians as Roy Eldridge, Buck Clayton, Billy Taylor, Dizzy Gillespie, Marian McPartland, Joe Newman, Peter Duchin, Sy Oliver, Skitch Henderson, and Mary Lou Williams. In 1976 she toured the western United States, western Canada, and Japan with the Mercer Ellington-led Duke Ellington Band. Throughout the 1970s, she worked as a regular with the Alvin Ailey Dance Company and for brief periods with the American Ballet Theatre, Royal Ballet, and Pennsylvania Ballet orchestras.

Ray's rich contralto voice and superb musicianship led to additional challenging and rewarding experiences as a concert chorister (in concert and recording studios), performing with such distinguished groups as the Schola Cantorum, Musica Aeterna, Camerata Singers, Leonard DePaur Chorus, and the Bach Aria Singers. Ray was most visible (and audible) at both the 1978 and 1979 Women's Jazz Festivals in Kansas City. At the 1978 event she was the featured bassist and vocalist in a performance of "Mary Lou's Mass" at the Premiere Concert. At the 1979 event, Ray performed as bassist with the group Aerial, winners of the Combo Tape Contest and as bassist/leader of the seventeen-piece band Big Apple Jazz Women, representing the New York-based Universal Jazz Coalition. Ray "the singer" emerged as one of the Festival's top vocalists, performing Emme Kemp's "Tomorrow's Woman."

*   *   *

Following the International Sweethearts of Rhythm years, bassist EDNA SMITH (Edet) toured with the Vi Burnside all-female combo and later led her own trio. She then returned to the classroom, earning the B. Mus., M. Mus., M. A. and Ed. D., the first two degrees from Manhattan School of Music and the latter two from Teachers College, Columbia University. The acquisition of additional degrees coincided with her years of teaching in New York City elementary and secondary public schools. Between 1961 and 1967, Smith served as a music lecturer at the University of Nigeria. Returning to the States, she joined the faculties of Queens and Medgar Evers colleges, continuing to lecture and write, primarily on the topic "African and Afro-American Music."

*   *   *

"Original" Sweethearts leader, featured trumpeter, accordion-
ist, vocalist, and arranger EDNA ARMSTEAD WILLIAMS left
the band in late 1942. She continued her musical activities
as a free-lancer, which included appearances with bands
fronted by such established leaders as Noble Sissle and Andy
Kirk. Making its debut at Los Angeles' Zanzibar in the fall
of 1945 was the racially integrated, all-female Edna Williams
Sextette (trumpet, alto and tenor saxophones, piano, bass,
and drums). A September 1945 article in the Afro-American
stated that "[t]his remarkable all-round musician ... for years
head of the famed Sweethearts of Rhythm aggregation ... is
marking time with the sextette until she can bring the other
crew-women to the coast." ("All Girls' Combo in Coast
Debut"--September 1, 1945, p. 8). Often referred to as one
of the nation's most versatile musicians, Williams recorded
"Body and Soul" for Victor in 1946, with four other "competent girl musicians" (trumpet plus violin, piano, bass and
drums), but died before its release. A reissue of this recording can be heard on the Stash Release (1978) "Women in
Jazz: All Women Groups" (ST-111).

*   *   *

As noted earlier, ANNA MAE DARDEN WINBURN (Pilgrim)
brought to the International Sweethearts of Rhythm a wealth
of musical experience, as well as beauty and charm. It was
announced in May 1948 that Anna Mae Winburn would retire
from the profession, following her early June marriage.
Her spouse-to-be was the popular entertainer Duke Pilgrim.
In 1950, Port Royal, Tennessee native Winburn pulled together
what remained of the International Sweethearts of Rhythm (following Rae Lee Jones's death) and with her husband as manager, revived the band's activities--with many new faces, of
course. She called the group Anna Mae Winburn and Her
Sweethearts of Rhythm. Working out of New York City, with
Universal Attractions serving as booking agent, the group
(often only a combo) remained active until 1956. Also between 1948 and 1956, Winburn gave birth to four children.

IN REMEMBRANCE

"I don't think I've met half dozen whites who
know who the International Sweethearts of

Rhythm were--but throughout all these years,
black people have never forgotten us...."
                                          --Roz Cron*

"Elite art" composer and Tufts University's Fletcher
Professor of Music THOMAS JEFFERSON ANDERSON wrote
the following:

> I remember 1940 as the year I failed the 7th grade
> at Benjamin Banneker Junior High School. At that
> time my father was a professor at Howard Univer-
> sity and I spent my afternoons at the Howard The-
> ater listening to the great bands of the era: Jimmy
> Lunceford, Duke Ellington, Erskine Hawkins, Count
> Basie, The International Sweethearts of Rhythm,
> Earl Hines, Cab Calloway and many others. These
> bands played for stage shows that were interspersed
> with third and fourth rate movies. After the movie
> one could hear them tuning up behind the large ma-
> roon velour curtains. Then the voice would say,
> "And now ladies and gentlemen, The International
> Sweethearts of Rhythm." As the curtain slowly
> opened we in the audience heard music of an un-
> usual nature. The first tune was always fast and
> the visual image of these beautiful women executing
> the technical demands of a first rate arrangement
> or "cutting the page" as we use to say is quite
> vivid in my mind to this day. I had been prepared
> to expect something of importance when I purchased
> my ticket and saw the bus with the inscription "The
> International Sweethearts of Rhythm." I had also
> been prepared by hearing the drums, tenor sax,
> trumpets, and trombones warm up on riffs and solo
> licks before the curtain opened. Yet one is never
> ready for that first piece which is a show stopper
> before the show begins.
>   My favorite band of this period had been Jimmy
> Lunceford. His group was the model. The Sweet-
> hearts of Rhythm were competitive. So were the
> other bands of the time. Their arrangements were
> always first rate, the ensembles well executed, and
> solos always interesting. They played with energy;

---

*Terry Teachout, "Sweethearts Delight Jazz Enthusiasts,"
The Kansas City Star, March 24, 1980, p. 15.

yet it was their physical beauty that attracted my
eye--a group of women the color of the rainbow.
Here I sat in a segregated audience and was wit-
nessing a performance by women who looked like
they were from all over the world. This was my
first visual experience with integration--my glance
into what the civil rights movement would be about
approximately two decades later. This advanced
visual image of what the United Nations would become was indeed impressive and these women working together to make music only further served to
emphasize what could happen in other areas in the
future.

As I now think back on the processes of accul-
turation and the procedure of being a part of a
particular environment with its accompanying institutions, I am always most appreciative for the year
1940.

                                   Medford, Massachusetts
                                   July 1982

                      *   *   *

A veteran of Count Basie's band, tenor saxophonist PAUL
QUINICHETTE remembered,

Those girls were good! They made Phil Spitalny
look like a fool, and they messed up Ina Ray Hutton
when she had a band, too. They came from all
over, those girls, and they were playing! ...
[T]hey had a big old matron, like a warden, and
she'd lock those girls up at night!

                                   From Stanley Dance's The
                                   World of Count Basie. New
                                   York: Scribner's, 1980,
                                   p. 300.

                      *   *   *

Educator/Administrator LEOTA J. GIBBS recalled,

As a young professional, I lived and worked in
Kansas City when there was a proliferation of
clubs on and near 18th and Vine. On weekends,
young adults would "clubhop" and spend the most

time at the liveliest spot. On one of these occasions, I do not recall the club, the Sweethearts of
Rhythm was being featured. We were so taken by
their poise, beauty, and the sweetness of their music,
that we spent our time at that one night spot.

Petersburg, Virginia
July 1982

* * *

Richmonder BOYD "JUNIE" ALMOND played bass with (Robert)
Snookum Russell's band, a group that worked out of Florida.
According to Almond,

Russell's band "battled" on a few occasions with
the Sweethearts and they outplayed us each time.
One battle took place in Mobile, Alabama and another at the Savoy in New York City. We toured
with them in Texas. It wasn't easy for us men
to be whipped each time by a group of girls. But,
those girls could play.

Richmond, Virginia
August 1982

* * *

Sweethearts's former musical director EDDIE DURHAM expressed his feelings about the group to jazz pianist Marian
McPartland:

People couldn't believe it was women playing, so
sometimes when the curtain opened I'd make off
that I was playing and the girls were just panto-
miming. Then I'd stop, and people could see they
really were playing. I simplified things for them
as much as possible.... I had to train the Sweethearts, but at the Apollo nobody believed girls
could play that way.

Quoted from Marian McPartland's "The Untold Story of
the International Sweethearts
of Rhythm," 1980, p. 5.
(Material to be used in the
book Jazzwomen, Oxford
University Press.)

* * *

Music educator C. ("Charlie") LAWLER ROGERS reminisced,

> I grew up in Charlottesville, Virginia. It was dur-
> ing the era of segregation and most of the athletic
> and musical happenings took place at Washington
> Park. This was also the place where "Negroes"
> went for talent shows and dances. I recall when
> Billy Eckstine brought his band to play for a dance
> at Washington Park. Prior to the dance, the guys
> in the band played a game of basketball with Jeffer-
> son High School students. The guys practiced and
> played their games in the park because there was
> no gymnasium for blacks.
>   The zenith of my nostalgia of Washington Park
> was when I got a chance to see and hear the Inter-
> national Sweethearts of Rhythm. The band's reputa-
> tion as an excellent performing organization pre-
> ceded it. The girls' coming caused great excite-
> ment in the black community.
>   The audience listened, danced and applauded
> with tremendous enthusiasm through the evening.
> Who could forget the lyrical and rhythmic solos of
> tenor saxophonist Vi Burnside. The same kind of
> respect was accorded the Sweethearts as that given
> to the big named male bands--and rightly so.
>   As the years passed, I often wondered what
> happened to them. No one ever wrote about
> them.
>
>   Wilmington, Delaware
>   August 1982

* * *

Symphony violinist and music educator THOMAS BRIDGE recalled seeing the International Sweethearts of Rhythm many
times at the Paradise Theatre in Detroit and the Regal Theatre in Chicago. He recently gave this assessment:

> The Sweethearts put on an enjoyable show. Theirs
> was a novelty act; they were an attraction. This
> was the first time audiences had seen that many
> black women, playing instruments traditionally con-
> sidered masculine. It took a while to adjust to the

idea, but once the audience did, it was with them
all the way.

Petersburg, Virginia
February 1982

*   *   *

Retired postal worker CHARLES B. CARTER, JR. remembered when his all-male social club Le Grande (known also
as The Sour Kats) brought the Sweethearts to Richmond, Virginia for an appearance at the open air Market Inn.   After
checking with the few members still alive, Carter guaranteed
the year to be 1939 (pre-separation from Piney Woods Country Life School).   As remembered by Carter,

That band compared favourably with most male
bands of the period.   We tried to get them back,
but their schedule wouldn't permit.

Carter also remembered that this was one of those
occasions when ticket sales got out of hand due to a lack of
control.   According to Carter,

One of our members was a printer.   We suspected
that he printed--and sold--a few extras.

Richmond, Virginia
June 1982

*   *   *

Retired North Carolina school administrators ELIZABETH
DUNCAN KOONTZ* and JOSEPH C. DUNCAN (sister and
brother) offered a joint memory since they were nearly "the
same in age and socially involved with the same peer group":

Salisbury was and still is a small college town with
about a twenty percent black population.   Thus we
had few places to hold dances.   Thompson's Garage
(a real garage, cleaned up to be used as a dance
hall) is where the "Negro Bands" performed.   It

_____
*Koontz was also former director of the Women's Bureau,
U.S. Department of Labor, and national president of the
National Education Association (NEA).

was there that the International Sweethearts of
Rhythm performed, on more than one occasion.
We believe it was "Smiling Billy Stewart," a native of Salisbury, who brought them. He operated
out of Florida in the area of entertainment. We
could always count on a full house since the college kids came from the five predominately black
colleges within a radius of sixty miles. These
were in addition to townspeople from nearby. We
were disappointed when we learned that they were
no longer on the circuit. They were a novelty
(being an all-female band), but they were good
musicians and role models for young black girls
who saw in them possibilities for themselves.
They played the contemporary dance music to our
liking. They were simply terrific; they looked
good and fascinated their audiences. Our recollection is that they were billed as a band that began
at a college in Florida.

                              Salisbury, North Carolina
                              September 1982

                    *   *   *

Trombonist, university professor, and current research associate at the National Institute of Education (Washington,
D.C.) CLAIBORNE T. RICHARDSON offered the following
reflection:

During the early 1940s, I was very active as a
jazz musician in the State of Virginia. The war
years brought many outstanding black musicians
(male) to Fort Lee, Virginia, because Fort Lee
was a band training unit for the Army. Hearing
good jazz played by musicians from famous bands
was commonplace. The touring civilian bands were
frequently booked into the Petersburg Fairgrounds
and dance halls in both Richmond and Petersburg,
Virginia. This is where I first heard The Interna-
national Sweethearts of Rhythm. I was especially
attracted to this group because of the uniqueness
of seeing and hearing an all-female band during this
period of male domination. An all-female jazz
group was unheard of. The question was always
"Can they play like men?" Answering that question
on a nightly basis were such excellent Sweetheart

players as Vi Burnside (tenor saxophone); Tiny
Davis (trumpet), who I remember often used the
rotary valved type that looked like something out
of a museum; Ina Belle Byrd (trombone); and leader
Anna Mae Winburn who was a very attractive woman
with a dignified beat. I gathered that these ladies
truly enjoyed their work and got a "big kick" out
of playing and traveling. They were always beauti-
fully attired in their evening gown styled uniforms
and had a swing style à la Basie.

Springfield, Virginia
October 1982

*   *   *

Sociologist CHARLES U. SMITH, currently Dean of Graduate
Studies at Florida A & M University, remembered,

I was just starting out in higher education (as a
freshman at Tuskegee Institute). That band played
just the kind of music we college students wanted
to hear, i. e. music we could dance to. We were
all lindy hoppers and jitterbuggers. Those girls
were pioneers in the women's liberation movement,
certainly with no such intent. Vi Burnside was as
good as any tenor saxophonist of the day. Drummer Pauline Braddy could also hold her own. Those
girls were forty years ahead of their time.

Tallahassee, Florida
October 1982

*   *   *

Educator/Historian JOHN HENRICK CLARKE, associate professor of African-American History, Hunter College, recalled,

I first saw the International Sweethearts of Rhythm
when they played at the Apollo Theatre. Later I
was stationed at Kelly Field in Texas. As I recall,
on two occasions the band had evening engagements
in nearby San Antonio and came out earlier in the
day to entertain the GIs. What an impact they had
on the black soldiers, even before going to Europe
to entertain the troops over there. They were a
unique group--real innovators, equal to any male

band of the period. They were in charge of themselves and their music.

New York City
October 1982

*   *   *

According to English and Afro-American Studies professor
ALICE JACKSON STUART (Middlesex County College, Edison,
New Jersey),

Do I remember the International Sweethearts of
Rhythm? You should have asked "How well do I
remember them?" I think the year was 1938.
I was Dean of Women at Bethune Cookman College--
steeped in a marvelous educational experience with
Mary McLeod Bethune. This was my first awareness of Piney Woods Country Life School and its
president. The band arrived in this huge make-
shift bus. It was during the summer. They stayed
on campus. First Laurence Jones made a speech
about Piney Woods, then the band played. It was
just great hearing and seeing a black women's jazz
band. I also heard them either at the Hippodrome
or Market Inn in Richmond, Virginia. Then, too,
I saw them play at the New York City World's Fair
(1940).

Plainfield, New Jersey
October, 1982

*   *   *

Public school teacher YVONNE JONES of Elmsford (New
York) Senior High School reminisced,

This brings back memories of pride, wonder, and
admiration. It was almost unbelievable that a group
of girls could dare compete with the named male
bands of the day. Their music was exceptionally
pleasing to the ear. I was frequently a part of the
cheering audience at various places.

Elmsford, New York
October, 1982

*   *   *

Reedman, arranger, string teacher (Orleans Parish Schools)
CAREY LAVIGNE remembered,

> I went into the Navy in 1942. So it was between
> 1939 and 1941 when I first met President Laurence
> Jones. He was quite a guy. I was in New Orleans
> playing lead sax with Herbert Leary's band and do-
> ing much of Leary's arranging. Jones came in
> wherever we were playing and heard a medley of
> waltzes that he liked. He approached Leary about
> securing the arrangement for his lady's jazz band
> at Piney Woods. Leary told him that he had to
> negotiate with me. I arranged some waltzes for
> his band and a few other things over a period of
> four or five months. I had to negotiate with some
> lady at the school--whose name I can't recall. The
> problem was getting paid. I got paid something,
> but certainly not what I was promised. That's why
> I stopped arranging for them. As for the band, it
> was a well organized group. They could play and
> they were always superbly attired.

> New Orleans, Louisiana
> October 1982

*   *   *

NELLIE E. BASS, sister of the band's organizer wrote the
following, "In Retrospect":

> The International Sweethearts of Rhythm, the "brain
> child" of the late Dr. Laurence C. Jones, was a
> big hit with the public from the beginning. Many
> people at Piney Woods worked as booking agents,
> many using their own cars for travel. Not only
> was the band a big hit because of the novelty of
> being girls, but they could really play. There
> were more requests for return dates than could be
> filled.

> Jackson, Mississippi
> November 1982

*   *   *

Wrote Salisbury State College's professor of sociology and
anthropology ALFRED K. TALBOT, JR.,

As a teenager growing up in New York City generally and Harlem specifically, I danced to the music
of those talented young ladies at three of Harlem's
best known ballrooms: the Renaissance, the Alham-
bra, and the Savoy, somewhere prior to 1943. My
boyhood friends and I marvelled at the sophisticated
musicianship of the "Sweethearts," who to us were
a real entertainment phenomenon because they were
able to hold their own in an era of such big band
superstars as Duke Ellington, Count Basie, Louis
Armstrong, Jimmy Lunceford, and Fletcher Henderson.

> Salisbury, Maryland
> October 1982

*   *   *

Chairperson and Associate Professor of African American
Studies (at the University of Maryland Baltimore County)
DAPHNE HARRISON offered this "brief but faded" memory
of the Sweethearts:

The beautiful ladies in long satiny gowns, who
played like I dreamed of playing someday, were
always a special treat when we went to the movies.
Such features as "Harlem Cowboy" with Herb Jef-
fries might be preceded by a Sweethearts short.
I also remember how much more exciting it was
to watch them than Phil Spitalny's All-Girl band.
Evelyn and her singing violin were no match for
the hot saxophones of the Sweethearts.

> Baltimore, Maryland
> November 1982

APPENDIX A

_____

THE BLACK WOMAN IN HISTORY

BOOKS

The Black Woman, ed. by LaFrances Rodgers-Rose (Sage Publications, 1980).

Bogle, Donald, Brown Sugar: Eighty Years of America's Black Superstars (Harmony Books, 1980).

Brown, Hallie Quinn, Homespun Heroines and Other Women of Distinction (Aldine Publication Co., 1926).

Cherry, Gwendolyn; Ruby Thomas; Pauline Willis, Portraits in Color: The Lives of Colorful Negro Women (Pageant Press, 1962).

Daniel, Sadie Iola, Women Builders (The Associated Publishers, 1931).

Dannett, Sylvia, Profiles in Negro Womanhood (Educational Heritage, Inc., 1964).

Davis, Lenwood C., The Black Woman in American Society: A Selected Annotated Bibliography (G. K. Hall, 1975).

Handy, D. Antoinette, Black Women in American Bands and Orchestras (Scarecrow Press, 1981).

Ladner, Joyce, Tomorrow's Tomorrow: The Black Woman (Doubleday, 1972).

Lerner, Gerda, Black Women in White America (Vintage
    Books, 1973).

McKenzie, Marjorie, 50 Years of Progress for Negro Women
    (Pittsburgh Courier Reprint, 1950).

Majors, M.A., Noted Negro Women (Donohue and Henneberry,
    1893).

The Progress of Afro-American Women: A Selected Bibliog-
    raphy and Resource Guide, compiled by Janet L. Sims
    (Greenwood Press, 1980).

Scruggs, L.A., Women of Distinction: Remarkable in Works
    and Invincible in Character (Scruggs, 1893).

Sterling, Dorothy, Black Foremothers: Three Lives (The
    Feminist Press, 1979).

Terrell, Mary Church, A Colored Woman in a White World
    (Ransdell, Inc., 1940).

Williams, Ora, American Black Women in the Arts and Sci-
    ences (Scarecrow Press, 1978, revised and expanded edi-
    tion).

ARTICLES

Cole, Johnetta, "Affirmation of Resistance: A Response to
    Angela Davis" (Woman: An Issue, ed. by Lee R. Edwards,
    et al., Little, Brown and Company, 1972).

Davis, Angela, "Reflections on the Black Woman's Role in
    the Community of Slaves" (Woman: An Issue).

Ebony, Special Issue--The Black Woman (August 1977).

Ebony, Special Issue--The Negro Woman (August 1966).

Garvey, Amy Jacques, "The Role of Women in Liberation
    Struggles" (Woman: An Issue).

Giddings, Paula, "Highlights of the History of Black Women,
    1910-1980," (Crisis, December 1980).

Lynch, Mary A. "Social Status and Needs of the Colored

Woman" (The United Negro: His Problems and His Progress, D. E. Luther Publishing Co., 1902).

Strong, Augusta, "Negro Women in Freedom's Battles" (Freedomways, Winter 1966).

Thomas, James Eugene, "The Role of Negro Women in the Battle for Equality" (Negro Digest, February 1964).

"Women Leaders" (Ebony, July 1949).

APPENDIX B

ALL-BLACK FEMALE INSTRUMENTAL
ENSEMBLES, 1880-MID 1940s

1880s
  The Colored Female Brass Band--East Saginaw, Michigan
  Female Drum Corps--Pittsburgh, Pennsylvania

Turn of the Century
  Female Symphony Orchestra--Cambridge, Massachusetts
  William Nickerson's Ladies Orchestra--New Orleans

First Decade
  Hallie L. Anderson's Ladies Orchestra--New York City
  N. Clark Smith's Ladies Mandolin and String Instrument
    Club--Chicago
  N. Clark Smith's Ladies Orchestra--Chicago

Second Decade
  Estella Harris' Jass Band--Chicago
  Marian Pankey's Female Orchestra (Jazz)--Chicago
  George Bailey's Female Brass Band--Indianapolis, Indiana
  Marie Lucas' Lafayette Theatre Ladies Orchestra--New
    York City
  Madam Corilla Rochon's Ladies Symphony Orchestra--
    Houston, Texas
  Martin-Smith School Ladies' Staff Orchestra--New York
    City

Early and Mid 1920s
  Professor Walden's Ladies Band--Cleveland
  The Silver Seal Ladies Orchestra--Cleveland
  Papa Waddles Female Brass Band--Omaha, Nebraska

Girls' Orchestra--Florida Agricultural and Mechanical
    College, Tallahassee, Florida
Girls' Drum and Bugle Corps--Florida Agricultural and
    Mechanical College, Tallahassee, Florida
Poro College Ladies Orchestra--St. Louis
Arabic Court Saxophone Band--Chicago

Late 1920s and Early 1930s
Negro Women's Orchestral and Civic Association--New
    York City
Olivia Porter Shipp's Jazz-Mines (Jazz)--New York City
Excelsior Temple Band--Brooklyn, New York
Colored Women's Band--Chicago
American Creolian Orchestra (Jazz)--New York City
Lil Armstrong's All-Girl Orchestra (Jazz)--New York City

Mid 1930s and Early 1940s
NYA Colored Girls' Orchestra--Mobile, Alabama
Harlem Playgirls (Jazz)
Dixie Sweethearts (Jazz)
Eddie Durham's All-Girl Band (Jazz)
Harlem Rhythm Girls' Corps (Jazz)--New York City
Sepian Lassies of Harmony (Jazz)--St. Paul, Minnesota
Prairie View College Co-Eds (Jazz)
Darlings of Rhythm (Jazz)
Bennett College Orchestra--Greensboro, N.C.

PIONEER BLACK FEMALE INSTRUMENTALISTS-- BAND/ORCHESTRAL AFFILIATION (Pre-1940)†

KEY

(1) Family Orchestra
(2) Lafayette Theatre Ladies Orchestra
(3) Chicago Colored Women's Band
(4) Excelsior Temple Band
(5) The Vampires
(6) Della Sutton's All-Girls Band
(7) Negro Women's Orchestral and Civil Association
(8) American Creolians
(9) Cleveland Women's Orchestra
(10) Martin-Smith Music School Orchestra/Ladies Staff Orchestra
(11) Mainstream--Male Dominated Orchestras
(12) Harlem Playgirls
(13) Dixie Sweethearts
(14) Nickerson Ladies Orchestra
(15) N. Clark Smith's Ladies Mandolin & String Club/Ladies Orchestra
(16) Lil Hardin Armstrong's All-Girl Orchestra
(17) Marian Pankey's Female Orchestra
(18) Estella Harris' Jass Band
(19) Colored Female Brass Band (East Saginaw, Michigan)
(20) Bailey's Female Brass Band

(*) indicates group leader.

---

†For additional information see D. Antoinette Handy, Black Women in American Bands and Orchestras (Scarecrow Press, 1981).

STRING PLAYERS

Violin
    Pamora Banks (12)
    Grazia Bell (11)
    *Mae Brady (11)
    Marjorie Ferrell (11)
    Elizabeth Foster (plus mandolin & bass) (1)
    Mildred Franklin (2)
    Marie Guilbeau (14)
    Emma Harris (14)
    Ruth Jackson (10)
    Penelope Johnson (10)
    Lelia Julius (12)
    Florence Lewis (14)
    *Gertrude E. Martin (10) (11)
    Pamela Moore (12)
    Mazie Mullen (7)
    Julia Lewis Nickerson (plus cello) (14)
    Gertrude Palmer (18)
    Alberta Riggs (15)
    Angelina Riviera (10)
    (Mrs.) Jesse Scott (1)
    Dorothy Smith (9)
    Jean Taylor (12)
    Marie Wayne (2) (10)

Viola
    Maude Shelton (2)

Cello
    Minnie Brown (2) (10)

String Bass
    Marge Backstrom (12)
    Jamesetta Humphrey (11)
    Lillian Humphrey (11)
    Gertrude H. Martin (7) (11)
    *Olivia Porter Shipp (plus cello)   (2) (7) (10) (11)
    Gwen Twiggs (13)

Harp
    Myrtle Hart (1)
    Olivette Miller (11)

Guitar/Banjo/Ukulele
    *Minnie ("Memphis Minnie") Douglas (11)

Laura Dukes (11)
*Vanzula ("Van") Carter Hunt (11)
Betty Lomax (7)
Fanny Wiley (1)

WIND PLAYERS

Cornet/Trumpet
*Viola Allen (19)
*Estella Harris (18)
*Leora Meoux Henderson (2) (5) (7) (11) (16)
*Gertrude Irene Howard (3) (15)
 Gertrude Hughes (11)
 Laurie Johnson (11)
 (Mrs.) Roper Johnson (20)
*Dolly Jones (Armendra) (11) (16)
 Dyer Jones (11)
 Nettie Lewis (20)
 Carrie Melvin (plus violin) (11)
 Alice Proctor (13)
 Mary Shannon (12)
 Mattie Simpson (11)
*Valaida Snow (11)

Saxophone
 Margaret Backstrom (12)
 Mildred Creed (11)
 Lula Edge (12)
 Gertrude Grigsby (11)
 Ophelia Grigsby (11)
 Hattie Hargrow (20)
 Elizabeth King (12)
 Helen Murphy (11)
*Alma Long Scott (8) (16)
 Gladys Seals (7)
*Isabele Taliaferro Spiller (plus trumpet) (4) (11)
 May Yorke (11)
 Irma Young (1)

Clarinet
 Bea Acheson (11)
 Geneva Moret (11)

Trombone
 Nettie Goff (11)
*Marie Lucas (2) (11)

Susie Stokes (20)
Della Sutton (6) (7)
Anna Wells (20)

Baritone
Ada Low (20)

Tuba
Ella Clifford (20)

PERCUSSIONISTS

Lottie Brown (2)
Jennie Byrd (13)
Alice Calloway (2)
Mary Alice Clarke (11)
Clothilde Hart (1)
Hazel Hart (1)
Bettie May (11)
*Marian Pankey (17)
Beverly Sexton (11)
Florence Sturgess (2)
Maggie Thompson (19)

BIBLIOGRAPHY

BOOKS

Bogle, Donald. Brown Sugar: Eighty Years of America's
Black Superstars. New York: Harmony Books, 1980.

Bradford, Perry. Born with the Blues. New York: Oak
Publications, 1965.

Carter, Consuella. A Pictorial History of the Tiger Band.
Published by the author, 1976.

Coggan, Blanche, et al. Prior Foster: Pioneer Afro-
American Educator. Published by the authors, Lansing,
Michigan, 1969.

Dance, Stanley. The World of Count Basie. New York:
Scribner's, 1980.

Day, Beth. The Little Professor of Piney Woods. New
York: Julian Messner, 1955.

Driggs, Frank. Women in Jazz: A Survey. Brooklyn, N.Y.:
Stash Records, Inc., 1977.

DuBois, W.E.B. The Souls of Black Folk. Greenwich,
Conn.: Fawcett Publication, 1961. (Originally, Chicago:
A.C. McClurg, 1903.)

Ellison, Ralph. Shadow and Act. New York: Random
House, 1964.

Feather, Leonard. The Book of Jazz. New York: Bonanza
Books, 1965.

218

Fernett, Gene. Swing Out: Great Negro Bands. Midland,
    Mich.: Pendell, 1970.

_____. A Thousand Golden Horns. Midland, Mich.:
    Pendell, 1966.

Handy, D. Antoinette. Black Women in American Bands and
    Orchestras. Metuchen, N.J.: Scarecrow Press, 1981.

Handy, William Talbot, Sr. Up from Gallatin: An Auto-
    biography. Published by the author, 1975.

Happy Hours in the Tour of the Cotton Blossom Singers.
    Piney Woods, Miss.: Piney Woods Country Life School,
    n. d.

Hartshorn, W. N., ed. An Era of Progress and Promise,
    1863-1910. Boston: Priscilla, 1910.

Hatch, James V., ed. Black Theater USA: 45 Plays by
    Black Americans, 1847-1974. New York: The Free
    Press, 1974.

Important Facts About Piney Woods Country Life School.
    Piney Woods, Miss.: Piney Woods Country Life School,
    n. d.

James, Doris. My Education at Piney Woods School. New
    York: Fleming H. Revell, 1937.

Johnson, Charles S. The Negro in American Civilization.
    New York: Henry Holt, 1930.

Johnson, James Weldon. Black Manhattan. New York:
    Alfred A. Knopf, 1930.

Jones, Laurence C. The Bottom Rail. New York: Fleming
    H. Revell, 1935.

_____. Piney Woods and Its Story. New York: Fleming
    H. Revell, 1922.

_____. The Spirit of Piney Woods. New York: Fleming
    H. Revell, 1931.

Keepnews, Orrin, and Grauer, Bill, Jr. A Pictorial History
    of Jazz. 2nd ed. New York: Crown Publishers, 1971.

Kinkle, Roger D. The Complete Encyclopedia of Popular
   Music and Jazz, 1900-1950. New Rochelle, N. Y.:
   Arlington House, 1974.

Little Journeys to Piney Woods, comp. by Laurence C. Jones.
   Piney Woods, Miss.: Piney Woods Country Life School,
   n. d.

McKenzie, Marjorie. 50 Years of Progress for Negro Women.
   Pittsburgh Courier Reprint, 1950.

Miller, Paul Eduard. Yearbook of Swing. Chicago: Down
   Beat Publishing Co., 1939.

Negro Education: A Study of the Private and Higher Schools
   for Colored People in the United States. Bureau of Education, Department of Interior, Washington D.C.: Bureau
   of Education, 1917.

The Negro Handbook, compiled and edited by Florence Murray.
   New York: Wendell Malliet, 1942.

A Pictorial History of the Piney Woods Country Life School
   (Fortieth Anniversary, 1910-11 to 1950-51). Piney Woods,
   Miss.: Piney Woods Country Life School, n. d.

Piney Woods Catalogues. 193? and 1938.

Placksin, Sally. American Women in Jazz: 1900 to the
   Present. New York: Seaview Books, 1982.

Purcell, Leslie Harper. Miracle in Mississippi: Laurence
   C. Jones of Piney Woods. New York: Carlton Press,
   1956.

Quarles, Benjamin. The Negro in the Making of America.
   New York: Macmillan, 1964.

Sampson, Henry T. Blacks in Blackface: A Source Book on
   Early Musical Shows. Metuchen, N.J.: Scarecrow Press,
   1980.

Sewell, George Alexander. Mississippi Black History Makers.
   Jackson: University Press of Mississippi, 1977.

Simon, George T. The Big Bands. Rev. ed. New York:
   Collier, 1974.

Tirro, Frank. Jazz: A History. New York: W.W. Norton,
1977.

Wilmer, Valerie. As Serious As Your Life: The Story of
the New Jazz. Westport, Conn.: Lawrence Hill, 1980.

ARTICLES

"Adjustment in Bands, Acts Ahead--Glaser," Afro-American,
January 4, 1947, p. 7.

"All Girls Band in W. Virginia," Chicago Defender, July 20,
1940, p. 20.

"All Girls' Band Sets Attendance Record at the Regal,"
Chicago Defender, October 24, 1942, p. 21.

"All-Girl Ork to 'Battle' Henderson on One-Nighters," Down
Beat, March 1, 1942, p. 2.

Allen, Henry. "End of an ERA," Washington Post, July 8,
1982, D1.

"Andy Kirk's Pianist Hears Greatest Femme Sax Section,"
Chicago Defender, December 20, 1941, p. 20.

"Anna Mae Winburn and Band Please Centennial and Dancing
Public," Omaha Star, September 3, 1938, p. 5.

"Arrest Members of All-Girl Band; School Prexy Irked,"
Jackson Advocate, October 17, 1942, p. 7.

Barnard, Eunice Fuller. "Home--Job--Or Both? The
Woman's Problem," The Nation, June 2, 1926, pp. 601-
602.

Bennett, Lerone. "No Crystal Stair: The Black Woman in
History," Ebony, August, 1977, pp. 164-170.

Bilbo, Theodore G. "An African Home for Our Negroes,"
The Living Age, June, 1940, p. 330.

Bontemps, Arna. "The Negro Contribution to American
Letters," The American Negro Reference Book, ed. by
John P. Davis. Englewood Cliffs, N.J.: Prentice-Hall,
1966.

222   Sweethearts of Rhythm

Cooper, Gypsie. "Can Women Swing?" The Metronome, September 1936, p. 30.

"Death of Rae Lee Jones," The Omaha Star, September 9, 1949, p. 2.

"Deaths and Funerals ... for Rae Lee Jones," Omaha Evening World-Herald, September 6, 1949, p. 30.

Denis, Paul. Published in Women in Music, Vol. IV, No. 7, April 15, 1939.

Dexter, Dave. "12 Great Negro Bands in New Jazz Anthology Album," Down Beat, April 1, 1941, p. 14.

"Did Not Cause Band to Leave," Pittsburgh Courier, May 24, 1941, p. 20.

Dodson, Neil. "Musicians Earn Their Living by the Hard Route," Afro-American, March 15, 1941, p. 14.

_____. "Sweethearts Not Seeking Husbands," Jackson Advocate, January 31, 1942, p. 7.

DuBois, W. E. B. "Close Ranks," The Crisis, July 1918, p. 111.

_____. "Negro Education," The Crisis, February 1918, pp. 173-175.

Dugan, James, and John Hammond. "In Retrospect ... An Early Black Music Concert, from Spirituals to Swing," The Black Perspective in Music, Fall 1974, pp. 191-208.

"Editor's Study," Harper's Monthly Magazine, January 1910, p. 313.

Feather, Leonard. "The Memories of Sweethearts," Los Angeles Times--Calendar, April 13, 1980, p. 64. (Same article, "The Sweetheart [sic] Hold School Reunion at Piney Woods," The Clarion Ledger/Jackson Daily News, April 20, 1980, Section I, p. 4.)

_____. "Women's Jazz Festival," Down Beat, July 1980, p. 58.

Fossum, Bob. "Girls Shouldn't Play Too Much Jazz, Says Ada," Down Beat, December 1, 1942, p. 14.

"Girls' Band Flees Dixie After Tiff with School, " Afro-
    American, April 26, 1941, p. 13.

Gossett, Hattie, and Carolyn Johnson. "The Politics of
    Power Instruments in Jazz, " The Boston Jazz Coalition,
    January/February 1980, pp. 1-2.

Handy, D. Antoinette. "Conversation with Lucille Dixon,
    Manager, Symphony of the New World, " The Black Per-
    spective in Music, Fall 1975, pp. 299-311.

"Harold Nichols and Girl Orchestra Star Acts at the Apollo, "
    New York Age, February 5, 1944, p. 10.

Harrison, Alferdteen. "We Were Professionals" (Interview
    of Lou Holloway), Southern Exposure, Fall 1980, p. 19.

Haynes, Elizabeth Ross. "Two Million Negro Women at
    Work, " Southern Workman, February 1922, p. 65.

"Hearts' Founder Dies in Denver, " Afro-American, September
    17, 1949, p. 8.

Hentoff, Nat. "The Women of Jazz, " The Chronicle Review,
    April 30, 1979, p. R20.

Heylbut, Rose. "The Hour of Charm, " The Etude, October
    1938, p. 639.

Hohl, Paul. "Kansas City's Women's Jazz Fest Superior
    by Far to First Two. " Billboard, April 5, 1980, pp. 66,
    69.

"How the Public Received the Journal of Negro History, "
    The Journal of Negro History, Vol. I, No. 2, April 1916,
    pp. 230-231.

Hughes, Langston. "The Negro and American Entertainment, "
    The American Negro Reference Book, ed. by John P.
    Davis. Englewood Cliffs, N.J.: Prentice-Hall, 1966,
    p. 833.

_____. "The Negro Artist and the Racial Mountain, " The
    Nation, June 23, 1926, p. 694.

"International Sweethearts Big Hit in Detroit, Mich. " Jackson
    Advocate, May 1, 1943, p. 3.

"Jazz Festival Will Feature Women," Richmond Times Dispatch, November 20, 1977, p. J-10.

Jones, Laurence C. "Dixie Music Lovers Like All Girls Band." Chicago Defender, February 24, 1940, p. 20.

_____. "Piney Woods Prexy Gives School's Side of Bolt Taken by Sweethearts of Rhythm," Pittsburgh Courier, May 3, 1941, p. 21.

"The Jubilee of Jubilees at Fisk University," Southern Workman, February 1922, pp. 73-80.

Koball, Burt. "Women in Jazz," International Musician, July 1975, p. 12.

Life, Special Report, 1976.

McCarthy, Jim. "A Jazz Band Flees," Afro-American, May 3, 1941, p. 13.

McPartland, Marian. "The Untold Story of the International Sweethearts of Rhythm," 1980. (In the book Jazzwomen, to be published by Oxford University Press.)

Maher, Jack. "Leave It to the Girls!" Metronome, December 1956, pp. 18-19.

"Managing the Cotton Blossom Singers," The Pine Torch, April 1928, p. 2.

Minor, Bill. "Piney Woods School, Death of a Dream?" The Capital Reporter, December 15, 1977, pp. 1, 6.

Montgomery, Aminah. "Spelman College, A Century of Service to Women Who Achieve," The Black Collegian, April/May 1981, pp. 90-93.

Moss, Carlton. "The Negro in American Films," Freedomways, Spring 1963.

"Mrs. Raylee [sic] Jones, Dies at Lutheran Hospital," Omaha Star, September 9, 1949, p. 1.

"Orchestra Hi-Way Pullman." Chicago Defender, September 16, 1939, p. 19.

Patrick, Melvin C. "GI's Line Up Mile Long to Greet Sweethearts [of] Rhythm," Afro-American, October 6, 1945, p. 23.

Phifer, Claude. "Four Fatal Fires," The Pine Torch, October 1933, p. 3.

The Pine Torch (Message from the President), July-September 1978, p. 1, and Fall 1980, p. 3.

"Piney Woods School Celebrates Seven Decades of Student Service in '79," The Pine Torch, January-March 1979, p. 1.

" 'Rays of Rhythm' Orchestra Replaces 'Sweethearts'," Afro-American, May 10, 1941, p. 14.

Rea, E. B. "Encores and Echoes," Afro-American, March 31, 1945, p. 8.

_____. "Sweethearts Set Tour of Europe," Afro-American, May 10, 1947, p. 8.

Rogers, Tommy W. "The Piney Woods Country Life School: A Successful Heritage of Education of Black Children in Mississippi," Negro History Bulletin, September/October 1976, p. 614.

Rowe, Billy. "All Girl Orchestra Is Getting Prepared to Crash the Big Time," Pittsburgh Courier, May 31, 1941, p. 20.

Schuyler, George. "The Negro-Art Hokum," The Nation, June 16, 1926, p. 662.

"17-Girl Band Which Quit School at Piney Woods, Rehearses for Big Time," Pittsburgh Courier, April 19, 1941, p. 21.

Shalvoy, Lorraine. "Women's Week Will Stress Job Goals," The Kansas City Star, March 20, 1980, p. 9.

Smith, Isadora. "The Girls Go Swell at Savoy," Pittsburgh Courier, September 29, 1941, p. 20.

Smith, Viola. "Give Girl Musicians a Break!--Idea," Down Beat, February 1, 1942, p. 8.

226   Sweethearts of Rhythm

Southern, Eileen. "In Retrospect: Black Prima Donnas of
the Nineteenth Century," The Black Perspective in Music,
Spring 1979, p. 95.

Stein, Shifra. "Festival Proves Jazz Prowess of Women,"
The Kansas City Times, March 17, 1978, p. 8C.

_____. "Jazz Festival Gives Women Performers a Show-
case," The Kansas City Star, March 18, 1979, pp. 1E,
9E.

"Sweethearts of Rhythm," The Chicago Defender, June 22,
1940, p. 20.

"Sweethearts of Rhythm Click in South and West," Chicago
Defender, January 20, 1940, p. 20.

"Sweethearts of Rhythm Get Welcome in Dallas," Chicago
Defender, January 27, 1940, p. 20.

"Sweethearts of Rhythm Manager Dies," Chicago Defender,
September 10, 1949, p. 1.

"'Sweethearts of Rhythm' Set New Box Office Record," New
York Age, August 30, 1941, p. 10.

"Sweethearts of Rhythm's Success Is Yarn of Opportunity
Cashed In," Chicago Defender, February 10, 1945, p. 13.

"Sweethearts to 'Battle' Henderson Soon," Down Beat, April
1, 1942, p. 5.

"Sweethearts Will Do One-Reel Movie Short," Down Beat,
May 6, 1946, p. 12.

"Swinging Rays of Rhythm Is Newest, Hottest Band on Tour,"
Chicago Defender, January 21, 1942, p. 20.

"The Swinging Rays Triumph," Chicago Defender, December
6, 1941, p. 21.

"They Make Music in Baltimore," Our World, April 1954,
pp. 48-53.

"This Girl Band Is Much Too Much with Swing and Jitter,"
Chicago Defender, June 15, 1940, p. 20.

"UJC Salutes Women in Jazz at Birdland June 26-29, " The Jazz Catalyst, June 1978, pp. 1, 8.

"Vi Burnside, World's Greatest Female Saxophonist, Dies Here, " Afro-American, December 5, 1964, p. 15.

Vollers, Maryanne. "Women's Jazz Festival Makes a Joyful Noise, " Rolling Stone, May 18, 1978, p. 19.

"A Vote for D.C., " Chicago Defender, July 13, 1940, p. 21.

Wade, James S. "A Holiday Message from the President, " The Pine Torch, October-December 1981, p. 2.

Watson, Ted. "War Provides 'Break' for All-Girl Bands, " Jackson Advocate, May 22, 1943, p. 7.

"Why Girl Bands Don't Click, " Jet, February 11, 1954, pp. 60-62.

Wilson, John S. "It's Women's Turn at the Jazz Festival, " New York Times, July 3, 1981, C 14.

_____. "Salute to Women in Jazz to Open, " New York Times, June 25, 1978, p. 39.

_____. "Women in Jazz, Past and Present, " New York Times, June 11, 1978, pp. D 25, 38.

"Women's Lib in New York, " The Black Perspective in Music, Spring, 1974, p. 107.

Wong, Willie Mae. "Nazis Gone, Germans Rave Over 'Sweethearts of Rhythm' Band, " Chicago Defender, September 8, 1945, p. 14.

MISCELLANEOUS SOURCES

Completed Questionnaires

Pauline Braddy
Lorraine Brown
Yvonne Busch
Toby Butler
Juanita Clark

Rosalind Cron
Lucille Dixon
Helen Jones
Evelyn McGee
Yvonne Plummer
Johnnie Mae Rice
Marion Estelle Simmons
Anna Mae Winburn

Correspondences

Nellie E. Bass--9/7/77, 3/21/81, 10/27/82
Pauline Braddy--9/2/77, 9/14/82, 9/27/82
Consuella Carter--8/31/77
Esther Louise Cooke--9/28/78, 11/1/78, 11/8/78
Lucille Dixon--7/3/75, 6/9/78, 5/14/81
Helen Jones (Memo via Consuella Carter, received at
    Lyons, Mississippi)--5/28/79
Geneva Perry--7/23/82
Claude Phifer--7/24/77, 7/26/77, 9/22/78, 5/5/82,
    10/9/82
Carline Ray--4/7/79
Anna Mae Winburn--4/8/80
Carol Comer (to "Original" Sweethearts)--Women's Jazz
    Festival, Inc.--1980

Interviews and Telephone Conversations

"Saluted" Sweethearts, Women's Jazz Festival, May 22
    and 23, 1980, Kansas City, Missouri--Judy Bayron,
    Pauline Braddy, Ione and Irene Grisham, Helen Jones,
    Evelyn McGee, Johnnie Mae Rice, Helen Saine, Willie
    Mae Wong
James R. Benton--3/24/80
Pauline Braddy--12/77, Washington, D.C., 5/25/82
Lorraine Brown--6/26/78, New York, N.Y., 8/24/78
Yvonne Busch--11/3/82, New Orleans, Louisiana
Consuella Carter--5/28/79, Lyons, Mississippi
Ernestine "Tiny" Davis--7/1/78
Lucille Dixon--7/26/75, 7/27/75, 6/26/78, New York,
    N.Y.; 7/25/82
Evelyn McGee--7/25/81
Etta Moten (Barnett)--10/23/82, Baltimore, Maryland;
    10/25/82
Geneva Perry--6/2/82
Claude Phifer--8/9/78, Mendenhall, Mississippi; 3/14/82,
    Piney Woods, Mississippi; 9/27/82

Yvonne Plummer--10/28/78, Virginia Beach, Virginia
Carline Ray--7/25/81
Dollye Robinson--3/15/82, Jackson, Mississippi
Helen Saine--7/1/78
Jesse Stone--5/22/80, Kansas City, Missouri
Anna Mae Winburn--4/18/80

Other

Brochures, Fliers, Booklets, Pamphlets--Piney Woods
    Country Life School, Piney Woods, Mississippi
STASH Records: ST-111, "All Women Groups"; ST-112,
    "Pianists"; ST-109, "Jazz Women: A Feminist Retro-
    spective"
Women's Jazz Festival Program, Kansas City, Missouri,
    1980

INDEX

(Underscored page numbers refer to photographs.)

231

Washington Park (Charlottesville, Va.) 202
Washingtonians (Duke Ellington) 64
"Water Boy" 48
Waters, Ethel 51, 55, 61; see also Ethel Waters and Her
    Ebony Four; Ethel Waters and Her Jazz Masters
Webb, Chick 68
Webb, Robiedell 150
Westchester Philharmonic 194
Western University Chorus 123
"Where the Bands Are Playing" 171
Whipper, Leigh 56
White, Annie ("Baby") 103, 113, 119-120
White, Charles 54
White, Clarence Cameron 53
White, George L. 49
White, Joshua 55
"Why Girl Bands Don't Click" 114
Wichita Jazz Festival 1
"Wife of His Youth and Other Stories of the Color Line" 45
Wilberforce University 136
Wiley College 128, 136
William Nickerson's Ladies Orchestra 65
Williams, Bert 50
Williams, Clarence 52
Williams, Cootie 53
Williams, Edna Armstead 121, 123, 125, 127, 143, 157,
    198
Williams, (Mr. & Mrs.) Jack 127
Williams, Mary Lou x, 2, 51, 58, 64, 150, 152, 197
Williams, Pauline Braddy see Braddy, Pauline
Williams, Spencer 50
Williams's (Edna) Sextette 198
Wilson, Edith 56
Wilson, John S. 3
Winburn, Anna Mae Darden 9, 11, 13, 14, 20, 22-23, 25,
    28, 114, 157, 161, 167, 174, 176, 177-179, 184, 198,
    205; see also Anna Mae Winburn and Her Sweethearts of
    Rhythm
Windsor Club (Ft. Lauderdale) 136
Wings over Jordan 54
"Women Blow Their Own Horns" 194
"Women in Jazz" 4
"Women in Jazz: All Women Groups" 198
Women in Music 131
Women's Bureau, U.S. Dept. of Labor 203
Women's Heritage Series (Rosetta Records) 63
Women's Jazz Festival, Inc. ix, 1-5, 8-9, 22, 28-29,
    197

F